Genesis of American Nationalism

**Topics in
United States
Diplomatic History**

Consulting Editor

Norman A. Graebner
University of Virginia

Genesis of
American Nationalism

Richard W. Van Alstyne / CALLISON COLLEGE
UNIVERSITY OF THE PACIFIC

Blaisdell Publishing Company

A DIVISION OF GINN AND COMPANY

WALTHAM, MASSACHUSETTS / TORONTO / LONDON

To My Grandchildren: Peter, Tom, Marshall, Allyn, Lisa.

Preface

While writing my last two books, *The Rising American Empire* (Oxford and New York, 1960; Chicago, 1965) and *Empire and Independence. The International History of the American Revolution* (New York, 1965), I became aware of the splendid collection of rare books available at the Henry E. Huntington Library and Art Gallery, San Marino, California. This collection proved invaluable, especially in connection with the second of the above books. It helped give inner meaning to the Revolution: an ambition for empire on the American part, a gnawing fear on the British side that American success would place Britain's own independence in jeopardy. France, it was felt, would emerge the real victor in the contest. Clever footwork on the part of British statesmen, strengthened by a resounding naval victory over the French in the Caribbean in April 1782, redressed the balance of power in Britain's favor and brought the Americans, independent in law but hardly in fact, again within the range of British influence.

When some five years ago Professor Graebner kindly invited me to contribute a volume to his series, I immediately thought of the Huntington Library's riches, which were then at my daily command; so I proposed a study of this literature to the end of analyzing the sources and evolution of an American ideology. I began by exploring the ideas of Sir Walter Raleigh and ended with the letters, writings, and speeches of men like John Quincy Adams, Edward Everett, Horace Mann, and Timothy Dwight. When I reached the year 1826 I stopped, persuaded that an American national creed by this time had been formulated and propagated. Very little if anything that could be labelled unique has been added to the American *Weltanschauung* since this year of the celebration of the fiftieth anniversary of national independence.

The Library's collection of rare books being catalogued chronologically, I was able to proceed methodically year by year over a period exceeding two and a quarter centuries; and all told I drew on more than nine hundred volumes in the collection. These varied in size from comparatively thin pamphlets to multivolumed sets, but obviously too numerous to be listed in a bibliography for this book. Those works from which I drew directly are of course cited in the footnotes, but the whole body of the literature was vital in the making of this book. In addition I scrutinized the several collections of published papers, in particular the inimitable edition of the *Jefferson Papers*, the *Diary* and letters of John Adams, and the *Writings of John Quincy Adams*. My analysis of the ideas and sentiments of these three men who were principals in the making of an American ideology rests almost exclusively on their collected works. Where necessary, though to a limited degree, I relied upon the books and articles of historians and other writers; and references to these secondary authorities are to be found scattered through the footnotes.

R. W. V. A.

Contents

Introduction   1

1

The Idea of Empire in the Eighteenth Century   3

The idea assumes shape and meaning: the Elizabethan English and
   the New World   3
New England: the American Israel   7
Patriotism and war: the memory of Rome   11
The Empire in thought and in action: from Daniel Defoe (1707) to
   Benjamin Franklin (1751)   17
Benjamin Franklin and Dr. John Mitchell: living space and encir-
   clement. The Protestant interest   51

2

The Revolution and Its Mythology   58

The virtuous republic and its world mission   58
Territory and Union: America the Empire of Reason   64
Thomas Jefferson: his creed and his ambitions   67
The vision of empire in the Pacific   78
Thoughts on the Constitution: Jefferson, Adams, and Madison   92
Some myths of the Revolution   95
John Quincy Adams: the Revolution, a sacred memory; the Dec-
   laration of Independence, the sacred text   110

3

A Rising American Nationalism   115

    John Quincy Adams's statesmanlike ideas   115

    An Englishman and a Frenchman react to the American scene in the 1790s   126

    Jefferson and his prejudices   130

    The deification of George Washington   135

    The central paradox: thirst for power, dream of an agrarian paradise   142

    Jefferson in the shoes of Defoe   148

    The illusion of "neutral rights"   151

    John Quincy Adams again: his fears and hopes   154

    A tonic to nationalism: the second war with Britain   158

    Piety, patriotism, republicanism: America as an amalgam of ancient Rome and Israel   169

Index   185

Genesis of American Nationalism

Introduction

The three parts into which this book is divided are to be read as one connected whole, the imperial idea being central and overriding. From the Elizabethan English the Americans absorbed the idea that the New World was theirs to conquer and possess; Spain and France were trespassers to be excluded by any means possible, and the aboriginal Indian to be displaced in order to make room for a migrating Protestant population from the British Isles. Protestant England and Scotland were thought of as an unlimited source of migrants to America, where their progeny would ultimately spread over both continents. Accordingly it became Britain's "duty" to employ all its strength in behalf of its American colonists. Benjamin Franklin developed the classic argument for this idea in his widely read essay, *Observations Concerning the Increase of Mankind*. The Americans must have room to expand, and Britain must help them get the room.

Imperial-minded Americans were by this time beginning to identify themselves with ancient Rome and its idea of patriotism or civic virtue. This was a change from the attitude of the preceding generation, which scorned patriotism as the ideological tool of aggressive war and unscrupulous business. Jonathan Swift regarded it with contempt, Bishop George Berkeley and others denounced it as a cloak for corrupt adventurers and politicians, while Alexander Pope thought a patriot a fool. Patriotism was still a "dirty word" in the middle of the eighteenth century. Oliver Goldsmith in his *Citizen of the World*, first published in 1762, made fun of it and linked it with drunkenness and partisan politics. The term stuck to the Whigs, both English and

1

American, who were the party of business and war. But as a student of Machiavelli, the sixteenth-century Florentine patriot, Viscount Bolingbroke revived the concept of the old Roman, a man of high principle and unsullied virtue. An exile from English political life who despised the Whigs, Bolingbroke earned fame as a political philosopher. His writings gave him a following from men as different as Franklin, Jefferson, John Adams, and His Majesty King George III. Bolingbroke's most influential work was his essay, *Idea of a Patriot King,* in which, like Machiavelli, he vested patriotism in the prince or ruler.

In addition to Bolingbroke and Machiavelli the books of the Roman historian Livy enriched the minds of eighteenth-century readers. The picture that Livy drew of the virtuous Roman Republic waging war on its enemies appealed to minds like John Adams who saw in republican America the reincarnation of ancient Rome. The analogy occurred often to Adams, who saw too that virtue in America would gradually degenerate into corruption as it had in ancient Rome.

Equally suggestive was the success of the Romans in building a far-flung empire. In planning for the destruction of Quebec in 1750 Governor William Shirley of Massachusetts drew the analogy of Carthage and pictured America as the New Rome. Once the French lost Quebec, a vast inland empire lay exposed to conquest. Eventually France was forced out, but the Patriots of 1776, who completed the change in usage of the word, discovered that Quebec was still a troublesome thorn in their flesh. However, for many years thereafter it remained an article of faith with the Americans that Quebec (or Canada, as it was soon to be called) would ultimately be absorbed into their continental empire. Meanwhile Rome continued as a living memory, furnishing an example to the United States, as Henry Clay put it, on how to make itself master of the world. Patriotism, wedded to commerce and the Christian religion, would bring fulfillment to the American world mission.

The Idea of Empire in the Eighteenth Century

1

I

"All the world is becoming commercial," wrote Thomas Jefferson in 1784. "Was it practicable to keep our new empire separated from them, we might indulge ourselves in speculating whether commerce contributes to the happiness of mankind. But we cannot separate ourselves from them. . . . We must then in our own defence endeavor to share as large a portion as we can of this modern source of wealth and power. . . ."[1] Washington, to whom Jefferson was here writing, had the same conviction. We have laid "the foundation of a great empire," the general had publicly declared. We have not done so "in a gloomy age of ignorance and superstition, but at an epoch when the rights of mankind were better understood and more clearly defined than at any former period." The next step must be a union of the states: "It is only in our united character, as an empire, that our independence is acknowledged, that our power can be regarded, or our credit supported among foreign nations."[2]

---

[1] Julian P. Boyd (ed.), *The Papers of Thomas Jefferson,* 17 vols. (published Princeton, N. J.: Princeton University Press, 1950–65), *VII,* p. 26.

[2] John C. Fitzpatrick (ed.), *The Writings of George Washington from the Original Manuscript Sources 1745–1799,* 39 vols. (Washington, D. C.: Government Printing Office, 1931–1944), *XXVI,* pp. 334–337; Thomas Condie, *Biographical Memoirs of the Illustrious Gen. George Washington* (Brattleborough, 1814), pp. 152, 159.

In these concise and lucid sentences the two most eminent leaders of the American Revolution showed they understood what they had accomplished, and expressed their views on the opportunities that lay ahead. Central to their thinking was the idea of empire. The word itself came naturally to them because it was common currency in the eighteenth century, and the idea which it expressed was native to the British and the American Colonial mind since the days of the early settlements.

Sir Walter Raleigh and his fellow Elizabethans, active in exploration, trade, and colonization in the closing decades of the sixteenth century, originated the idea. Raleigh fancied himself the conqueror of South America, setting up an imaginary "Emperor of Guiana" as a tributary to the English Crown and opening the Orinoco River to English colonization. Others, notably Sir Humphrey Gilbert, Raleigh's half-brother, and a number of wealthy businessmen with the means to speculate, looked more to North America as better suited for colonization. Newfoundland and the coast south from the St. Lawrence to the Spanish Floridas interested them especially. The Newfoundland fisheries were already a solid source of wealth, and the inviting harbors and milder climates farther south suggested the possibilities of permanent colonies. Interest extended upwards from businessmen like Edward Hayes, the self-made merchant of Liverpool, to the highest members of Queen Elizabeth's court. Probing voyages, aimed at finding suitable locations, started at least as early as 1570, many of them inspired by Richard Hakluyt, the geographer in whose mind exploration and colonization were two parts of the same operation. Sir Walter himself tried planting a colony off the North Carolina coast in 1584.[3]

All overseas trading ventures of the sixteenth century, as well as a

---

[3] David B. Quinn, *Raleigh and the British Empire* (New York, Collier Macmillan, 1962), pp. 159 ff., and *ibid.,* "Edward Hayes, Liverpool Colonial Pioneer," Trans. Historic Society of Lancashire and Cheshire, *III,* 1959, pp. 25–45. Sir Walter Raleigh, *The Large, Rich, and Beautiful Empire of Guiana,* V. T. Harlow (ed.) (London, 1928). The original work was published in 1596. Two and a half centuries later Sir Robert Schomburghk, a geographer and surveyor, explored the Orinoco after reading Raleigh. In 1848 Schomburghk got out an edition of Raleigh's book for the Hakluyt Society of London.

growing number of domestic concerns doing business inside Tudor England, were chartered monopolies. From the established practices of the trading monopolies the idea passed easily and naturally to the problem of overseas colonization. Only venture-capital put up by a small group of entrepreneurs could accomplish the task. Thus when colonization actually started, as it did in 1607 under the auspices of the Virginia Company of London, it was meant to have a free field. Sharing the area with competitors was not to be thought of: each enterprise took the precaution of getting a certain part of the country reserved exclusively for itself. The idea of exclusive colonization applied, of course, even more to foreigners than it did to potential English competitors. It was axiomatic with the Elizabethan English that the New World — all of it, North as well as South America — would eventually fall to them. Spain and, at the time, the much more modest interests of France, would be crowded out. Rome and its distant colonies furnished the classic example — garrisons of soldiers placed strategically, followed by their families and developing into civilian colonies. The leaders of Elizabethan England were increasingly confident that they were the modern Romans. And like Rome, England would be the leader of the civilized world. England's mission, wrote Raleigh in all seriousness, was to rescue the natives of America from Spain, teach them the liberal arts of civility, and propagate the doctrines of the "true" Protestant religion.[4]

A realistic observer, Raleigh recognized the function of war in the process. It was important to enlist the aid of the aborigines in the use of weapons. In an essay published posthumously Raleigh described war as "natural, customary, arbitrary, voluntary, and necessary," and he attempted an analysis of what he called "the mystery of invasive warre." If two nations meet on the same plain, he wrote, "the more mighty will seek to take from the other." If they be divided by mountains, they will fight for the mastery of the passes; if rivers flow between them, they will contend for the bridges. "Yea, the sea itself must be broad, barren of fish, void of islands, else it will yield plentiful quarrels." Natural war, Raleigh concluded, is caused by want of room upon the earth, and he was prepared for a

---

[4] Quinn, *ibid.*, p. 159.

liberal definition of this phrase. Arbitrary war sprang from many other motives, the most honest being fear of injury and desire to head off danger.[5] Thomas Hobbes, in his great classic treatise *The Leviathan,* elaborated upon these ideas not long after — Hobbes belonged to the generation following Raleigh's, and his writings were part of the intellectual heritage of the eighteenth century in both England and America.

All of these ideas propounded by the Elizabethan English passed into the minds of the eighteenth-century Americans who, as we shall see, adapted and changed them to meet their own requirements. The concept of a British empire began taking shape while yet England and Scotland were separate countries. John Selden used it in an influential treatise written first in Latin and then translated and published in English in 1652.[6] Dedicating his book to Parliament, the "supreme autoritie of the nation," Selden developed an historical argument that "the Seas, flowing about this Island, hath before the old Roman invasion and since, been . . . an inseparable appendant of the *British Empire.* . . ." Parliament, he asserted, was "the founder of the most famous and potent *republic* in the world," whose survival depended upon keeping the Dutch at arm's length, then England's most dangerous rival. Without dominion over the surrounding waters, which he depicted on a map showing the coast of Europe extending like a half-moon around Britain, the island would be "a great prison," and its inhabitants so many captives and vassals of their neighbors. To the term *empire* Selden applied its simplest Latin meaning: a dominion or a sovereignty. But Selden was less fearful of being "imprisoned" than he was of seeing the English losing the race for overseas trade, and so he claimed the adjacent seas for the British Empire.

Oliver Cromwell, who now assumed the reins of power, put punch into Selden's legal disquisition by defeating the Dutch at sea. Moreover, Cromwell took up Raleigh's idea of a pincer action against

---

[5] Sir Walter Raleigh, *Judicious and Select Essays and Observations* (London, 1650). The quotations are from the second essay.

[6] John Selden, *Of the Dominion or Ownership of the Sea,* translated from the Latin into English by Marchmont Needham.

Spain in the New World, using his Navy to capture Jamaica and so drive a wedge into the Spanish Caribbean. Cromwell termed his plan his Western Design, but it was a restatement of Raleigh's ideas; and in the meantime, with English colonization progressing rapidly in America, popular usage readily expanded the idea of the "British Empire" to take in the overseas colonies. So the British Empire developed in the course of the seventeenth century into a Roman-like structure, not merely a local sovereignty but a vast and growing complex of island colonies and mainland settlements with continental ambitions.

Meanwhile, other books spread the gospel of empire. While published in London, several of them were written either by colonists in America or by men who had been to the Colonies. Writing on Sir Francis Drake and boasting that he did so "especially for the stirring up of heroick spirits," one author in 1635 took pains to describe New Albion on the far northwest side of North America and to remind his readers that that country belonged to them, because Drake had been there. William Wood, who had migrated to America, wrote a successful book on *New England's Prospects,* giving a unique but by no means inaccurate description of New England as an island or a peninsula situated between the St. Lawrence and the Hudson, the Great Lakes in the background. A third writer, after four years in New England, returned home in 1642 to let religious dissenters know how they could, by emigrating, escape further oppression at the hands of the bishops; and still a fourth, who had been in the thick of the war with the Pequot Indians, wanted his readers to know that the Colonists had been right in waging war on the aborigines.

But the men who best reflect the attitudes of the early Puritans are their famous governors, William Bradford of Plymouth and John Winthrop of Massachusetts Bay. Bradford's *History,* republished as recently as 1952, is one of the great books of American literature, contributing powerfully to making legendary heroes out of the Pilgrim "fathers." England, he tells us was "the first of nations" to be adorned by the light of the gospel "after the gross darkness of popery . . . had covered and overspread the Christian world."

Seventeen years after landing on Plymouth Rock, the Pilgrims were engaged in a war of annihilation against the Pequots. These Indians, "a stout and warlike people," had tried in vain to win the support of their neighbors, the Narragansetts, against the white man. They used "pernicious arguments," as Bradford put it, pointing out that the whites would overspread the country and deprive the red men of their lands. Then they attacked alone, but met with swift reprisal. The men from Plymouth took their fort by quick assault, and then: "standing together, with the wind all was quickly on a flame, and thereby more were burnt to death than was otherwise slain. It burnt their bowstrings and made them unserviceable. . . . It was a fearful sight," Bradford observes,

> "to see them thus frying in the fire . . . and horrible was the stink and scent thereof; but the victory seemed a sweet sacrifice . . . thus to enclose their enemies in their hands and give them so speedy a victory over so proud and insulting an enemy." [7]

The remnant of the tribe then fled in terror.

Plymouth's neighboring, but not *neighborly*, Colony of Massachusetts Bay was for the time being unaffected by native wars, but found itself involved with French Papists. Hostility between two rival claimants to the governorship of Acadia brought one of them, a M. La Tour, to Boston in search of aid. The ministers, Winthrop tells us, were greatly perturbed at the prospect of helping Papists, who were not to be trusted: Catholics did not feel obliged to keep faith with heretics. But the governor took a secular view: La Tour had *an interest* in keeping faith; the religious issue was "but accidental," but even so, the French under him might be converted to "the love of truth." "Solomon tells us," replied Winthrop's opponents, "that he that meddleth with a strife which belongs not to him takes a dog by the ear, which is very dangerous."

But the governor found biblical texts to support his side of the argument too, and went ahead with aid to La Tour without further consultation. La Tour being weaker than his rival, Winthrop seems to have had in mind a program of "divide and conquer," thereby converting the small French settlement into a dependency of Massa-

---

[7] William Bradford, *Of Plymouth Plantation, 1620–1647,* a new edition by Samuel Eliot Morison (New York: Knopf, 1952), pp. 3, 290–296.

chusetts. But he was fated to be disappointed. A lend–lease arrangement whereby La Tour got four vessels and sixteen pieces of ordinance for a rental of £200 per month was not enough to bring him victory. With support from France, the rival governor established himself in power at Port Royal, and La Tour fell back on Winthrop's hospitality in Boston. Between the lines of Winthrop's account, which is our only source, we gather that, in spite of the internal dissension aroused by the presence of the dubious guest, Winthrop expected an ultimate victory. He kept La Tour for more than a year, but the whole thing turned sour when the Frenchman sailed away in 1646 to engage in piracy.[8] So ended the first attempt from Massachusetts to create an ascendancy over the Acadian French.

Massachusetts got its first real taste of Indian warfare in 1675, when the tribes under the leadership of a chief whom the Colonists called King Philip attempted a general massacre of the whites. This time the danger was so serious as to call forth the united energies of the New England Colonies — the Indians, it was asserted, had taken five years to accumulate enough guns, powder, and bullets to wage war, and the Colonists took fourteen months to break them down. Three books giving an account of the war were soon published, and each author took pains to justify the conflict from the standpoint of the whites. The first one was by a merchant of Boston who assured his readers in England that the land had been bought from the Indians for good value. But, conceded this writer, when the Indians woke up to what was happening to them they resolved on war. The merchant, in other words, saw the wrath of the red men as a normal expression of human nature. The other two books were by clergymen who reflected the established Puritan view that New England was the American Israel, its white inhabitants the chosen people of God or, as John Winthrop had quaintly put it, the "City upon a Hill" to whom the whole world looked for redemption. Making a reference to the Dutch publicist, Grotius, whose treatise on war and peace had developed the concept of the "just war," the Rev. William Hubbard spoke

[8] Winthrop's Journal, "History of New England," 1630–1649. J. K. Hosmer (ed.), 2 vols. (New York: C. Scribner's Sons, 1908), *II*, pp. 105 ff., 130, 136–137, 178, 275.

of the Indians' defeat as "a good omen unto Israel when the government of the tribes falls into such hands as have understanding in the
times to know what Israel ought to do." Hubbard's book, originally
a sermon preached before the governor, council, and deputies, con-
tains the first map of New England ever cut and marks the towns
that the Indians had attacked. Increase Mather, foremost of the
Boston clergy, began his book with the assumption that "the Lord
God of our Fathers" had given us rightful possession of the heathen
people, who had plotted mischievous devices against "the English
Israel." The Indians themselves, Mather asserted, did not pretend
that we had done them wrong, so of course the war against them
was "just." [9]

Only thirteen years later New England found itself engaged in an
even more serious Indian war, wherein the tribes were being openly
backed by the French from Canada. This was the first of the inter-
colonial wars that were to recur over a period of three quarters of a
century. Indians and Canadian French having struck suddenly at the
frontier town of Deerfield and massacred its inhabitants, Cotton
Mather, who had fallen heir to his father's pulpit, exhorted "the
people of God" to make a swift counter-attack. The emergency
called for "a brisk sally forth upon the French territories, which must
else be a perpetual obstacle to the thriving of these plantations. . . .
Who is on the Lord's side?" Mather demanded. "Who is for Jesus
against Satan, and who is for the true Christian, Protestant religion
against Popery and Paganism? . . . Take your choice, my dear countrymen; but there is no room to be indifferent." [10] Governor Bradstreet
and the General Court rose to the occasion, launching a full-scale
invasion of Acadia. But Quebec, far up the St. Lawrence, was the
main center of French power in America; English expeditions, cheered

---

[9] *The Present State of New England . . .* faithfully composed by a merchant
of Boston (London: 1675); W. Hubbard, *A Narrative of the Troubles with the
Indians . . .* (Boston: 1677); Increase Mather, *A Brief History of the War with
the Indians . . .* (Boston: 1676).

[10] Cotton Mather, *The Present State of New England . . .* (Boston: 1690);
and for a searching study of the Puritan "chosen people" concept see Loren
Baritz, *City on a Hill. A History of Ideas and Myths in America* (New York:
John Wiley & Sons, 1964), pp. 3–46.

on by the Colonies, had raided it before, and Massachusetts tried it again in 1691. "Our Israel," however, was not strong enough to cope with the French by itself; and the English, preoccupied by a war in Europe, were not yet ready to take up plans for overpowering the French in the New World. In 1707 Massachusetts made its first direct appeal for English naval support, and soon thereafter a grand pattern of empire, aiming at the elimination of the French and the Spanish, began taking shape.

II

Meanwhile, Puritan ideas of an American Zion in the wilderness were matched by certain great English writers of the eighteenth century. Bishop George Berkeley exceeded the aspirations of even John Winthrop and William Bradford in his famous poem of 1726, of which the last three stanzas run as follows:

> There shall be sung another golden age,
> The rise of empire and of arts,
> The good and great inspiring epic rage,
> The wisest heads and noblest hearts.

> Not such as Europe breeds in her decay;
> Such as she bred when fresh and young,
> When heavenly flame did animate her clay,
> By future poets shall be sung.

> Westward the course of empire takes its way;
> The four first acts already past,
> A fifth shall close the drama with the day;
> Time's noblest offspring is the last.

Berkeley's idealistic conception found an echo in the phrase "Empire for Liberty," which Jefferson coined near the end of the century. An Anglican bishop with a broad and philosophical bent, Berkeley reached minds like Franklin's and Jefferson's to which the dogmas of New England Puritanism could make no appeal. But Berkeley was as good a puritan as John Winthrop, albeit a pleasanter personality and a more cosmopolitan spirit. And theological hair-splitting aside, his social values were like Winthrop's without the latter's political ambitions. After the Peace of Utrecht (1713) a wave of wild speculation swept over Western Europe, bursting in the great South Sea Bubble of 1720. Berkeley was so shocked at what he saw that he wrote an "Essay Towards Preventing the Ruin of Great Britain," and mentally he turned to the New World as a place to make a new start. Subsequently he spent more than two years in America, where his philosophical works were published.[11] Like the Puritans, he stressed simplicity of manners and, with the South Sea affair especially in mind, decried all get-rich-quick schemes in contrast to the slow, moderate gains of honest work.

By this time the old Roman concept of patriotism was receiving attention; but Berkeley, observing the contemporary English scene, rejected it. The seventeenth-century Puritans were unfamiliar with the term, although their idea of virtue, by which they meant simplicity, frugality, and devotion to the common interest, conformed to Berkeley's. The poet, Alexander Pope, could write: "A patriot is a fool in ev'ry age;" and Berkeley, in a slim volume entitled *Maxims Concerning Patriotism,* identified patriots with the gambling portion of society which he disliked so intensely. "Gamesters, fops, rakes, bullies, stock-jobbers: alas! what patriots!" he exclaimed contemptuously.[12] Overseas trading was highly speculative by nature, and the manipulation of company stocks, of which the South Sea Company was the most conspicuous, gave the stock jobber, or speculator, a bad odor.

Old English society devoted to the land could not abide the thought: the stockjobber personified corruption and moral decay, as Berkeley described it. He undermined the foundations of society. At

---

[11] *Complete Works,* 4 vols. (Oxford: Clarendon Press, 1901), *IV,* 321–338; Benjamin Rand, *Berkeley's American Sojourn* (Cambridge, Mass.: Harvard University Press, 1932).

[12] *Complete Works, IV,* pp. 561–563; Edmund S. Morgan, "The Puritan Ethic and the American Revolution," *William and Mary Quarterly,* 3rd ser., *XXIV* (1967), pp. 3–43.

the same time the pushing world of business, bent on territorial and commercial expansion overseas and politically identified with the Whig Party, was "patriotic" — it stood for the growth of the Empire, which entailed more wars with France and Spain. Of this the country gentry who rallied round the Tory Party felt deeply distrustful. A half century later, when the American Revolution was in full swing, King George III registered this same attitude of distrust: whiggery was stockjobbery, and patriotism was no better. As a youth, the king was thoroughly indoctrinated with the prejudices against business; but as a man keenly interested in agriculture — he was known affectionately as "Farmer George" — he won the hearts of the country gentry.

Two other writers, apparently more widely read than Bishop Berkeley and so more influential in expressing or shaping attitudes, appear in the literature of this generation. The first was John Trenchard, whose four-volume work known as *Cato's Letters,* came out in a series of magazine articles in several of the weekly British journals before publication in book form in 1723–1724. Starting with a fierce attack on stockjobbers, that "dirty race of money changers," Trenchard conveyed the idea that England was corrupt:

> Poor England! What a name art thou become! a name of infatuation and misery! How art thou fallen! how plundered! And those that have done it would, to keep their spoil, agree to assist others to squeeze out thy last dregs, and to suck out thy remaining blood.

Basic to the argument of this book is the premise, often repeated, that "the world is govern'd by men, and men by their passions; which being boundless and insatiable, are always terrible when they are not controuled." The only safeguard is wise government, and although the author is not sanguine that this can be achieved, he turns to Roman history for his examples and to Machiavelli for advice on how intelligent, self-restrained government can be realized. "All men are born free," Trenchard decided. "Liberty is a gift which they receive from God himself; nor can they alienate the same by consent. . . ." But, looking to Machiavelli's practical experience for guidance, Trenchard recognized that "scarce any man is as good as he himself or his party make him, or as bad as his enemies represent him. . . . The subjects which men understand least," he wrote, continuing to paraphrase the Italian, "are generally what they talk of most. . . . Few men who have ever been in possession of power have known what to do with it, or ever understood the principles upon which all power is founded; and their mistakes have made endless havoc amongst mankind." Much admired and studied for his insights into statecraft, Machiavelli remained as one of the great teachers of eighteenth-century thinkers from Trenchard and Bolingbroke to Franklin, John Adams, and Jefferson.[13]

Cato's Letters, moreover, linked war and conquest with internal corruption and revolution.

> What is got by soldiers, must be maintained by soldiers; and we have . . . already seen the frightful image of a military government. . . . The Romans, when they had extended their conquests so far and wide that they were forced to keep provincial armies to awe and preserve the conquered countries, became a prey to those armies. . . .

Like the old Roman whose name and eloquence he assumed, Trenchard fought bitterly against territorial ambitions, which he viewed as born of the machinations of the trading companies; but he hoped in vain for a return to virtue through a society of small landowners and merchants.

Henry St. John, Viscount Bolingbroke, was less prone to denunciation than Trenchard, though basically they shared the same ideas. Bolingbroke was possibly the most interesting, attractive, and influential personality in eighteenth-century England, fascinating to such diverse characters as Voltaire, John Adams, Thomas Jefferson, and the young prince who in 1758 became King George III. Jonathan Swift wrote of him as[14]

---

[13] Cato's Letters, 4 vols. (London: 1723–1724), I, pp. 25, 65, 266; II, p. 43; III, pp. 84, 118, 136–148, 201. Also W. B. Gwyn, The Meaning of the Separation of Powers. An analysis of the doctrine from its origin to the adoption of the United States Constitution (New Orleans, La.: Tulane University Press, 1965), pp. 82–99; and H. Trevor Colbourn, The Lamp of Experience. Whig History and the Intellectual Origins of the American Revolution (Chapel Hill: University of North Carolina Press, 1965), passim.

[14] In the Journal to Stella, Letter 33, "Works," Temple Scott (ed.), (London: 1897), II, p. 273. Also Zoltán Haraszti, John Adams and the Prophets of Progress (Cambridge, Mass.: Harvard University Press, 1952), pp. 49–79.

the greatest young man I ever knew: wit, capacity, beauty, quickness of apprehension, good learning, and an excellent taste; the best orator in the House of Commons, admirable conversation and good nature, and good manners; generous, and a despiser of money.

Bolingbroke was the close friend of Alexander Pope, who prepared his writings for publication. So deeply did his thoughts sink into Pope's mind that they reappear, even in the words used, in the latter's didactic but absorbing poem *An Essay on Man.*

Bolingbroke, however, was not in rhythm with the times: he negotiated the moderate Treaty of Utrecht which terminated the long War of the Spanish Succession, and so angered the Whigs for cheating them out of a total victory over the Bourbon powers that he had to leave the country. In France he linked his fortunes with the exiled followers of the Stuart kings and, while subsequently permitted to live and write in England, he remained permanently barred from public life. This handicap did not impair the very great and lasting literary influence of the "Ishmael of his Age."

Like the author of *Cato's Letters,* Bolingbroke harked back to Machiavelli for his model, elaborating upon the Florentine in his famous essay *The Idea of a Patriot King.* While detesting the Whigs as factious and unscrupulous, and antipathetic to their aggressive policies abroad, Bolingbroke advanced the concept of patriotism by centering it in the ruler. "Patriotism," he wrote, "must be founded in great principles, and supported by great virtues. . . . To espouse no party, but to govern like the common father of his people, is so essential to the character of a Patriot King, that he who does otherwise, forfeits the title. . . . Party is a political evil, and faction is the worst of all parties." [15] A deist and a skeptic, Bolingbroke had scant patience with religion; hence the Dissenters, who were the religious activists of the eighteenth century in England and America, condemned him. But Jefferson and Adams did not feel this way: both were avid students of Bolingbroke's ideas on religion and politics. Next to Voltaire, Bolingbroke probably had no stauncher admirer

---

[15] Henry St. John, Viscount Bolingbroke, *Letters on the Spirit of Patriotism* . . . (London: 1749), pp. 100, 148. *Also* his *Letters on the Study and Use of History,* 2 vols. (London: 1752).

than John Adams. Bolingbroke reflected deeply on the nature of history, as did Adams, and postulated a mixed type of government, with power divided between the king, the aristocracy, and the representatives of the people as the only practical way of coping with the passions. A rich heritage of political philosophy, reaching back to Aristotle, lay behind these ideas. Pope expressed them thus in verse:

> 'Till jarring int'rests of themselves create
> Th'according music of a well-mixed State.
> Such is the World's great harmony, that springs
> From Order, Union, full Consent of things!
> Where small and great, where weak and mighty, made
> To serve, not suffer, strengthen, not invade,
> More pow'rful each as needful to the rest,
> And, in proportion as it blesses, blest,
> Draw to one point, and to one centre bring
> Beast, Man, or Angel, Servant, Lord, or King.
> *For Forms of Government let fools contest;*
> *Whate'er is best administered is best.*

"Absolute monarchy," declared Bolingbroke, "is tyranny, but *absolute democracy is tyranny and anarchy both*," and to this Adams said a hearty amen. Adams never altered his mind on the subject. "The fundamental article of my political creed," he wrote Jefferson many years after, "is that despotism, or unlimited sovereignty, or absolute power, is the same in a majority of a popular assembly, an aristocratical council, an oligarchical junto, and a single emperor. Equally arbitrary, cruel, bloody, and in every respect diabolical." [16]

---

[16] Italics in these excerpts inserted for emphasis. Adams to Jefferson, Nov. 13, 1815, in *The Adams–Jefferson Letters*, Lester J. Cappon (ed.), 2 vols. (Chapel Hill: University of North Carolina Press, 1959), *II*, p. 456. *Also* Zoltan Haraszti, *John Adams and the Prophets of Progress* (Cambridge, Mass.: Harvard University Press, 1952), p. 58; and W. B. Gwyn, *The Meaning of the Separation of Powers* . . . . (New Orleans, La.: Tulane University Press, 1965), pp. 100–131.

III

These anti-imperial ideas, embodying distrust of armies, business and politics, encountered a powerful stream of imperial thought which swept along through the eighteenth century gathering strength, as it were, from tributary rivers flowing into it from both Britain and America. "An undiscover'd Ocean of Commerce" lies open before us. The statement comes from Daniel Defoe, the famous author of *Robinson Crusoe*. England, Defoe added, is "now the center of the world's commerce. But I have not said this because it is England, but because it is true; and I must have been partial against England, rather than for it, if I had said otherwise." Defoe wrote this in 1728, near the end of his life, but he had said it before many times. Trade was his religion, as he almost boasted:[17]

> Our interest is our trade; and our trade is, next to our liberty and religion, one of our most valuable liberties. If our neighbors pretend to slam the door against our commerce, we must open it; and that by force, if no other means will procure it. To invade our commerce is to invade our property, and we may and must defend it.

Scottish and American merchants felt much the same way: if they were to realize their own ambitions, they had to have English help. Years before the Scots had sent out an expedition to occupy and colonize the isthmus of Panama, then called Darien, in the heart of the Spanish Empire. Ordinary Scots put their savings into the scheme, and William Paterson, the leading financier of Edinburgh who had been prominent in 1690 in the founding of the Bank of England, not only invested in the enterprise but sailed with his wife on the expedition. Once established on the isthmus, the Scots expected to intercept the gold and silver coming from Peru enroute to Spain; and, as the English explorer, William Dampier, who had rounded Cape Horn,

---

[17] *A Plan of the English Commerce*, xii; *Atlas Maritimus & Commercialis, or a General View of the World* . . . (London: 1728); John Robert Moore, *Daniel Defoe, Citizen of the Modern World* (Chicago: University of Chicago Press, 1958), pp. 311–312.

made clear, a settlement in Darien would lead to a direct route to the South Sea or Pacific Ocean.

An Edinburgh writer, publishing in 1699 after the expedition had sailed, put the case to the English: together they could penetrate the Spanish Empire, advance into the Pacific and secure control of the seas. For the English this would mean a decisive advantage for their East India Company over its French and Dutch competitors. More immediately, it would mean a wider market for English goods in Scotland and Scottish-sponsored colonies. For the Scots it would mean the sure confidence that aid from the stronger and wealthier country to the south would bring them. The two countries had the same king, but for practical purposes he was an English monarch, not a Scottish, residing in Westminster, not in Edinburgh. An English failure to rise to the bait could well force Scotland into the arms of France, where it had been in the days of Queen Elizabeth.[18]

These arguments found their mark south of the border. English and Scottish businessmen were already mixed up together and committed to the "Protestant interest" in enmity to the Catholic world on the Continent. Daniel Defoe was an outstanding representative of this interest: to his way of thinking union with Scotland was a necessary first step in the coming struggle with France for world empire. So, when in 1706 the proposed Union, with its corollary of a single British Parliament in place of two separate parliaments, became an issue in practical politics, Defoe was an ideal agent for the English government. He knew Scotland probably better than any other Englishman, and he proved indispensable in making the final arrangements leading to the Act of Union in 1707.[19]

Meanwhile, writers had begun to draw attention to the overseas Colonies and their potential for empire. A few of these authors were native-born Americans, while all the rest could boast of extensive experience in America. An anonymous writer who had fought in the Indian wars of New England published in 1692 a comprehensive vol-

---

[18] A Defence of the Scots Settlement at Darien . . . and arguments to prove that it is the interest of England to join with the Scots . . . (Edinburgh: 1699).
[19] John Robert Moore, Daniel Defoe, Citizen of the Modern World (Chicago: University of Chicago Press, 1958), pp. 176–196.

ume entitled *The English Empire in America*. The book included all the colonies from Newfoundland to Jamaica, giving a full description of each colony, its history and economy, and leaving the reader with an impression of the possibility of unlimited expansion in the years to come. Two little books, one written from Boston, the other from New York, described the capture of Acadia and the raid on Quebec which Sir William Phips had staged from Boston in 1690. French interest in Canada, these writers agreed, was not to be feared; the "honester side," meaning the English, had several advantages when the time came for the next attempt.[20]

But most influential was a two-volume work published in London in 1698 by Father Louis Hennepin, a Franciscan who had lived for eleven years in America. Hennepin had gone originally to Quebec. From there he had travelled inland with La Salle and then down the Mississippi to its mouth. Whether justly or not, he felt that he, rather than La Salle, had found the great river; and, aggrieved by the treatment he received upon his return to France, he exiled himself to Utrecht in the Netherlands, where he wrote his book in English and dedicated it to King William III. Writing of his journey through 4,000 miles of wilderness and including in his book a number of fine maps and illustrations, Hennepin glowed with pleasure at the country he had seen. It was, he said, larger than Europe, and "nothing is there wanting to lay the foundation of one of the Greatest Empires in the world." [21] Defoe, who centered his thoughts on the West Indies, acknowledged his debt to Hennepin for making known the importance of the great river system of North America; and Benjamin Franklin, not slow in catching the vision of empire, got his first impressions of the great valley from Hennepin's book.

Two other French works were put out at this time in translation by London publishers. Baron Lahontan, a former governor of the French colony in Newfoundland who had exiled himself to England, wrote two volumes containing twenty-three maps and cuts, on the

---

[20] *An Account of the Late Action of the New Englanders* . . . (London: 1691); *A Journal of the Late Actions of the French at Canada* . . . (London: 1693).
[21] *A New Discovery of a Vast Country in America* . . . Father Louis Hennepin, 2 vols. (London: 1698).

French possessions in North America. Lahontan was grateful to the English for sheltering him. He was enjoying, he said, "a sort of liberty that is not met with elsewhere. . . . Of all the countries inhabited by civilis'd people, this alone affords the greatest perfection of liberty." Another French writer, the Sieur Raveneau de Lussan, in a book on the buccaneers that went through two editions, diverted attention to the South Seas. Then a native Virginian, Robert Beverley, found a London publisher for his impressive book on *The History and Present State of Virginia*. Beverley dedicated his book to Robert Harley, the leading Whig politician and patron of Defoe, crediting Harley with an appreciation of the great value that Virginia held for England. And in a sense Beverley started a revival of interest in "the learned and valiant Sir Walter Raleigh," whose "incomparable book, *The History of the World*," had been written just a century earlier while Raleigh was a prisoner in the Tower.[22]

Raleigh's name conjured up memories. Defoe wrote a short biography of the Elizabethan (1719), and then in 1740 William Oldys published a lengthy biography which remained standard for many years. The British Empire was Raleigh's great idea. The French in North America were intruders, their colonies in Acadia and on the St. Lawrence were fit objects for attack and annihilation whenever the opportunity arose. In the English mind this idea was a fixation, and the Colonists in America were the first to try putting it into operation.

Directing attention especially to the American Colonies and encouraging English people to emigrate to them, was a comprehensive and authoritative two-volume work written by John Oldmixon and published in 1712. Oldmixon had the help of Herman Moll, a geographer who made the maps for the book, and subsequently a handsome edition was put out in the German language. Oldmixon wrote from his own experience and intensive reading: he travelled the Atlantic coast from Acadia to South Carolina, corresponded with other writers who either lived in their respective Colonies or at least were person-

---

22 Robert Beverley, *The History and Present State of Virginia . . . By a native and inhabitant of the place* (London: 1705).

ally familiar with them, and before publishing he showed his chapters to his various correspondents. Like Defoe, Oldmixon was a staunch supporter of the Union with Scotland, and to the doubters at home who bewailed the drain of population to the Colonies he held out the prospect of new markets for English manufacturers. The Empire was a unity, all the parts of which were important: the Colonies, as they filled with people, would make England prosperous. Besides, asked the author rhetorically, without them how could we break into the Spanish Empire? Jamaica, he added with a backward glance at Cromwell, was the key to the Spanish Main.[23]

All these ideas of an expanding empire in the New World, where there would be no room for the French and Spanish, found fertile soil in the powerful business interests centered in London around the turn of the century and allied with the Whig government of Queen Anne which was fighting the War of the Spanish Succession. By 1710 this war had piled up a national debt of nine million pounds, irking the country squires who bore the main burden of taxation and worrying the conservative financiers of the Bank of England lest the war end in national bankruptcy. Government-sponsored lotteries, with tickets selling as high as £100 apiece, helped pay for the out-of-pocket expenses of the war. Working with Robert Harley, Defoe's old patron, a group of speculators incorporated as the South Sea Company, the biggest of all such schemes. The company would relieve conservative minds of anxiety: it would take over the national debt, giving its stock in exchange. In return it was granted a monopoly of the trade with the South Sea, it being assumed that somehow or other Spain and France would be phased out. The geographer, Herman Moll, published a book describing the coasts, countries, and islands "belonging" to the South Sea Company. Moll was an accomplished cartographer whose maps were to lend authority to a number of books, in addition to Oldmixon's, on the New World. For his own book he drew a fine map in color showing all of South America, the

---

[23] John Oldmixon, *The British Empire in America . . .* , 2 vols. (London: 1708). The German edition was issued in Leipsig in 1744.

islands of the Caribbean or North Sea as it was then called, New Spain, the "island" of California, New Mexico, and Florida. Supposedly all of these were company lands.[24]

In this same year, 1711, Captain Woodes Rogers returned from an arduous, but brilliant round-the-world voyage financed by the merchants of Bristol. Rogers was out almost three years, in the course of which he took much booty from the Spaniards including the capture of the Manila galleon off the coast of California. His book, published in 1712, was a highly readable volume describing the incidents of the voyage including the finding of the castaway, Alexander Selkirk, on the island of San Fernandez off the Chilean coast. Selkirk's real name, it was said, was Selcrag, and he had been on the island for four years and four months. Defoe picked the story up and made it into his *Robinson Crusoe,* first published seven years later. Like Raleigh, Defoe was more interested in Guiana, however, so he located Crusoe's island off the mouth of the Orinoco and had his hero live there twenty-eight years.

According to Woodes Rogers, the French as allies of Spain were rapidly taking over the trade of South America, supplying the goods that the Spaniards did not have and taking hard metal in payment. But, with England superior at sea, Rogers saw no difficulty in getting this business away from France. Fired with enthusiasm for the South Sea Company, Defoe had already written in this vein. France, England's principal enemy and rival, must be ousted from the South Sea and England must push farther into the West Indies and claim California, which belonged to it by virtue of Sir Francis Drake's discovery. The American Colonies would share in these benefits, as would the Royal African Company, through the sale of Negroes. Jamaica was already an entrepôt for the slave trade, where the victims were sold to the Spaniards at 200 pieces of eight per head. No such opportu-

[24] John Carswell, *The South Sea Bubble* (London: Cresset, 1961), pp. 1–59; Virginia Spencer Cowles, *The Great Swindle* (New York: Harper, 1960), pp. 73–99; Lawrence Poston, "Defoe and the Peace Campaign, 1710–1713," *Huntington Library Quarterly,* XXVII (1963), pp. 1–20; Herman Moll, *A View of the Coasts, Countries and Islands within the Limits of the South Sea Company* . . . (London: 1711).

nity had ever before arisen, Defoe insisted. The gains would amply recompense the long, tedious, and expensive fatigues of the war.[25]

The South Sea Company turned into a gigantic postwar swindle, the directors unloading new stock on the gullible public and driving up the price to fantastic heights until the bubble finally burst in 1720. But Defoe's confidence in the future of the British Empire remained unabated. He saw himself in Raleigh's shoes, paying tribute to that "Father of Improvement" and striving to reawaken the war spirit against Spain. When next he wrote on the subject, in 1727, he had familiarized himself with the naval operations of Cromwell in the Caribbean and had mastered the principles of sea power. He knew the sailing times and the routes followed by Spanish vessels: on the outward voyage from Cadiz to the Canaries, where the *flota* broke up some of the galleons bearing away for Cartagena on the Main, others destined for Hispaniola and Vera Cruz; on the return the entire fleet massed at Havana, indisputably the best port in the West Indies, and from thence it moved northward to catch the winds blowing eastward from the coast of the Carolinas. "The superiority by sea is the thing that we lay the whole weight upon," Defoe declared, "and being masters of the sea is that which the sum of affairs depends upon." One English squadron posted off the harbor of Porto Bello would lock up Spanish money "so that tho' it be in their possession, yet it is out of their reach." Another squadron in the Gulf of Florida would intercept the homeward-bound Spanish ships. And, Defoe wrote in all seriousness:

'Tis my stated opinion (speaking without national prejudice) that England is so far from being in danger by a war with Spain, that it would be no loss to us if we never had any peace with them; and I believe we have much more to say for a continued war with Spain than the Spaniards have for a continued war with the Turks and Moors.

---

[25] Daniel Defoe, *A True Account of the Design and Advantages of the South Sea Trade* . . . (London: 1711); *ibid., An Essay on the South Sea Trade* . . . (London: 1712); Captain Woodes Rogers, *A Cruising Voyage round the World* . . . (London: 1712); Captain Edward Cooke, *A Voyage to the South Sea* . . . , 2 vols. (London: 1712); and John Robert Moore, *Daniel Defoe, Citizen of the Modern World* (Chicago: Chicago University Press, 1958), pp. 213–214.

And then, perhaps with tongue in cheek, he observed:

> Trading nations seek no conquest, aim at no increase of power, or aggrandizing of persons or families. Great Britain is rich and strong, and opulent enough in her own wealth, power, and commerce. She seeks no more than a peaceable possessing her just rights, and preserving to her people the free extending their commerce, that they may trade in peace with all the world, and all the world with them.

The next year, 1728, Defoe published a new book which he called *A Plan of the English Commerce*, an eloquent plea against passing up the opportunities knocking at England's door. He asked:[26]

> As for new Colonies and conquests, how do we seem entirely to give over, even the thoughts of them, tho' the scene is so large, tho' the variety is so great, and the advantages so many? On the contrary, we seem to forget the glorious improvements of our ancestors, such as the great Drake, . . . and above all, the yet greater Sir Walter Raleigh, upon the foot of whose genius all the English discoveries were made, and all the colonies and plantations, which now form what they call the English Empire in America were settled and established.

During this same year there appeared the large and very impressive *Atlas Maritimus et Commercialis, or a General View of the World,* for which Defoe was reputed to have written the preface. The *Atlas Maritimus* was a triumph of cartography, its maps being drawn according to a new projection advocated by the astronomer Edmund Halley; and in addition it was encyclopedic in the information it gave of the geography, the history and the trade of Great Britain, of the countries of Western Europe, of the coast of Guinea and the organization of the slave trade, and especially of America from Greenland to Cape Horn and up the west coast as far as California. America, declared the *Atlas,* is "a prodigy of wealth, immeasurable in its quantity, inexpressible in its value." [27]

---

[26] Daniel Defoe, *An Historical Account of the Voyages and Adventures of Sir Walter Raleigh* . . . (London: 1719); *ibid., The Evident Advantages to Great Britain* . . . *from the Approaching War* . . . (London: 1727). *A Plan of the English Commerce* is to be found in the Shakespeare Head Edition of *Defoe's Selected Writings,* 14 vols. (Oxford: Blackwell's, 1927), XIII.

[27] *Atlas Maritimus* . . . , *ibid.,* pp. 99 ff., where Defoe also picturesquely characterizes America as "a chain'd slave to Europe."

Meanwhile, more French books, appearing in translation, familiarized English readers with the Mississippi valley. Travel books, a Paris bookseller reminded his patrons in 1714, were in great demand. La Salle's journey down the river was described in a book published in London in that year, a second edition following only five years later. Both editions included fine, large maps of the valley and of the Caribbean area. An even more ambitious work was a 327-page volume, with maps and charts, narrating a voyage to the South Sea and along the coasts of Chile and Peru. The author, an engineer to the king of France, disguised himself as a trader, his object being to make hydrographic observations and to draw exact plans of the ports and fortresses under Spanish control. Edmund Halley wrote a postscript for the English edition of this book.[28]

By this time the speculative craze, more heated if possible than that in England, had seized hold of the French, and was mixed up with colonization. The Scotsman, John Law, who had learned the gambler's art in Bath, England, came to Paris to tell the French how they might pay off their war debt with paper money and become rich in the doing. Law took over the derelict Mississippi Company, amalgamated it with the Banque Générale, and bought the national debt with shares of the company. Like the South Sea directors in London, he kept pyramiding the stock, promising high returns from the supposed earnings of the company in America, and exciting French people into selling their lands in order to acquire shares in the company. Actually, the Mississippi Company did engage in some colonizing activity in Louisiana. New Orleans was founded under its auspices in 1717.

A disillusioned Scotsman, who said he had been employed as a clerk in Law's Paris *Comptoir,* wrote the story of the "Great Mr. Law" and of the collapse that occurred in Paris in 1720. Law's machinations, charged this author, brought greater calamities in two years than twenty-six years of war had accomplished previously, and the

---

[28] *A Journal of the Last Voyage perform'd by Monsr. de la Salle . . . with an exact map of that vast country . . .* (London: 1714); *The Travels of Several Learned Missionaries of the Society of Jesus . . .* (London: 1714); M. Frezier, Engineer, *A Voyage to the South-Sea . . .* (London: 1717) a report to the King; *Mr. Joutel's Journal of his Voyage to Mexico . . . ,* 2nd ed. (London: 1719).

London publisher of the book sought to comfort English victims of the South Sea Bubble with the remark that the French and Dutch had been worse fools than they. This protest literature, of which *Cato's Letters*, we recall, was a leading example, shaped an attitude of bitterness. The stockjobber henceforth played the villain's rôle, such as "Wall Street" was to play repeatedly in later American history whenever hard times descended upon the nation.[29]

Internal boom and collapse, however, made only a temporary impression on the English mind, at least that part of it which was predisposed in favor of imperial growth. Defoe, we recall, was not at all daunted by the momentary set-back; and in 1725 a London publisher found it worthwhile to bring out in translation a very readable Spanish work in six volumes written by the historiographer to his Catholic Majesty, giving the history, geography, and social structure of all the Spanish colonies in America.[30]

IV

Meanwhile, Colonial Americans were able, through London publishers, to get their ideas before the English public. John Lawson, surveyor-general of North Carolina, published two books in 1709 and 1714, respectively. With eight years of experience, Lawson determined to impress the English with the value of his province, and he complained vigorously of the systematic way in which the French were going about their task of exploring the wilderness and building an influence over the Indians. In 1721, barely a year after the Bubble, the Board of Trade responding to various pressures from the Colonies, especially from Pennsylvania and New York interests, issued a far-reaching report favoring a general advance into the Mississippi. By this report the British government rejected proposals emanating from Paris since the Peace of Utrecht, that the two powers agree to a

---

[29] John Carswell, *The South Sea Bubble* (London: Cresset, 1961), pp. 77–101; Virginia Spencer Cowles, *The Great Swindle* (New York: Harper, 1960), pp. 100–116; *The Memoirs, Life and Character of the Great Mr. Law . . .* written by a Scots Gentleman (London: 1721).

[30] *The General History of the Vast Continent and Islands of America . . . ,* Antonio de Herrara, historiographer to His Catholic Majesty . . . , 6 vols. (London: 1725).

permanent boundary along the watershed of the Alleghenies. As the French saw it, this watershed formed a *natural* boundary, wherein the wilderness would remain a buffer between the British coastal empire and the French interior which nature had rendered tributary to the St. Lawrence.[31]

The Board of Trade's report, however, was much too mild to suit the thinking of Daniel Coxe of Carolina, who put his views forcefully before the English public the following year. Coxe had fourteen years of experience in America, and he identified himself as the son of the proprietor of Carolina, the man he claimed had really discovered the Mississippi. The French had no business in that country, he insisted, and he was indignant that the frontiers of the English Colonies lay naked and open to attack for nearly two thousand miles. To meet this danger the Colonies should form a coalition or union under a supreme governor and a general council made up of two deputies elected annually from each colony.

Fearful of being hemmed in from the rear, Coxe wanted immediate action from Britain. The French should be required to abandon their positions on the Mississippi and the Gulf of Mexico, and since they were still weak, now was the time to expel them. Prudence and policy, wrote Coxe, should prompt us to keep a balance in America as well as in Europe. Let the French stay north of the St. Lawrence: they had been checked in Europe, they should be checked in America. Or if Britain would not go it alone, let her make common cause with Spain. The Spanish too, Coxe believed, had good reason for checking French encroachment.

Here Coxe voiced a sentiment that was to have a place in the American mind for approximately a century: of the two Bourbon powers, Spain was the weaker, and was therefore to be preferred as a neighbor. As he put it:

Nothing seems more proper and reasonable than for that great river [the Mississippi] to be the settl'd and acknowledged boundary and partition between the territories of Spain and Great Brit-

---

[31] John Lawson, *A New Voyage to Carolina* . . . (London: 1709); *ibid., The History of Carolina* . . . (London: 1714); and on the Board of Trade's Report see R. W. Van Alstyne, *The Rising American Empire* (New York: Oxford University Press, 1960), pp. 13–16.

ain on the northern continent of America, Nature seeming to have form'd it almost purposely for that end, as will be evident to those who shall give themselves the trouble of viewing the annexed map. And at the same time they'll perceive how the French have worm'd themselves into a settlement between the English and Spanish plantations on pretence of a vacancy; and with an assurance scarce to be parallel'd, have set bounds to the dominions of both.

And if the French were not stopped — if they engrossed the Indian trade and stunted the English Colonies, Britain itself would suffer: it would eventually lose its markets in America; shipping and manufacturing would shrink accordingly; land values would fall; Britain would recede to the level of a second-rate power. This thought began to make a dent on the English mind: Britain's own fortunes were tied to America's. Coxe wound up with an absorbing description of America, drawing attention to the Mississippi and the Great Lakes and imaginatively suggesting a possible future connection between America and China.[32]

So long as the French kept to the country north of the Great Lakes these Southern writers appeared satisfied, but Northern interests let it be known they could be appeased only if France were expelled from the whole continent. The Scotsman, Samuel Vetch, who had been on the over-ambitious expedition against Darien in 1699, found a more effective outlet for his energies in New York and New England. With the Union between England and Scotland now established, and with the leading families of New York and Massachusetts at his back, Vetch was in a strong position to advance his ideas with the Board of Trade in London. This he did in 1708 in a closely reasoned paper on "Canada Surveyed." Vetch stated his thesis as:

The French Dominions upon the Continent of America, briefly considered in their situation, strength, trade and numbers, more particularly how vastly prejudicial they are to the British interest, and a method proposed of easily removing them.

He then returned to Boston from where, during the next three years, he led in two systematic attempts to conquer Canada. Neither of these invasions, however, succeeded.

---

[32] Daniel Coxe, *A Description of the English Province of Carolina* . . . (London: 1722).

Meanwhile, Vetch's friend and contemporary, Jeremiah Dummer, a native of Boston who had made his home in London, undertook to put the case to the British public. Like Vetch and Sir William Phips who had made the previous attempt of 1690 on Canada, Dummer argued that the cause of empire hinged on getting the St. Lawrence. With it in British hands, he declared, the future was assured:[33]

> All persons that have the least knowledge of the affairs of America need not be inform'd of the necessity there is for dislodging the French at Canada, to secure our commerce and colonies on the Northern Continent, where the English in New England and New York are daily encroach'd upon by the French and Frenchify'd Indians; and being only in possession of a slip of land on the coast, are in danger of being driven out of the Country, if the French power encreases, which it has continu'd to do these hundred years; and the encouragement the French Government gives their plantations, shews that there's little likelihood of our gaining the ground we have lost, if we can preserve what remains.

Dummer found it hard to understand why the several expeditions, especially the last one in 1711 which was well manned and equipped, should have failed. With Canada would go the beaver trade and, above all, the fisheries which, he roundly asserted, were worth more than the mines of Mexico or even of Peru. Through them Britain would get a stranglehold on the markets of Spain; and without a share in the fisheries France would see its sea-going commerce disappearing. Eighteenth-century politicians and writers held the Newfoundland fisheries of supreme importance: not only were they the source of great wealth, but they were "the nursery of seamen," a phrase repeated so often as to become a stereotype. Without this "nursery" a seagoing, commercial nation could not compete.

Meanwhile, the long war of the Spanish Succession came to an end in 1713 in a series of treaties signed at Utrecht; and New England was only partially appeased by the annexation of Acadia, which the

---

[33] Jeremiah Dummer, *A Letter to a Friend . . . on the Late Expedition to Canada . . .* (London: 1712), p. 7; G. M. Waller, *Samuel Vetch, Colonial Enterpriser* (Chapel Hill: University of North Carolina Press, 1960), pp. 94–206, 219–234; Richard W. Van Alstyne, *Empire and Independence. The International History of the American Revolution* (New York: John Wiley & Sons, 1965), pp. 2–3.

British incorporated as the Colony of Nova Scotia, with Vetch as its first governor. Cape Breton Isle to the north remained in French hands, however, and insured continued French control of the St. Lawrence, especially after the erection of the stone fortress of Louisbourg. This and the permission granted the Acadians to keep their homes, instead of being forced into exile as Vetch for one proposed, were thorns in the flesh of the anti-Catholic Puritans of Boston. The Reverend Daniel Neal reflected their resentment in a two-volume *History of New England*, published in London in 1720, the year of the Bubble. Neal himself never visited America, but he got his information and his ideas, as he acknowledges in his preface, from New England clergymen, especially from Cotton Mather; and his book reads as though he were himself a resident of Boston. Cape Breton, he charges, was "basely" relinquished to the French, though it was a place of the greatest importance to our English settlements. Neal's volumes made such an impression in New England that they earned him an honorary degree from Harvard.[34]

These views were underscored by a pious New England writer and disciple of Cotton Mather. His name was Samuel Penhallow, and his book, *The History of the Wars of New England with the Eastern Indians,* was published in Boston in 1726. Indians and French were now firmly linked together in the New England mind. New England was like Israel in the land of Canaan, surrounded by a barbarous foe; and since the French put weapons in the Indians' hands and spurred them on to massacre the English, they were the real enemy. Disappointed with the previous failures to subjugate Canada and adopting a tone of reproach toward England for not lending a strong enough hand, Penhallow called for another invasion. In Canada itself he saw little value, but its reduction would benefit the whole British Empire. Referring to "the ingenious Mr. Dummer," Penhallow agreed that:

the consequence would be very valuable; for as it [Canada] extends above one thousand leagues towards the Mississippi, it would require a vast consumption yearly of the English manu-

---

[34] Daniel Neal, *The History of New England . . . to the Year 1700,* 2 vols. (London: 1720). A posthumous edition in 1747 was greatly expanded.

factury to support it; there being so great a number of several nations that live behind, which bring down vast quantities of furs of all sorts, as amount to an incredible sum. But Her Majesty's royal aim . . . was not so immediately to advance a trade, as the security and peace of her good subjects in North America; being thoroughly apprised that so long as the French inhabit there, so long the English would be in hazard.

In New York opinion was less aggressive, though Governor Burnet built Fort Oswego on Lake Ontario in 1726 as a check upon the French. The Iroquois being traditional friends of the English, the problem was to keep them from drifting into the hands of the dreaded enemy to the north. This was different from the view of Puritan New England with its unbroken record of border warfare. But there was nervousness lest the Indians be lured away and then, as the versatile Cadwallader Colden put it, the consequences would be dreadful. Colden was an alert middle-aged Scotsman, with a very wide and distinguished circle of friends both in the Colonies and in England; he was an influence in the life of the young Benjamin Franklin, with whom he corresponded for many years thereafter; and while not so ready as the New Englanders to make war, he was committed to the program of inland expansion destined by its very nature to drive the Indians and the French closer together.[35]

Another big war starting against Spain in the Caribbean in 1739 provided a fresh tonic for expansion-minded writers. William Oldys published his timely biography of Sir Walter Raleigh, recalling the Elizabethan's exploits at great length; and other British writers, denying that Spain had any right to be in the New World at all, took up the problem of capturing the key Spanish ports in the West Indies — Porto Bello, Cartagena, Havana.[36] Maps and plans of these harbors appeared in London bookstores in 1740, and it was expected that they would be captured.

---

[35] Samuel Penhallow, *The History of the Wars of New England* . . . (Boston: 1726), pp. 67–68; C. Colden, *The History of the Five Indian Nations* . . . (Philadelphia: 1727); and for Colden's extensive correspondence and influence on other important men of the time see his *Papers*, 7 vols., in *Collections of the New York Historical Society*.

[36] In addition to Oldys' biography, a work of 576 pages, London publishers issued at least five other books on this subject in 1740–1741.

A fourth edition of a popular work, *The History of the Buccaneers of America,* in two volumes, stimulated interest in plundering the Spaniards. The editor, Alexander O. Esquemeling, was a Dutchman who had once sailed with the French; and the book was a collection of stories, originally written in different languages, putting the exploits of the freebooters in an attractive light and describing the countless opportunities for taking prizes. The Welshman, Sir Henry Morgan, had once sacked Porto Bello and burned the city of Panama, and the British exceeded the other nationalities in numbers of free-booters. Piracy, the editor pointed out, flourished best in the West Indies: the many uninhabited islands with good harbors and a natural supply of fresh water and provisions insured the pirates of a refuge from troublesome men-o'-war; and every year large sums were remitted to England, the fruit of their operations. From the West Indies pirate expeditions roved all over the South Atlantic and even into the Indian Ocean. Some of the older pirates retired to live the good life on the island of Madagascar, but most of them, the author added as an afterthought, found themselves suddenly in the next world.

Admiral Edward Vernon captured Porto Bello in 1740, but Vernon was cool to the idea of conquest on the mainland. As a naval officer, he maintained that Britain could more easily achieve ascendancy by stationing men-o'-war to control the passageways into the Caribbean. Nevertheless, an offensive under his command was launched from England the following year, Cartagena being its objective. An expeditionary force of 3600 men from Philadelphia, promoted enthusiastically by Benjamin Franklin and the governor of Pennsylvania, joined in this campaign. The attempt failed, however, and Vernon was made the scapegoat. But perhaps involuntarily writers on the economics of the Caribbean came to his support. Thus the merchant, John Campbell, after carefully studying the Spanish authorities, depicted Spain as a sieve. Though in possession of the best parts of America, the Spanish were impoverishing themselves on military defense while the other nations took over their commerce. Goods and manufactures sold in the Spanish Colonies came almost entirely from these other nations, and had to be paid for in bullion. Except for the commissions earned by Spanish merchants, the profits were all drained away. Moreover, the small islands of the Dutch, the Danes, the French, and the British in the West Indies were all valuable as entrepôts for smuggled goods.[37]

William Perrin, much in the style of Defoe, argued that the future lay in keeping ahead in trade and navigation, and in the progress the French were making in this respect they were the real source of danger. Perrin voiced an idea that was to be repeated often: namely, that France harbored a grand design of universal monarchy, and might achieve it by obtaining superiority in overseas commerce. The French had one-third of the Spanish colonial trade, Perrin asserted, and through it they would render Spain politically subordinate. He noted they had captured the advantage in the British sugar trade by under-selling the British West Indian planter in the American market. In another ten years they would be first in the all-important woollen trade, and Britain would become subject to France for its supply of bullion. Moreover, Perrin anticipated that the French would try to sow dissension between Britain and its American Colonies. The Colonies were Britain's principal source of strength, but if they were allowed to drift into French hands, they might eventually declare their independence.[38]

V

Meanwhile, with France again in the war and superseding Spain as the main enemy, New England thrilled to the news of a decisive victory to the north. Louisbourg, the "dagger" which the French had pointed at them from Cape Breton Isle for a quarter of a century, surrendered after a forty-nine-day siege to a combined land force from Boston and a British task force from the West Indies. This fortress being one of the greatest military marvels of its time, its capitulation was the more surprising. Governor William Shirley was

---

[37] John Campbell, *A Concise History of the Spanish America . . . collected chiefly from Spanish writers* (London: 1741). *Also* Richard Pares, *War and Trade in the West Indies, 1739–1763,* (New York: Barnes & Noble, 1963); R. W. Van Alstyne, *The Rising American Empire* (New York: Oxford University Press, 1960), pp. 147–148.

[38] William Perrin, *The Present State of the British and French Sugar Colonies, and our own Northern Colonies considered . . .* (London: 1740).

the moving spirit behind this offensive, and Shirley thought not merely of the wounds the dagger might inflict in its stabs at New England shipping, but also of the brilliant prospect for conquest that the fall of the fortress would open up.

The Reverend Thomas Prince of Boston's South Church was among the first to catch the new spirit in a sermon dedicated to Shirley on July 18, 1745, a bare month after the victory. After 17 pages of giving thanks to God, Prince got down to the more mundane business of discussing the economic and strategic value of Cape Breton. Adopting the traditional attitude that the French were intruders on the continent, and that the Tory ministry had committed a "base" act in giving the island back to them in 1713, Prince enumerated Cape Breton's assets: it had the best pit coal in North America; a trade had sprung up between it and the French West Indies; it was squarely in the center of the fishery; it commanded the entrance to the bay and river of Canada; and it lay near the track of all the trade between Europe and the British mainland Colonies. The clergyman then drew a fanciful picture of the "thousands of people" he said were swarming into the island from the French homeland, and he cautioned:

> It seems highly probable that if the peace continued much longer, there would be in a few years' time such a multitude of French inhabitants, as with the growing numbers in the bordering continent of Nova Scotia and Canada, with the addition of the Indian nations, would exceedingly vex and waste, yea, endanger the conquest of our English Colonies.

Nor was the significance of the victory lost upon the English. *The Gentleman's Magazine,* most popular of the London periodicals, gave a full account in its July issue and published a hymn on the subject, the second stanza of which runs as follows:

> Beyond the wide Atlantick Sea
> She rises first to crown our toils;
> Thither to wealth she points the way,
> And bids us thrive on Gallic spoils.

And John Trenchard, the author of *Cato's Letters,* took the opportunity to repeat his former strictures on the vice of Old England and contrast it with the virtue of the New England people. "Justice and virtue," he declared, "seem to have taken their residence" among the latter whose sagacity and bravery reminded him "of the ancient Romans leaving the plow for the field of battle, and retiring after the conquest to the plow again." [39]

Louisbourg and Cape Breton remained much in the public eye on both sides of the Atlantic for the duration of the war. Oftentimes the Boston weekly newspapers republished articles previously printed in the London press. The rising of the Scottish clans under Bonnie Prince Charlie, the last of the Stuart Pretenders who had lived in exile in France, and their bold invasion of England in the hope of seizing the throne from the Protestant king, George II, brought the war home to the English. Charles Edward Stuart was "the Popish vagrant"; and Popery, tyranny, massacre, and murder were nouns which had a common meaning to the English mind. A poem on "Liberty" in *The Gentleman's Magazine* for November 1745 catches the spirit of the times:

> Arm, Britons, arm, your country now demands
> Not empty speeches, but vindictive hands:
> Shall a mad, Highland crew, rebellious race,
> In British hearts fair virtue's lines efface?
> Shall Popish tyranny pollute the throne
> Where sacred liberty so long has shown?
> Forbid it, Heaven, let ev'ry *Briton* cry,
> And ans'ring Heaven forbid it from the sky!
> Is there a wretch, by freedom bless'd, so vile
> To wish that freedom banish'd from this isle?
> On him may Pop'ry, rags and bondage wait,
> Curs'd in his wish with all the plagues of fate
> But be the men whom liberty inspires,
> Whose patriot souls paternal ardour fires,

---

[39] Thomas Prince, *Extraordinary Events the doings of God . . .* (Boston: 1745). Trenchard's opinion appeared first in *The Gentleman's Magazine* and was copied in the Boston *Weekly News Letter*, Nov. 14, 1745. For a graphic description of the siege of Louisbourg, written by Roger Wolcott, a participant, see *Collections of the Connecticut Historical Society, I*, pp. 131–160.

> Who'd fight, like William, in their country's cause,
> And die all gard'ners to defend her laws:
> Be these with freedom, peace and plenty crown'd,
> Blest in this age, and to the last renowned.

To minds in both Old and New England France was "a restless and fatal enemy" led by "the popish, cruel, ambitious . . . house of Bourbon." Exclaimed the *Boston Evening Post:* "What murders she commits on her quiet neighbours as well in peace as in war." And from Pennsylvania came a demand that the French be pushed west of the Mississippi. "Nothing but a wide river, or inaccessible mountain, are sufficient to separate us from such Monsters in nature . . ." it was asserted. But to achieve all this and bring France and Popery to heel Cape Breton was essential. In its issue for November 20, 1746 the *Boston Weekly News Letter* devoted its entire front page to an article reprinted from the *Westminster Journal* on the subject. The London writer supplied fourteen reasons for keeping the island, what it would do for the British Empire, and how severely it would hurt France and all other Catholic countries. "All the Papists in Christendom," he wrote, "will depend upon us for their fast-day provisions, and must pay us a greater tax, for their superstition, than they pay even to the Pope himself." Coincidentally, in Boston the Rev. Thomas Prince in an anniversary sermon was rounding up similar arguments, reciting the achievements of the French monarchy over the preceding century and a half and demanding its expulsion from the New World.[40]

Two other New England writers followed Prince's lead in 1747 but, because their books were published in London and intended for English readers, they take on special significance. One of these authors disguised himself behind the pseudonym Massachusettensis; the other was William Bollan, Governor Shirley's son-in-law and the Colony's agent in Britain. A book by a French Jesuit, Pierre de Charlevoix, recounting his experiences in the interior of North America, was

---

[40] Prince, Charles Chauncy and other Boston ministers preached annual Thanksgiving sermons during the remaining years of the war in commemoration of the fall of Louisbourg. Both the *News Letter* and the *Boston Evening Post* gave the subject constant attention, borrowing news items, poems and editorial articles from the London press.

published in translation in London the same year. Bollan, in particular, drew on Charlevoix as well as other French writers. Both Massachusettensis and Bollan wanted Canada and the Mississippi hinterland for the British Empire; both described at great length the forts built by the French and the alliances and intrigues with the Indians; both stressed the machinations of the priests, who told the Indians that the Savior of the World had been a Frenchman murdered by the English; and both suggested that racial intermixing between French and natives would ultimately be detrimental to the English Colonies. Both were sure that the French intended "in proper time to push us all into the ocean."

But the point which these writers were most anxious to drive home was the importance of keeping Cape Breton. The island held the key to the St. Lawrence and likewise the key to the North Atlantic. Obviously Bollan and Massachusettensis bent their efforts toward winning over the English. In the theory of sea power French thinking was more advanced than British. Louis XIV's keen-minded minister, Jean-Baptiste Colbert, almost a century earlier had perceived the value of Cape Breton when tied to the French home base at Brest. Firmly secured by a supporting fleet, it would give France command of the sea. But Colbert's successors in the eighteenth century, especially Cardinal Fleury who served Louis XV after the Peace of Utrecht, had been too cautious: Fleury had laid out large sums in fortifying Cape Breton but, not wishing to provoke another grand alliance against France, he had been laggard in building a fleet. In exploiting the fisheries, however, the French had been ahead of the English. Fishing was a valuable segment of the French economy, and it utilized the services of over 25,000 young fishermen who, at the end of their period of indenture, qualified for employment in the Navy. In a word, France possessed all the factors necessary for command of the seas except a fleet, and that could still be built.

But in English hands Cape Breton would bring unity and strength to the Empire. The British Colonies now reached from the northern extremity of Newfoundland to the sugar islands; their value was measurable not solely in terms of economics, but by the influence and position they gave to Great Britain. All the parts of the Empire were interdependent; and if the Colonies were lost, bluntly declared

Massachusettensis, Britain would lose its own independence too. This was an idea capable of exerting powerful influence on the English mind. But there were skeptics who doubted the good faith of New England. The more the latter flourished, the more it would be inclined to separate from the mother country. William Bollan regarded this view as widely held, and so he went out of his way to answer it. Supposing New England did feel so disposed, he queried, it would have to turn to some other power for help. It would never be strong enough to stand alone. France was the one alternative, but how could a people who so detested Popery, slavery and arbitrary power make such a choice? In a word, it was unthinkable. On the other hand, to annex Cape Breton would lead to unlimited opportunities. Through the fisheries Britain would tap the treasure of France and Spain, and its king "would soon become the greatest prince in Europe, and his people have the most extensive and enriching trade." [41]

In 1749, the year after the war, a book of exceptional importance made its appearance in Boston. The author was William Douglass, and he entitled his book *A Summary, historical and political, of the first Planting, Progressive Improvements, and Present State of the British Settlements in North America.* Parts of the book had already been published — in the *Boston Weekly News-Letter,* in Franklin's *Pennsylvania Gazette,* and elsewhere. A second volume was made available four years later, and then came two London editions in 1755 and 1760 respectively. Douglass was a Scottish physician who had lived for thirty years in America, and he addressed himself to the people of Europe who, he considered, had only vague notions of America.

He was refreshingly candid on his personal background and preferences, rejecting orthodox Christianity and treating the Bible as "a most valuable collection of moral precepts, sometimes delivered in plain literal sentences, but generally by way of mystery, fable, allegory, allusion, and the like." His enemies attacked him for advancing "the

---

[41] Massachusettensis (author unknown), *The Importance of Cape Breton considered . . .* (London: 1746); William Bollan, *The Importance and Advantage of Cape Breton truly stated . . .* (London: 1746).

most complete and undisguis'd system of atheism . . . ever dar'd to be publish'd in a Christian country." Philosophically he was close to Bolingbroke: he dissociated himself from any political party, though saying he was a "genuine Whig" — one who was for keeping a balance of power between the several branches of government, in contrast to a republican who was for abolishing the prerogatives of the king and giving unlimited power to the people through their representatives in the legislature. Towards Catholics, however, he shared to the full the prejudices of Puritan Boston and characterized the Church as pernicious and subversive.[42]

Like Neal and Oldmixon, to whom he paid his respects, Douglass looked back in anger to that "infamous" treaty of Utrecht, and denounced the "abandoned, wicked ministry" which had given the French more even than they had expected. "The French," he observed, "are the common nuisance and disturbers of Europe; and will in a short time become the same in America, if not mutilated at home, and in America fenced off from us by ditches and walls, that is, by great rivers and impracticable mountains." France, that is to say, had to be checked, even dismembered, both in Europe and America, if there was to be peace. And like the clergyman, Thomas Prince, Douglass ignored the facts of immigration by insisting that the French were "more capable of swarming into their colonies than we are." Of course, he wanted Canada and Cape Breton incorporated in the British Empire; and he reiterated the sentiment now common in New England that the French population of Nova Scotia was undesirable and in some way had to be got rid of. The idea of deporting these people en masse had already been bruited, though it was puzzling to know where to send them. Both Douglass and Governor Shirley showed they were giving thought to the matter.[43] Douglass also took pains to assure his readers they need have no fear

---

[42] Two whole issues of the Boston News Letter, June 10 and 16, 1748, were given over to attacks on Douglass.

[43] Correspondence of William Shirley . . . , Charles Henry Lincoln (ed.), 2 vols. (New York: Macmillan, 1912), I, pp. 273–280, 404–405 (Hereafter Shirley Correspondence). William Douglass, M. D., A Summary, historical and political, . . . and Present State of the British Settlements in North America, 2 vols. (Boston: 1749), I, pp. 201–210, II, pp. 112 ff.

that the American Colonies would want to declare their independence.

VI

May heav'n on Britain long propitious smile,
And lasting tenure grant of Breton's isle.

The couplet, which first appeared in *The Gentleman's Magazine* for December 1746 and then was copied in the *Boston News-Letter*, epitomizes nicely the wartime appraisal of Cape Breton. For a short time the island enjoyed parity with Gibraltar, which the British had taken from Spain in 1704. But early in 1748 rumors of the approaching peace appeared in print: Cape Breton was to be exchanged for Madras in India, which the French had captured, and France was to renounce for good the support Versailles had for so many years given the exiled Stuarts and their Jacobite followers. This last was a concession of great importance to the English: it strengthened the Protestant interest, which was the cornerstone of the Revolution of 1688, and lessened the danger of future internal insurrections of which the Jacobite uprising of 1745 had been an eloquent reminder. These terms became common knowledge — they were repeated several times in both the London and Boston papers — and they were incorporated in the peace treaty signed at Aix-la-Chapelle in October 1748.[44]

Louisbourg, the one spectacular military event of this war, became at some later time — perhaps a hundred years or more after the event — a symbol in American historical folklore. Historical myths merit the closest examination: they shape, or rather misshape attitudes and accordingly can have long-range consequences. Though difficult to trace, and sometimes inexplicable, the historical myth is nevertheless a very common psychological phenomenon. The Louisbourg myth is a prime example: it is supposed to demonstrate the cold-blooded indifference of Britain to its American Colonies, a repudiation, even

---

[44] *News Letter,* Feb. 4, March 10, June 2, Aug. 25, Sept. 15, 1748; *Evening Post,* Aug. 1, Sept. 12, 26, Dec. 26, 1748.

an insult to the pride of New England in its military achievement. In other words, the decision to hand back the fortress to France is alleged to have so outraged feeling in America, especially in New England, that it planted the seed for the Revolution that broke out a quarter of a century later.

During the ten months when the pending cession was public knowledge, however, it was accepted virtually *without a murmur.* Such open indignation as was expressed actually originated in London, only to be reprinted in the Boston press. In spite of the thrill of victory in 1745, the expedition had been regarded in New England with mixed feelings. Shirley had had a hard time persuading the Massachusetts Assembly in the first place to support the enterprise; and *at no time* in 1748 or thereafter did the Assembly express itself on the British decision to return the fortress. Shirley had influential enemies who disliked the monetary inflation which his ambitious schemes entailed, and news received in Boston in November 1748 that Parliament had voted Massachusetts the sum of £183,649 in hard cash as reimbursement was of course welcome. Through an agent in London, Shirley had lobbied for this opportunity; and when in due course the cash arrived on a warship — 217 chests of Spanish dollars and a hundred barrels of copper coin — his opponents compelled the governor to employ it in calling in the depreciated paper currency.[45]

Shirley himself seems to have lost interest in Louisbourg. He shifted his attention to a project for cooperating with New York in capturing Crown Point on Lake Champlain. Crown Point too possessed great strategic value: its capture would open Canada to invasion. But to start on this larger scheme he needed still more British naval assistance. Shirley understood and appreciated the help he had received from Commodore Warren in 1745 — Warren's task force had made the Louisbourg expedition practicable; and Warren was the first to send word to Boston that the garrison holding Louis-

---

[45] *Shirley Correspondence, I,* pp. 401–405, 478–480, 499–504. Benjamin Franklin in 1745 eagerly responded to Shirley's appeal for aid, but registered no protest later against Louisbourg being returned. Leonard W. Labaree (ed.), *The Papers of Benjamin Franklin,* 10 vols. published (New Haven, Conn.: Yale University Press, 1959–1966), *III.* Hereafter *Franklin Papers.*

bourg would be transferred to Chebucto Bay, the splendid harbor to the south on the coast of Nova Scotia.

Warren's intelligence was correct: the British government, prior to the treaty of Aix-la-Chapelle, committed itself to defending Nova Scotia. It did not favor an all-out war for the expulsion of France from North America. In June 1749 a British expedition disembarked in Chebucto Bay to found the new permanent base of Halifax, and this was accepted as a satisfactory substitute for Louisbourg. Shirley and William Pepperrell had meanwhile taken ship for London, where they found a powerful ally in Lord Halifax. What passed between these men is unknown, but soon thereafter New England merchants were awarded contracts for provisioning the garrison at Halifax and Shirley's idea of displacing the Acadian French began to receive an airing. In Boston the new colony got full publicity from the newspapers, which gave it their approval and recognized it for what it was: a complete offset to the French garrison stationed once again on Cape Breton Isle.[46] As a symbol of outraged pride, Louisbourg belongs strictly to the realm of folklore.

VII

Two books published in London reflect the new view. Otis Little, the author of the first one which was republished in Boston, fulsomely praised the New England Colonies, pointed to the advantages of fortifying Nova Scotia in place of Louisbourg, and stressed the need to infiltrate a Protestant population that would swamp the Acadian French. Nova Scotia, as the author described it, would become a valuable adjunct to New England. Little was surveyor-general for the new colony, and the Boston papers came immediately to his support. The *Post* credited him with influencing the British government, and the *News-Letter* devoted its whole front page to a description of the country which it borrowed from the *London Magazine*.[47]

---

[46] *Shirley Correspondence, I*, pp. 499–504; Boston *Weekly News-Letter*, June 10, 29, July 20, Aug. 17, 31, 1749, Jan. 25, Feb. 1, Mar. 29, 1750; Boston *Evening Post*, June 26, July 10, 1749.

[47] Otis Little, *The State of Trade in the Northern Colonies Considered; with . . . a particular description of Nova Scotia* (London: 1748).

Little was unusually vehement in trying to dispel the notion, apparently now quite general in the United Kingdom, that New England would break away. These people are all Protestants, he told his English readers. They abhor Popery. Were they ten times more populous and wealthy, nothing could induce them to revolt; neither love of liberty, force of oppression, burden of taxes, nor desire to become more powerful could impel them to struggle for independency. To do so they would have to get help from a foreign state. To whom could they apply? "No people in their senses would subject themselves to the French, Spaniards or Dutch," and he added:

> should they aim at absolute Independency, the expense of defending themselves would infinitely exceed any they have yet been subject to, and indeed, they could not subsist without the protection of their Mother Country.

Following close behind Otis Little, Richard Rolt published a four-volume history of the war just terminated. Rolt's principal interest was in the military and naval operations of the war, so he gave a detailed and lengthy account of the Louisbourg expedition. But while lauding the victory and remaining also thoroughly distrustful of the French, Rolt saw no harm in handing back Cape Breton: Halifax was more than an offset and Nova Scotia would be opened to Protestants. The Boston papers took the same line, giving details to show how fast Halifax was growing, advertising maps and plans of the city and harbor, and even pointing out how superior it was to Louisbourg. And already the British goverment had dispatched several thousand Germans to establish the farming colony of Lunenburg to the south of Halifax.[48]

In 1753 William Douglass published his second volume. Douglass was highly pleased with the progress made in Nova Scotia, called Halifax a "uniform elegant town," and expressed indifference to the return of Cape Breton. But he accused the French of fresh encroachments and showed himself unalterably opposed to their remaining

---

[48] Richard Rolt, *An Impartial Representation of the Conduct of the Several Powers of Europe in the Late General War*, 4 vols. (London: 1749–1750), IV, 625.

on the St. Lawrence and so making themselves masters of the inland trade of the continent — "an incredible prejudice to the British nation," as he described it.

Douglass's influential volumes register opinions and attitudes prevailing by this time in both Britain and America. Books and pamphlets continued to flow, invoking still stronger adjectives expressive of anti-French feeling, insisting that only Great Britain possessed a rightful claim to the continent, and reiterating the peril in which both mother country and Colonies were alleged to stand if the French were allowed to remain. Five authors in particular were prominent: the Scotsman, James Houstoun, who in 1753 published a running historical account; the New Yorker, Archibald Kennedy, who published in that city in 1751 and again in 1754; the Bostonian, Dr. William Clarke, who shared his book with Benjamin Franklin in 1755; the retired American merchant, John Payne, in 1756; and the famous cartographer, Dr. John Mitchell, of both Britain and America in 1757.

James Houstoun's book is an autobiography written in part as a diary interspersed with occasional letters. The ill-fated Darien expedition of 1699 caught his fancy when he was a small boy of eight, and after he grew up he spent his life travelling in Asia, Africa, America, and most parts of Europe. His book records his views from the Union of Scotland with England in 1707 to the fall of Louisbourg in 1745. Houstoun viewed the Empire as a whole and saw no serious obstacle to its obtaining ascendancy in both the West Indies and North America. The northern Colonies in America, he recalled, had supported Admiral Vernon in 1740, and Jamaica, "one of the best jewels in the British Crown," had provisioned a numerous army and navy over a period of a year. "There's no nation in the world," he asserted, "so perfidious as the French," and no nation who adore their king as much as they do. The Spanish are different, he went on to say. They "have too exalted opinions of themselves to adore their King." They and the French "are as diametrically opposite to one another in their way of thinking as East is from West: So it must be a very unnatural union between these two nations." [49]

---

[49] *The Works of James Houstoun, M. D., . . .* (London: 1753), pp. 237, 268–369, 356 ff.

A previous writer, manifestly well informed on the island geography of the Caribbean, made essentially the same point. The rivalry between the French and the Spanish in that area had become so intense that an alliance between Spain and Great Britain was now advisable. Since Utrecht, France had so encroached in Santo Domingo and in the Leeward Islands, which formed a chain across the entrance to the Caribbean, that it was in a position to intercept both British and Spanish commerce. Jamaica was now virtually helpless, and against the superior strength of France, Spain was in danger of becoming a vassal state. But an expansion of the British Navy and an understanding with Spain would redress this imbalance.[50]

Both of these writers were attracted to the coming value of Nova Scotia. Jesuits from Canada had infiltrated the province and stirred the Indians to an implacable hatred of the English. Having heard from a correspondent in Louisbourg after the fortress had been captured, Houstoun described the wealth of the fishery on which the whole Papal empire depended, pointed to the enormous advantages accruing to both Old and New England if the British kept a stranglehold on the fishery, and suggested that Canada would be the next object of conquest and bring with it the control of the whole fur trade.

To Archibald Kennedy, a Scotsman by birth but now collector-general of customs and receiver-general in New York, the French were "the disturbers of the peace of mankind," whose national polity was "one continued train of chicane and deceit." And, he proceeded:[51]

> Our case at present is neither more nor less than this, viz., that the French are now drawing a line along the borders of our settlements in every province, from the mouth of St. Lawrence to the mouth of Mississippi, and building forts to secure the most convenient passes on the lakes that form the communication; by which they will effectually cut off all intercourse and traffick between us and the Indians inhabiting the inland coun-

---

[50] A Short View of the Encroachments of France . . . , Anon. (London: 1750). The work is obviously written with knowledge.
[51] Archibald Kennedy, Serious Considerations . . . (New York: 1754); Franklin Papers, IV, 117–121.

tries. . . . One great step, if not the greatest, to this grand Monarch's universal system, is that of being possess'd of this Northern
Continent. . . . The French lay their plans of this kind at a distance, but seldom lose the point in view.

Kennedy thought it very important to keep the Indians pacified and
got Franklin, his junior by twenty years, and Cadwallader Colden,
whose own book on this problem was now in its second edition, to
read his essay in advance of publication and give him their support.
This they both did, Colden memorializing the governor of the province and Franklin writing a letter to Kennedy's printer which the latter
published as an appendix. All three men favored a union of the
Colonies so as, in Franklin's words, "to form a strength that the Indians may depend on for protection, in case of a rupture with the
French"; and Franklin and Kennedy took the opportunity to express
their sentiments against the Germans who had been flooding into
New York and Pennsylvania. These people, they thought, were an
alien element who would do the Empire no good. Kennedy's aver-
sion to them dated back to 1711, when he commanded a company
in Colonel Vetch's army of invasion into Canada. The Germans in
his company showed no enthusiasm.

Franklin was even more outspoken in his dislike. Pennsylvania, he
feared[52]

will in a few years become a German Colony; instead of their
learning our language, we must learn their's, or live as in a
foreign country. Already the English begin to quit particular
neighbourhoods surrounded by Dutch, being made uneasy by
the disagreeableness of dissonant manners; and in time, numbers will probably quit the province for the same reason.
Besides, the Dutch under-live, and are thereby enabled to
under-work and under-sell the English; who are thereby ex-
treamly incommoded, and consequently disgusted, so that there
can be no cordial affection or unity between the two nations.
How good subjects they make, and how faithful to the British
interest, is a question worth considering. And, in my opinion,
equal numbers might have been spared from the British Islands
without being miss'd there. . . .

---

[52] *Franklin Papers, IV*, pp. 120–121.

Franklin had been reading a book by Joseph Robson, which he had recently purchased from England. Robson had spent six years on Hudson Bay, and reported on the competition the French were giving the English in the far north. The French controlled the heads of the rivers draining into the bay, and they would soon be in a position to claim the whole country and its fur trade as their property. Robson was irked at the Hudson's Bay Company for "sleeping at the edge of a frozen sea" while the French took over; and he was indignant lest Britain lose the continent by default. The Northwest, he insisted, was capable of sustaining a large population, but the company would do nothing. So he demanded:

> Are these countries and seas then perpetually to be locked up from Britain by a charter which is no longer supported by act of parliament? Is this vast continent, the due improvement of which would bring immense wealth to the nation, to lie uncultivated and unknown; or to be discovered, settled, improved, only by the French?

Robson also threw out another thought that other writers were beginning to express. Commerce and a formidable marine were great points in the polity of all the states in Britain's neighborhood, so that:[53]

> it is more than ever become her wisdom and her duty, not only to secure the possessions she already has, but to lay hold of every opportunity to multiply and enlarge them. *This and this alone will enable her to maintain the balance of Europe, and to preserve herself from becoming one day a tributary dependent upon some more active and vigilant power.*

In 1755 William Clarke, like Douglass a Boston physician with a flair for writing, published a pamphlet entitled *Observations on the late and present conduct of the French, with regard to their encroachments upon the British Colonies in North America. Together with remarks on the importance of these Colonies to Great Britain.* The pamphlet was especially timely because it appeared after the stinging

---

[53] Joseph Robson, *An Account of Six Years Residence in Hudson's Bay from 1733 to 1736, and 1744 to 1747* (London: 1752), italics added for emphasis. Robson had been surveyor to the Hudson's Bay Company.

defeat which the French and Indians had given General Braddock in the wilderness of Virginia. This disaster made a profound impression throughout the British Colonies: it intensified the fear that the French and Indians would really drive them into the sea.

Clarke himself had taken part in the Louisbourg expedition of 1745, and was a close friend of Governor Shirley. With the death of Braddock Shirley found himself in command of the British forces in America and had the responsibility for organizing three campaigns of prime importance: one to Nova Scotia with the object of arresting and deporting the Acadian French *en masse,* a drastic measure which had long been on his mind; another against Crown Point, which Clarke described as "so absolutely necessary to secure the friendship and fidelity" of the Six Nations; and the third against the French post at Niagara, which was the key to the Great Lakes.

After rehearsing the familiar story of French encroachments since 1713, Clarke stated his conviction that France was systematically aiming at possession of all North America which would result in the establishment of the universal Monarchy. He was especially apprehensive of a French offensive in Nova Scotia and Maine, "from hence the whole force of Canada might, in a few days, be poured into the Eastern Parts of the Colony of Massachusetts Bay, the great nursery of trees for masts, yards, and bowsprits of the Royal Navy." And he reacted to what today would be called "brain-washing": the success of French priests in luring away the Indians from their British connections and in creating unrest among the Acadian French. Cape Breton Clarke dismissed as of small importance by itself, but should the French master Nova Scotia with its commodious harbors, they could dispute the mastery of the seas. Such a disaster would be felt immediately: in the loss of the cod fishery, in the interruption of the trade route between New and Old England, in the loss of the forests which furnished masts and ships' timber, in the forced evacuation of the English settlements in Maine and western New York, and so on. An article which the *Boston Post* copied from a London newspaper put it even more sensationally: "our floating castles would be no more; and, instead of true religion, liberty and plenty, superstition and tyranny, hunger and nakedness, chains and wooden shoes would be the portion of Britons."

For Britain there were but two choices. Its existing grandeur and power were inseparable from its American Colonies, whose population was now doubling, mainly through natural increase, every twenty years. This rate of growth would continue as long as there was room to expand. But to make this possible and render the Colonies secure, strong reinforcements from Britain should be dispatched without delay. If, on the other hand, the initiative were left to the enemy:

> the trade and commerce of France, and with it her naval power, would increase to such a degree of superiority over that of Great Britain, as must entirely destroy her commerce, reduce her from her present state of independency to be left at last *nothing more than a Province of France*. The French Court are very sensible of this, and have long been pursuing such measures as may finally bring about this Event, tho' perhaps at a distant time.[54]

Clarke's ideas were, to be sure, common currency. Words like "freedom," "tyranny," "slavery" fell easily from the pens of various writers. Exclaimed a New York paper in a full-page article:

> Shameful it is indeed that our negligence should enable the inglorious Sons of despotic Tyranny to take the field with the British Sons of Heaven-born Freedom! Shameful to the last degree that they who have nothing to lose but their gilded chains should be more solicitous concerning the events of uncertain war.

Thomas Hutchinson had used almost the same language as Clarke in a paper he had written the year previously for the benefit of the delegates of the Albany Congress. Like Franklin and others, Hutchinson was trying to spur the Colonies into a union among themselves, the better to oppose the French; but the lethargy displayed at Albany rendered all the more urgent the appeal to the mother country for armd assistance. Clarke himself did not write on the spur of the moment; he had been pondering his ideas, making drafts, and writing letters to Franklin and Shirley for upwards of a year. Clarke and Franklin were almost of the same age. The geographer, Lewis Evans, who made a map intended to help Braddock on his march inland, felt

---

[54] William Clarke, *Observations . . .* (Boston: 1755). *Franklin Papers, V,* 250. Italics added.

as they did. To people who objected that the Colonies were already too large, Evans drily remarked: "If such an opinion prevails, an opportunity now offers of soon making them less." And if an independence movement was to be feared, Great Britain could avert it by backing the Colonies in their aspirations.[55]

Aaron Burr, president of the College of New Jersey, speaking on New Year's Day 1755 which was devoted to fasting and prayer against French encroachments, saw in French history a record of treachery, cruelty and unlimited ambition, and urged support of Governor Shirley, the accepted leader of the activist elements in the Colonies. John Huske, a native of New Hampshire and a Member of Parliament who enjoyed publishing outlets in both London and Boston, reiterated the claim that only Britain had a right to North America and joined in whipping the dead horse of British diplomacy at Utrecht for compromising with the French. William Vinal, preaching a sermon in Newport, Rhode Island, after learning of Braddock's defeat, denounced the French for being "of as bad a disposition as it is possible for human creatures to be of . . . They are become respectable and formidable in Europe; but they are ambitious, enterprising, subtil, deceitful, perfidious, and extremely cruel." The Reverend Charles Chauncy of Boston was equally warlike and resolved to embark on a program of conquest. But Chauncy concentrated his fire on the unfortunate Braddock rather than on the enemy. New England soldiers had done the fighting, but the posts of honor and profit had gone to British officers. Massachusetts, Chauncy asserted, had been the chief protector of all the American Colonies for more than a century; and now New England forces were taking a hand in emptying Nova Scotia of its French inhabitants. The deportation of the Acadians had indeed begun, to the satisfaction of Massachusetts, but Chauncy stands apart from these other writers in claiming so much credit for New England.[56]

---

[55] L. H. Gipson, *Lewis Evans* (Philadelphia: University of Pennsylvania Press, 1939).

[56] Aaron Burr, *A Discourse* . . . (New York: 1755); John Huske, *The Present State of North America* (London: 1755, reprinted in Boston); Charles Chauncy, *A Letter* . . . and *A Second Letter* . . . (Boston: 1755).

VIII

Meanwhile, in 1751 Benjamin Franklin had written an essay on population which he had shown to some of his friends, including Governor Shirley; and Shirley, seeing in the paper a telling argument in support of his expansion program, induced Franklin to have it printed as an appendix to Clarke's pamphlet. Even when first published, the appendix attracted more attention than the pamphlet — *The Gentleman's Magazine* reprinted extracts from it in its November 1755 issue. Clarke's arguments were already standard and the reading public in Britain, in Franklin's opinion, needed no further persuasion. But Franklin had something different to say. In the interest of imperial unity he had been advocating a free trade system within the Empire, Parliament to repeal the acts it had passed in restraint of American trade and manufactures and to admit Colonial representatives to its membership. By such a union, he hoped, "the people of Great Britain and the people of the Colonies would learn to consider themselves, not as belonging to different communities with different interests, but to one community with one interest." This, he believed, would "greatly lessen the danger of future separations."

Franklin centered his essay around the assumption that population increase is directly in proportion to free land. America having an abundance of land, its population would multiply, doubling as it had been every twenty years, while Europe being fully settled would remain comparatively stationary. Even so, "so vast is the territory of North America that it will require many ages to settle it fully." Meanwhile, a huge demand for British manufactures growing, a glorious market was "wholly in the power of Britain, in which foreigners cannot interfere." It was Britain's interest to provide more living room for people in America, meaning of course that it should aim at breaking the French hold on the interior. Fecundity is controlled only by the means of subsistence, and since there is no limit to the latter in America there is no end to which the population could grow. In another century, Franklin declared with obvious satisfaction, "the greatest number of Englishmen will be on this side the water." And then, he exclaimed:

What an accession of power to the British Empire by sea as well as land! What increase of trade and navigation! What numbers of ships and seamen! How important an affair then to Britain . . . and how careful should she be to secure room enough, since on the room depends so much the increase of her people!

Finally, saying that a nation "is like a polypus; take away a limb, its place is soon supply'd," Franklin, contradicting what he had previously said, advised the English they would not lose by emigration: the places at home left vacant by the emigrants would soon be filled. He repeated his dislike of the Palatinate Germans who were crowding into Pennsylvania, and declared quite frankly that he wanted only English people in America. He patronized the Scots by including them with the English, but let the Welsh and Irish go unmentioned. "Which leads me to add one remark: that the number of purely white people in the world is proportionably very small." [57] Small it truly was because, according to Franklin, only the English and the Saxon branch of the Germans were "white." The humor of this new twist to the "chosen people" concept seems to have gone unnoticed.

In *The French Encroachments Exposed . . . in Two Letters . . . recommended to the perusal of every honest Briton,* John Payne, a retired businessman living in America but publishing in London, put the case for perpetual war with the French, those "powerful robbers" to whom "all the back doors to our houses lye open." "Let us regain all that have been stole from us," Payne demanded, "and powerfully protect our country, people, and trade, by sea and land: this cannot impoverish our empire . . ." And since France had a "long premeditated scheme" of universal monarchy, Payne concluded:[58]

we would become a *French province,* and see that proud perfidious nation stand without a rival, distributing laws to all the maritime powers of Europe. We would . . . behold them universal lords of the sea, and bidding fair for the monarchy of Europe . . . We can at present quash their intrigues, we can ruin their marine, and drive them out of North America. This,

---

[57] *Franklin Papers, IV,* pp. 227–234; *V,* pp. 449–450; *VI,* pp. 216–217.
[58] London, 1756. Payne focused his attack especially on the Jesuits and their "wicked schemes."

if we do not embrace the present opportunity, shall perhaps be never again in our power to accomplish . . .

Of all these writers, the most judicious and best informed was the cartographer, Dr. John Mitchell, whose map of North America, first printed in 1755 after five years of preparation, made him the recognized authority on American geography. Mitchell, moreover, had lived in America, principally in Virginia, for at least twenty years before returning to England sometime in 1747 or 1748; and his association with leading men on both sides of the Atlantic who were firm believers in making common cause against the French gives the book that he published in 1757 an unusual distinction.

Starting with the thesis that the American Colonies were now not only a source of great wealth but were also necessary to the safety and defense of Great Britain, Mitchell brought to bear the full weight of his immense geographical knowledge to show how vulnerable the Colonies were in the contest then under way. He put his emphasis on the "prodigious water-carriage" of the St. Lawrence and the Mississippi, and described in great detail how it was possible to go by water from Hudson Bay to the Gulf of Mexico and the several routes that could be taken. Because Quebec and New Orleans were far apart, and settlement in between admittedly sparse, English people were not to imagine that the French would be unsuccessful. On the contrary, "they go from place to place all over America by water, while we have many long and chargeable journeys to make by land, before we can get at them." Then Mitchell enumerated the forts which the French had located at convenient distances, and showed how Crown Point on Lake Champlain, Niagara on the Great Lakes, and Duquesne at the head of the Ohio gave them a strategic grip on the continent. French strategy pointed at Nova Scotia and New York. Citing Charlevoix, Mitchell analyzed the commanding importance of the former: with this province would go the entire fishery, in terms of economics worth more than mines of gold and in terms of sea power invaluable for the control of the North Atlantic. With Crown Point and the Nova Scotian coast in their hands, the enemy could launch a successful offensive against New York.

If not stopped, the French would get all of North America and the West Indian sugar islands. Among the latter, they had encroached on the western portion of Hispaniola, which commanded the Windward Passage, and on some of the most strategically valuable of the Leeward Islands, notably St. Lucia, Dominica and Tobago in addition to their original possessions, Guadeloupe and Martinique. Ideologically Mitchell shared the belief now common that the French had no "right" in America at all. Only Britain had "a real and original right" to the continent, although the Spanish had a claim to the southwestern parts and the French to a small portion north of the St. Lawrence, where he would let them remain provided they were watched.

Like some of his predecessors, Mitchell reacted to "the false and groundless notion" influencing many people that the Colonies would rebel and throw off their dependence on Britain. There was no argument like experience, he wrote: the Americans by themselves were unable to resist a handful of French; without Britain's whole force and naval power behind them they could not survive. Another writer, who preferred anonymity but who also showed a first-hand knowledge of American geography, was equally emphatic: it was unnatural to suspect the Americans of rebellious intentions, and as ill justified as a man would be for refusing to build a house for fear of its being burned.[59]

These points were all brought out and stressed by Arthur Young in a succinct and forthright little volume he published in 1759. Young was a precocious writer — he was only eighteen at the time — and his many books and clear, strong point of view were to make him famous. This work bears the trademarks of both his elders, Mitchell and Franklin, and glows with satisfaction at the favorable turn the war had now taken. Louisbourg had again fallen, this time to a large British fleet and army, and Fort Duquesne Young knew to be in British hands. He had yet to hear of the fall of Quebec, which would make a dictated peace possible. Nothing short of total victory would suffice. Britain should exclude the French from the continent and take over all of the sugar islands. And there was no need to fear an inde-

---

[59] John Mitchell, *The Contest in America between Great Britain and France* . . . by an impartial hand (London: 1757); Anon., *A Letter to a Member of Parliament on the Importance of the American Colonies* . . . (London: 1757).

pendence movement in America. Let the Americans grow prosperous; encourage them to produce more of the things they could sell in the mother country in exchange for British manufactures; and promote a permanent union among them, with a governor-general and a separate parliament. Such measures would eliminate the causes of possible discontent.[60]

From the clergy of New England arose a chorus of praise for the victory, and a promise of peace and prosperity for the British Empire and the "Protestant interest" in the future. As the eminent Reverend Jonathan Mayhew expressed it, the Empire and the Protestant interest were mutual. Britain and the Colonies he viewed as absolutely inseparable. When a Protestant king and nation defeated the French monarchy, they also defeated the Church of Rome. Moreover, being aware of the successes the British had had in Asia, Mayhew prophesied that "the time is not far distant, when both the Roman papacy shall come to nothing and the gospel shall be propagated throughout the world." And another preacher exulted: Canada, "the North American Babylon, New England's rival," had fallen. France, "the mother of harlots," had long plotted to "crush the rising glory" of the English Colonies. She had seized possession of the two great rivers, prejudiced the natives, and sowed the seeds of Roman tyranny and superstition. She "drew out her breasts to her true sons," the Indians, supplied them with arms, powder, provisions and "that finish'd piece of armour," the scalping knife. From this date, September 8, 1760, the clergyman concluded, "we may date our happiness as a free and undisturbed people." [61]

"How chearfully has our Mother Country employed her riches and strength for the preservation of her tender and exposed offspring!" exclaimed the Reverend Samuel Cooper, another well-known Boston preacher.

---

[60] Arthur Young, *Reflections on the Present State of Affairs* . . . (London: 1759).

[61] Jonathan Mayhew, *Two Discourses* . . . *October 25, 1759* (Boston: 1759); and *ibid., Two Discourses* . . . *October 9, 1760* (Boston: 1760); Eli Forbes, *A Sermon preached October 9, 1760* . . . (Boston: 1761); Colbourn, *The Lamp of Experience*, (Chapel Hill: University of North Carolina Press, 1965), pp. 60–66.

What fleets and armies have been sent to our rescue. An obligation which ought to be remembered with filial respect and the warmest gratitude. To the British forces we have chearfully joined our own aid, even to the utmost of our ability . . .

Taking a backward glance to 1745, Cooper admitted that even after the capture of Louisbourg New England could not keep a single fortress in Nova Scotia without British assistance.

"Reflect upon our miseries had we been conquered by papists, tyrants and slaves," another minister admonished. But now the Indian trade is ours, a vast country lies open, our settlements may push out in safety on all sides. We shall convert the Canadians to the Protestant faith. And from the Reverend William Smith, provost of the College of Philadelphia, came the assurance that the best of all possible worlds lay ahead. Protestant Christianity, civil liberty, and humanity were identical; Popery, slavery, savagery were the antitheses. These being decisively beaten, the way lay open for extending "our empire far over this continent," and for the final propagation of Christianity and the sciences to the ends of the earth.[62]

Franklin, now Pennsylvania's agent in London, shared in the general exultation and confidently restated the ideas he had previously set forth in his essay on population. Mayhew, Cooper and no doubt other clergymen drew on this essay for their sermons. Influential English writers also put their pens to work. A new London edition of Father Charlevoix's *Journal* was put on the market in 1761. Among others bearing the stamp of authority and placing the blame for the war upon the French, was T. Jefferys, official geographer to the British government. Jefferys put out two books, each with a liberal number of maps and plans to illustrate his thesis. The first was on the French possessions in America, with special attention to the wealth of the Mississippi valley. "No part of the world seems more happily adapted to second the operations and improve the glory of a maritime power than this province of America." The second book was on the Spanish islands and mainland settlements. Jefferys wrote concise and meaty descriptions of all the Spanish colonies; fascinated his readers with

---

[62] William Smith, D. D., *Discourses on Public Occasions in America,* 2nd ed. (London: 1762).

a lengthy and interesting analysis of the Spanish commercial and defense systems; stated his opinion that Spain was now more feeble than it had been before Columbus; and suggested that since France, Spain's "cunning and deceitful" ally, had been reduced to the lowest extremity, nothing hindered the British from moving at will into Spain's vast dominions in both North and South America.[63]

Franklin, Jefferys and all these other writers saw eye to eye in this vision of world empire. Franklin, even better than Jefferys, appraised the geopolitics of the Mississippi valley. In the next war it could be used for a two-pronged attack that would sweep Spain from the New World — a base for "raising a strength . . . which . . . might easily be poured down the Mississippi upon the lower country and into the Bay of Mexico, to be used against Cuba, the French Islands, or Mexico itself." And, he continued:

> I have long been of opinion that the foundations of the future grandeur and stability of the British empire lie in America; and though, like other foundations, they are low and little seen, they are, nevertheless, broad and strong enough to support the greatest political structure human wisdom ever erected. . . . All the country from the St. Lawrence to the Mississippi will in another century be filled with *British* people. Britain itself will become vastly more populous, by the immense increase of its commerce; the Atlantic sea will be covered with your trading ships; and your naval power, thence continually increasing, will extend your influence round the whole globe, and awe the world![64]

---

[63] Thomas Jefferys, *The Natural and Civil History of the French Dominions* . . . (London: 1760); *ibid., A Description of the Spanish Islands and Settlements* . . . (London: 1762).

[64] Albert H. Smyth (ed.), *The Writings of Benjamin Franklin*, 10 vols. (New York, Macmillan, 1905–1907), *IV*, pp. 3–7; *V*, p. 46. Gerald Stourzh, *Benjamin Franklin and American Foreign Policy* (Chicago: University of Chicago Press, 1954), pp. 98–99.

The Revolution and Its Mythology

2

I

"The United States elevated to glory and honor." This was the theme which Ezra Stiles, president of Yale, chose for his sermon before the governor and assembly of Connecticut in May 1783. The sermon is an ideological masterpiece — a complete summation and synthesis of the ideas shaping up since the days of Raleigh and Winthrop and centering on America. It is 172 pages long. Nevertheless, it is to be assumed that it fell on attentive ears; the men who heard it had legislated compulsory taxation for the support of the Congregational clergy to which Stiles belonged. In Connecticut persons of other persuasions, especially Anglicans, found themselves handicapped.

Winthrop's "City on a Hill" and Cotton Mather's "American Israel" are uppermost in Stiles's thoughts, but blended with secular ideas of a "republic of virtue" which the minister had absorbed from his reading of Oceana, an allegorical study written by the English philosopher, James Harrington. Oceana was Cromwell's England, a republic wherein Congregationalists had triumphed over the bishops and executed the king, Charles I. Harrington postulated an "immortal commonwealth" where liberty meant the rule of reason over passion, a government of laws over men. The trail leads back to the ideal Republic of Plato and forward from Harrington to the thinkers of the American Revolution. For the ideal commonwealth a society of small landowners was a prerequisite, and the America of 1783 seemed to offer the great opportunity. Stiles began his sermon on this assumption. New England in particular, he insisted, had made a reality of Harrington's ideas.

But, in contrast to Europe, which Stiles held to be stagnating, America would grow and expand by virtue of a spreading population. Paraphrasing Franklin, the minister keeps recurring to this theme. The American population would be Protestant, and the number of English people would exceed all the others. Within two generations the United States would outnumber the population of Great Britain, by which time "the Lord shall have made his American Israel, high above all nations. . . ." Then Stiles outlines the national mission and sanctifies the marriage between commerce and religion:[1]

> This great American revolution, this recent political phenomenon of a new sovereignty arising among the sovereign powers of the earth, will be attended to and contemplated by all nations. Navigation will carry the American flag around the globe itself; and display the Thirteen Stripes and New Constellation at Bengal and Canton . . . and with commerce will import the wisdom and literature of the east. . . . A time will come when six hundred millions of the human race shall be ready to drop their idolatry. . . . They will then search all Christendom for the best model, the purest exemplification of the Christian church. . . . And . . . should American missionaries be blessed to succeed in the work of Christianizing the heathen, in which the Romanists and foreign Protestants have very much failed, it would be an unexpected wonder, and a great honour to the *United States*. AND THUS THE AMERICAN REPUBLICK, BY ILLUMINATING THE WORLD WITH TRUTH AND LIBERTY, WOULD BE EXALTED AND MADE HIGH AMONG THE NATIONS IN PRAISE, AND IN NAME, AND IN HONOUR. I doubt not this is the honour reserved for us. . . .

More guarded in his judgments but utopian nevertheless in his outlook was the widely respected English Non-Conformist minister, Dr. Richard Price. Of his claim to be a genuine exponent of the

---

[1] First published in 1783, this sermon went into a second edition in 1785. *See also* Edmund S. Morgan, *The Gentle Puritan. A Life of Ezra Stiles, 1727–1795* (New Haven, Conn.: Yale University Press, 1962), pp. 453–455. On Harrington see Charles Blitzer, *An Immortal Commonwealth. The Political Thought of James Harrington* (New Haven: Yale University Press, 1960).

American Revolution and its ideals there can be no doubt. All during the war Price had preached the American cause to crowded London congregations; the Continental Congress actually invited him to America in 1778; and, though he never came, Ezra Stiles's college, Yale, lost no time in 1783 in granting him an honorary degree. Price now put out a new tract entitled *Observations on the Importance of the American Revolution, and the Means of Making It a Benefit to the World.* Untainted with the commercial spirit but apprehensive that it would get the better of the Americans and lead to the same corruption and degeneracy which he decried in Europe, Price hoped that the United States, located on a sequestered continent, would lay the foundation of an empire which would prove "the seat of liberty, science and virtue." Next to the introduction of Christianity, he argued, the Revolution might turn out to be "the most important step in the progressive course of human improvement." Its blessings could become universal, and the time reached when "kings and priests shall have no more power to oppress." Lest the Americans fall to fighting among themselves, they should have a general government but, like the good doctrinaire type of English Whig that he was, Price expressed his distaste for the armed forces: an army was an instrument of tyranny, and if the United States would insulate itself against the quarrels of Europe, take advantage of its lands for settlement, and avoid the snare of commercial ambition, it would fulfill its mission.[2] In Dr. Price we hear again the voice of Bishop Berkeley; in the pages of Ezra Stiles we re-read the ambitious creed of the Protestant interest.

Meanwhile Benjamin Franklin with the support of John Stockdale,

---

[2] Dr. Price's *Observations* were first published in London in 1784 and reprinted the same year in Boston. The author expressed his hopes and fears in a letter to Jefferson, March 21, 1785. Then his original foreboding over the effects of luxury and money-grabbing, which he had heard were characteristics of the seaboard towns, deepened when he reflected on the evils of Negro slavery. "The friends of liberty . . . in Europe will be mortified, and an event which had raised their hopes will prove only an introduction to a new scene of aristocratic tyranny and human debasement," he wrote on July 2. Julian P. Boyd (ed.), *The Papers of Thomas Jefferson,* 17 vols. published (Princeton, N. J.: Princeton University Press, 1950–1965), *VIII,* pp. 52, 258–259. Hereafter cited as *JP.*

foremost among London publishers, returned to his well-worn theme of *lebensraum* in America. "Hearty young labouring men" who were good at husbandry could get on in a country where there was a "general happy mediocrity." Rich people who lived idly or bought paintings and other things that "are more curious than useful" were not wanted. After enjoying years of high living in London and Paris, — wine, women but apparently not song — Franklin preached the simple life of the cultivator and the workman. In Europe, he declared, "the youth are dragged up in ignorance of every gainful art, and obliged to become soldiers or servants, or thieves" (the association is interesting), if they were to make a living. In America they would find a hearty welcome: there was plenty of room and plenty of work, and they need have no fear of jealousy. Indifferent himself to religion, Franklin took pains to reassure his English readers on the subject. And he must have enjoyed the humor of writing that in America "atheism is unknown . . . ; infidelity rare and secret; so that persons may live to a great age in that country without having their piety shocked by meeting with either an atheist or an infidel. . . ." And apparently hoping to blot out the memory of Indian warfare, Franklin now had a good word for the "noble savage," depicting him as a model of civility and homely wisdom. When a preacher told the Indians of how "our first parents" had fallen because of eating an apple, he had the chief reply: "It is bad to eat apples. It is better to make them all into cider." [3]

As if to lend weight to Franklin's argument, an appealing little book issued from the press in America the same year, beckoning immigrants to Kentucky,

> the central part of the extensive American empire . . . where springs a harvest for the poor; where conscience ceases to be a slave, and laws are no more than the security of happiness; where nature makes reparation for having created man; and government, so long prostituted to the most criminal purposes, establishes an asylum in the wilderness for the distressed of mankind.

---

[3] Franklin, Two Tracts: *information to those who would remove to America* . . . (London: John Stockdale, 1784; another edition in 1794).

The well-known trapper, Daniel Boone, and several other men gave this book their support.[4]

The classic picture of America as an agrarian utopia comes from the pen of Michel Crèvecoeur, a Frenchman with an unusual career who had settled on a farm in New York soon after the close of the French and Indian War. Crèvecoeur had moved from Normandy, where he was born, to England, where he was educated, thence to Quebec, where he is believed to have served in Montcalm's army. Then in 1759, after the latter's defeat and death, he started on a lengthy tour of the American Colonies and in 1765, the year of the Stamp Act, he became a British subject. At some later time — just when appears not to be known — he wrote his famous *Letter from an American Farmer . . . to a Friend in England* which, issued first in London in 1782, went through a number of editions in English, French and German during the ensuing decade. Mathew Carey, an Irishman who developed a successful publishing business in Philadelphia, brought out the first American edition in 1793. Carey, after the manner of Franklin, had already tried his own hand at luring emigrants from the British Isles.

The point about this is that Crèvecoeur — he wrote under the pen name of Hector St. John so as not to betray his French origin to his English readers — depicted the idyllic life he had been leading on his New York farm *before* the American Revolution. Remaining aloof from the patriot party and expressing his disdain for their "perpetually bawling about liberty without knowing what it is," he aroused their enmity and they eventually drove him from his farm whence he found protection with thousands of other loyalist refugees under the British Army in New York City. But *none* of this background appears in the *Letter;* since it bears no date and uses the present tense, it has a timeless quality. "An humble American planter, a simple cultivator of the earth," as he chooses to describe himself, he tells his fictitious English friend that he has discovered "the most perfect society now existing in the world." As he warms

---

[4] John Filson, *The Discovery, Settlement and Present State of Kentucke . . .* (Wilmington: John Adams, 1784).

to his subject, he asks rhetorically, "What then is the American, this new man?" and gives his own answer:[5]

> He is an American who, leaving behind him all his ancient prejudices and manners, receives new ones from the new mode of life he has embraced, the new government he obeys, and the new rank he holds. . . . Americans are the western pilgrims . . . ; they will finish the great circle.

Such flattery did not fail to attract the interest of Benjamin Franklin, who befriended him in Paris. In 1783 Crèvecoeur returned to New York first to act as French consul and then to accept citizenship; but after only seven years he again departed for France, never to return. Carey's edition of Crèvecoeur's book came out *after* its author had left the country he had pictured as a paradise.

A fellow Frenchman, Brissot de Warville, who came in 1788 to travel but not to settle, wrote a somewhat similar panegyric. In a three-volume work published in Paris after his return, he dwelt on the virtues of a society of free cultivators, and advised the Americans to try to wipe out all traces of their British origins. This, he admitted, would be difficult — they spoke the same language — but by opening America as an asylum for all men they could make it different. Jealous of the strides the British were making in reestablishing their trade outlets in the country, Brissot studied how the French might retain a share. Wine was the best possibility, he decided:[6]

> Wine becomes a real want to those who have once been acquainted with it. Happy or miserable, rich or poor, everybody makes use of wine. Wine is the delight of the happy or of the rich. It helps the unfortunate to support his sorrow; the poor think they find it an equivalent for the food they are without.

---

[5] Page 47 of Carey's edition. Crèvecoeur and his writings have drawn periodic interest. *See,* for example, Moses Coit Tyler, *The Literary History of the American Revolution, 1763–1783,* 2 vols. (New York: G. P. Putnam's Sons, 1897), *II,* pp. 347–358. The original London edition (1782) was reprinted with a biographical introduction (New York: Fox Duffield & Co., 1904).

[6] Jacques Pierre Brissot de Warville, *Nouveau Voyage dans les Etats-Unis de l'Amerique Septentrionale, fait en 1788,* 3 vols. (Paris: chez Brisson, 1791); *Considerations . . .* (London: Robson and Clarke, 1788).

Variations upon the theme of "a great, lasting and happy empire" continued to find their way into print in the post-Revolution years. To make it a success the Mississippi must be secured; the great river was the key to the northern part of the continent. It was absurd to expect the Spanish to yield it, nor were treaties to be depended upon,

> for he that trusts to anything but the operation of their interest, is a poor politician; and he that complains of deceit, where there is an interest to deceive, will ever be considered as deficient in understanding.

The sentiment was Thomas Hutchins's, whose books on the interior, drawn in part from Charlevoix, identified him as geographer to the United States.[7]

Accompanying this idea of empire as territory was the idea of empire as union. Without a central power the Confederation would be "like a cask without hoops that may and probably will fall to pieces, as soon as it is put to any exercise which requires strength." The author had been reading Gibbon's *Decline and Fall of the Roman Empire*, published only a few years before. From small beginnings the Romans had risen to empire in territory, population and wisdom, but without a strong government they could not have accomplished all this. Similarly the Americans, with an extensive western territory to defend, would find themselves victims of conquest as the Romans had been at the hands of the Goths and Vandals, unless they formed a union. Independence was "one of the greatest events . . . in the history of mankind," but none of the "puny sovereignties" of the states could keep it. Only a union so strong as to keep internal broils in check could successfully lay the foundation of an empire.[8]

In a Fourth of July oration in 1787 the poet Joel Barlow, aware of

---

[7] Thomas Hutchins, *An Historical Narrative . . . of Louisiana and West Florida . . .* (Philadelphia: Robert Aitken, 1784); Thomas Brockway, *The European Traveller in America . . .* (Hartford, Conn.: Hudson and Goodwin, 1785).

[8] Pelatiah Webster, *Political Essays . . .* (Philadelphia: Joseph Cruikshank, 1791); Jonathan Sewall, An Oration . . . (July 4, 1788); Jonathan Jackson, *Thoughts upon the Political Situation . . .* (Worcester, Mass.: 1788). Webster was a student of public finance who had been publishing his essays since 1776.

the federal convention then meeting in Philadelphia, brought these several ideas together. The Revolution, he asserted, had been the achievement of sober reason and reflection. A nation of "laborious agricultural people . . . reasoned before they felt," while they discussed the acts of the British Parliament "in a cool and dispassionate manner." A federal government made permanent and foreign commerce placed upon a respectable footing, a hundred millions would populate the territory and be made happy. "Every free citizen of the American Empire," the orator declaimed, "ought now to consider himself as the legislator of half mankind. . . . The present is an age of philosophy; and America, the empire of reason." Building on this fanciful view of the new society, Barlow meanwhile composed a long epic poem in which Columbus, the hero of 1492, is depicted as a prophet who sees as in a dream the train of events culminating in the arrival of a "utopian harmony of mankind." [9]

Such a man turned into a very useful tool for the Scioto Land Company, a highly dubious enterprise with claims to nearly five million acres in southern Ohio. The company employed Barlow to promote its schemes in France, and sales went well until French newspapers began raising embarrassing questions. The bubble burst in 1792, Barlow himself managing to escape involvement in the scandal but somehow emerging as a man of wealth only two years later.

Climactic to this literature of the 1780's was *The American Geography* of Jedidiah Morse. A Congregational minister like Ezra Stiles, Morse — he was the father of the inventor of the telegraph — felt indignant that now the United States "have risen into Empire," Americans should still be leaning on European writers for their knowledge of geography. His was a practical contribution to independence, and he got his book out in time to coincide with the inauguration of the new national government under Washington. During the four previous years of study and writing he spared no pains to make his book a success: he travelled from state to state,

---

[9] Joel Barlow, *The Vision of Columbus* (Hartford, Conn.: 1787) amplified some years later as *The Columbiad.* On Barlow and the Scioto Company see *JP, XVI,* pp. 159–162.

communicated with men of science, read the works of the great explorers like Captain Cook who were opening up the Pacific Ocean, and enlisted the aid of men like Thomas Hutchins who had personal knowledge of the Mississippi valley. His first edition in 1789 was followed by two more, greatly enlarged, in 1792 and 1794, respectively, and the book continued to appear in new editions from time to time during the next quarter of a century. Moreover, a simplified version designed for children went through nineteen editions.

Holding it a truism that empire travels from east to west, Morse was confident that "her last and broadest seat will be America." The sciences and the arts will flourish here; civil and religious liberty will revive unhindered by the cruel hand of civil or ecclesiastical tyranny; mankind will be humanized under a government that "shall be calculated to protect and unite, in a manner consistent with the natural rights of mankind, the largest empire that ever existed. Elevated with these prospects," he thought, "which are not merely the visions of fancy, we cannot but anticipate the period as not far distant when the American Empire will comprehend millions of souls west of the Mississippi." Nor was it intended that the western boundary should stop at the river. Well informed on the value of New Orleans and hopeful of the overthrow of Spanish rule on the lower Mississippi, Morse stressed the ease with which a conquest could be effectuated. Moreover, he added:[10]

> Europe is already aware of the rising importance of America, and begins to look forward with anxiety to her West India Islands, which are the natural legacy of this continent, and will doubtless be claimed as such when America shall have arrived at an age which will enable her to obtain her right.

Thus anticipating the imminent expulsion of Europe, Morse reiterates the fixed idea that America belongs to the Anglo-Americans: after the states have united, national independence will come, and then the acquisition of a continent-wide empire with proprietary rights over the adjacent seas and islands.

---

[10] Morse's first edition was published in Elizabethtown, N. J.; the second and third by John Stockdale in London; later editions were published in both countries. The excerpts are from the first and third editions.

II

The mentality of Thomas Jefferson furnishes an open door to the hopes and ambitions and to the many contradictory attitudes and prejudices reflected in the American mind. Himself a man of sophisticated tastes and intellectual acumen, Jefferson liked to romanticize the ordinary dirt farmer as a paragon of virtue, and to imagine the future utopia that an agarian society would produce in America. Brissot de Warville's panegyric gave him great satisfaction, he told its author, particularly the passages which "proved" that American society will be "more virtuous, more free, more happy in agriculture" — the surest road to affluence and the best preservative of morals. With amusement we read the sentiment he expressed to another correspondent:[11]

> Were I to indulge my own theory, I should wish them [the states] to practice neither commerce nor navigation, but to stand with respect to Europe precisely on the footing of China. We should thus avoid wars, and all our citizens would be husbandmen. . . .

A lengthy letter Jefferson wrote from Paris to John Jay in 1785 illustrates the paradox, of which he himself seems to have been aware. After first boasting of all the land the United States possessed wherewith "to employ an infinite number of people in their cultivation," he continued:

> Cultivators of the earth are the most valuable citizens. They are the most vigorous, the most independant, the most virtuous, and they are tied to their country and wedded to its liberty and interests by the most lasting bands . . .

But as soon as a surplus of labor is reached, other outlets must be found; and Jefferson hoped, and apparently believed, that these would be upon the sea, for "I consider the class of artificers as the panders of vice and the instruments by which the liberties of a country are generally overturned." Inheriting from their mother country their taste for navigation and commerce:[12]

---

[11] *JP, VIII*, pp. 631–634; *X*, pp. 261–263.
[12] *Ibid., VIII*, pp. 426–428.

Our people are decided in the opinion that it is necessary for us to take a share in the occupation of the ocean, and their established habits induce them to require that the sea be kept open to them, and that that line of policy be pursued which will render the use of that element as great as possible to them. . . . But what will be the consequence? Frequent wars without a doubt. Their property will be violated on the sea, and in foreign ports. . . . These insults must be resented . . . or in other words, our commerce on the ocean and in other countries must be paid for by frequent war. . . . This reasoning leads to the necessity of some naval force, that being the only weapon with which we can reach an enemy. . . .

The paradox lies between the sentimental and the practical, but it is less real than it seems: no matter how much he indulged himself in the romantics of agriculture, Jefferson always made the choice in favor of national wealth and power. He is the complete embodiment of the nationalist statesman, seeking and trying every avenue to national advantage that comes into view, and prepared to take life as he observed it. "There is always war in one place, revolution in another, pestilence in a third interspersed with spots of quiet," he wrote almost at the same time. "These chequers shift places, but they do not vanish; so that to an eye which extends itself over the whole earth there is always an uniformity of prospect." [13] But America was different: unlike other nations it could not be tempted into wrong doing.

These attitudes, strengthened by certain prejudices, become clear as we examine Jefferson's career as minister to France during the five critical years from 1784 to 1789. Incidentally he benefited from a record-breaking Atlantic crossing: only nineteen days in a brig from Boston to Brest. Knowledge of the ineffectiveness of the United States and especially of the success the British were already experiencing in recapturing their American markets irked him. "All respect for our government is annihilated on this side of the water," he reported. "It is a dangerous opinion to us, and possibly will bring on insults which will force us into war." British animosity was at a new high, stronger by far than it had been during the war and secure in the confidence that British merchants had a corner on the trans-

---

[13] *Ibid.,* pp. 558–559.

atlantic carrying trade. "We are the lowest and most obscure of the whole diplomatic tribe." Such was Jefferson's pessimism near the end of his first month in Paris.[14]

Putting his mind on how to remedy this situation, he conceived of two possibilities, though in neither case did he hope for quick success. One was to get the Mediterranean trade started again. Prior to the war this had been a valued part of the American economy, but separation from Britain had meant the sacrifice of British naval protection and the French had been deaf to American wartime pleas for their aid against the African pirate states. A new approach to France on the subject Jefferson seems not to have considered, but he thought a Portuguese contact would be valuable. Portugal's own interests and its proximity to Morocco and the Straits of Gibraltar gave it an advantage against the pirates. Consular and even diplomatic relations with Portugal were worth soliciting. In addition Jefferson thought of Spain, which of course could help if so minded. But the one course he seriously proposed was to confront the pirates directly: either pay the tribute demanded or build a navy and make war on them. John Adams, now representing America in London, regarded the tribute as the wiser course for the time being; Jefferson preferred war. Actually neither of these was practicable, there being no general government in America with funds or ships at its command.[15]

The second possibility was to seek closer ties with France, relying on that country's position in the European power structure for "putting the bridle into the mouth of England." Jefferson had a quick eye for the strategy of the French ports, for none more than for Cherbourg. This was a new peninsular port on the coast of Normandy, admirably located for challenging the British in the Channel, and the French were lavishing attention upon it. When completed, they could base their whole navy upon it. "Nothing has ever been wanting to enable this country to invade that," he concluded, "but a naval force conveniently stationed to protect the transports." Linked

---

[14] *Ibid., VII*, pp. 501–502, 508–513.

[15] *Ibid., VII*, pp. 571, 637; *VIII*, pp. 444–446; *IX*, pp. 264–267; *X*, pp. 86, 123, 176–177.

with Dunkirk, farther to the northeast where the Channel narrowed, Cherbourg made invasion feasible.[16]

Next in Jefferson's interest came Honfleur, a small outport near Le Havre upon which the French government had conferred the franchise. Honfleur awakened Jefferson to the possibility of its becoming a port of entry for American rice and whale oil, and beyond that to the reopening of the direct trade with France which had abruptly terminated as soon as the war was over. Britain had never been a consumer of American rice, but the whole crop was customarily shipped to Cowes on the Isle of Wight where it was processed and then re-exported to its Continental markets. Wholly dependent on Britain for selling their rice, Jefferson's South Carolina friends snatched eagerly at the prospect of a French competitor capable of breaking the British monopoly. It pained the Charleston firm, Brailsford and Morris, for instance, to witness the ease with which American merchants fell back into their old habits of dealing only with British businessmen. American buyers, they admitted, were prejudiced in favor of English goods, but there was a wide market for French goods too if the French would only make the effort. Wines, brandies, fruits, linens, soap and other commodities in which the French excelled would be welcome and would balance the cost of marketing Carolina rice through France. It was a bitter pill, they said, to see how their recent enemies had taken over nine-tenths of their export business;[17]

> and in walking our streets, whether convinced by the dialect, or the names of those who supply our wants, that we should rather conceive ourselves in the Highlands of Scotland than in an American State, is the source of painful reflection to every citizen.

Unfortunately French indifference and failure to respond left the American merchants, their pride insulted, just where they had been before the Revolution — helpless in the coils of a well organized and aggressive British monopoly. Judging by the tone adopted by orators and tract writers of Boston, one may conclude that the same feeling of impotent rage prevailed in that part of the country, its shipping suffering from a postwar depression. England was the "harsh step-

---

[16] *Ibid., X,* pp. 240–241, 245, 247; *XI,* p. 33.
[17] *Ibid., XI,* pp. 40, 262–266; *XII,* pp. 263–264, 295–296, 298–301.

mother," whose wily policy was aimed at our impoverishment and ruin. British commercial agents "filled the continent," bringing with them every kind of goods which had formerly "given bread to our honest tradesmen." [18]

> The alarming prospects of speedy misery — the decline of our merchants — and the absolute ruin of our mechanicks — are representations by no means fictitious . . .
> The Crisis is now arrived! from this moment we may date our eternal infamy and ruin, if by supineness or dastardly fear, we let it pass. . . .

Overheated Protestant clergymen joined in to beat the dead horse of tyranny which that "priest-led, dissembling, execrable tyrant Charles I" was alleged to have perpetrated 150 years earlier; to deny that the Americans had ever had any help from the mother country in their "bloody wars with the savages"; to accuse the British merchants of provoking the French and Indian War in 1756; and especially to embroider the propaganda of the so-called "Boston Massacre." By making "Massacre Day" an annual occasion the Boston radicals had built up an elaborate legend around this episode wherein, as the late Professor Schlesinger has shown, street loafers and hoodlums emerged as folk heroes. The revolutionary printing firm of Peter Edes reprinted in 1785 all thirteen of the annual orations delivered on the subject since 1771; and the Reverend John Gardiner used his oratorical talents for picturing that "night of horror and of the blackness of darkness," when, "the innocent, unarmed inhabitants of this peaceful though much injured town then fell victims to the brutal violence of the mercenary slaves of George the III." [19]

Meanwhile John Adams in Britain was disposed to a more philosophic view. American trade having returned to its old channels, British merchants could see no reason for making concessions. Better than ever, the Navigation Acts worked to their advantage, at least in

---

[18] *American Commerce. Broadside. The Observer, extra.* Friday, April 15, 1785. Only two copies of this rare item are known to be extant; one at the Henry E. Huntington Library and Art Gallery, San Marino, Calif.

[19] John Gardiner, An Oration, July 4, 1785, Boston; [13] *Orations . . . [in] Boston to commemorate the evening of the fifth of March, 1770 . . .* (Boston: Peter Edes, 1785).

the short run. A tract written by Lord Sheffield, the biggest ship-owner in the kingdom, set the tone of British mercantile opinion and went quickly through six editions. The Americans were no longer privileged to share in the British carrying trade, and they were shut out of the important West Indian market.

Yet beneath this veneer of self-assurance Adams thought he detected uneasiness and injured pride. "The jealousies of old physicians and lawyers, of young and rising geniuses in their profession often stimulate them to acts of ingenerosity and injustice," and nations behaved in the same manner. There was more dread of America than there was of France or of Spain, and fear lest the American states form a union. "European ministers expect a great deal of trouble from America," Adams remarked, "and they all know that she will always prevail. We know too that we shall have a great deal of trouble from Europe; but I hope we are neither so impious, so inhuman, or so silly as to wish her annihilated." There was a strong propensity among the English to believe "that America is weary of her independence; that she wishes to come back; that the states are in confusion; Congress has lost its authority; . . . no laws, no order, poverty, distress, ruin and wretchedness."

But, on the other hand, the poverty among the masses in Europe, and the high cost of living were such as to create a desire to emigrate. Every government was sensible of this, and employed all the scribblers to abuse us. Adams was surprised when, in October 1786, Britain and France concluded a commercial treaty according each other most-favored-nation treatment; a French population of twenty-five millions provided a promising outlet for British manufactures, as he realized; but he concluded that the agreement could not long remain proof against the mutual jealousies of the two nations while preferring to believe, with striking inconsistency, that the treaty was really aimed at the United States, a mere "farce of political hypocrisy." [20]

---

[20] See John Adams, *Reels 111* (May 26, 1785–Feb. 28, 1786) and *112* (Dec. 3, 1785–Feb. 28, 1788), Adams Manuscripts. The quoted extracts are from sundry letters to John Jay and R. H. Lee, printed here by permission of the Adams Manuscript Trust.

Farce or not, the treaty was a product of the new economics of free trade taught by Adam Smith, and the more significant in that it was between two ancient rivals neither one of which would come to terms with the United States. Jefferson himself had spent two months in England trying to make some arrangement with the British government. "Their silence is invincible," he reported. They remained indifferent to negotiating any commercial treaty, and they were not planning on any political connection either.[21] The Americans were still in default on their prewar debts — a standing grievance to the British — and since the American market was wide open to British goods, from their standpoint no need for a treaty existed.

Jefferson returned to Paris in a bitter mood, feeling that the United States was little better than a vassal of Great Britain. If only the scales could be evened up by buying more from France, that[22]

> would cement an union with our friends and lessen the torrent of wealth which we are pouring into the laps of our enemies; for such the British are more generally and more rootedly at this time than at any moment of the war.

Personally Jefferson got on well with Vergennes — a great minister, he thought him, attentive and agreeable to do business with, aware of the United States as a weight against Britain but nevertheless lacking confidence in its government. So, despite French friendliness, manifested officially by their sending out a new minister, Eléonore F. Moustier, to Philadelphia, it led to no practical results. The Americans desperately needed the West Indian trade, one of their most lucrative prewar outlets; but the French no more than the British would give it to them.

In Jefferson's view Britain was the "natural enemy," ruled by "that ungracious, rascally court." Plainly he had lost his temper over his fruitless visit to London:

> That nation hates us, their ministers hate us, and their king more than all other men. They have the impudence to avow this, tho' they acknowledge our trade important to them. . . . I think

---

[21] *JP, IX*, pp. 397–399, 402.
[22] *Ibid.*, pp. 472–473.

their hostility towards us is much more deeply rooted at present than during the war.[23]

Outbursts like these recur several times in his letters, so that Jefferson's Anglophobia seems pathological in its intensity, traceable to deeper causes than the frustrations of his London visit. Perhaps the fires of the Revolution had burned so deeply into his vitals as to be inextinguishable, fanned undoubtedly by his personal losses suffered during the war. The Virginia tobacco planters had been hard hit. While occupying the state in 1781, Cornwallis's army had freed thirty of Jefferson's slaves and inflicted property damage aggregating three or four thousand pounds, according to Jefferson's own figures. Jefferson was still feeling bitter over this in 1788. History, he wrote the historian William Gordon, "will never relate the horrors committed by the British army in the *Southern* states of America." [24]

Late in January 1787 Jefferson decided to visit the south of France — "the land of corn, wine, [olive] oil and sunshine," as he wrote happily from Aix-en-Provence. Marseilles too pleased him very much, and besides having a look at the new Languedoc canal he wanted to explore the possibilities for trade with the French ports he had not yet seen. While in Provence he became an enthusiastic connoisseur of French wines; and a lengthy report he wrote home on the varietal Burgundies and Bordeaux suggests that he, like Brissot de Warville, hoped that here were products that could stimulate a Franco–American trade. Jefferson's Francophilia was as pronounced as his opposite feeling toward Britain. "Nothing should be spared on our part to attach this country to us," he told Madison:[25]

It is the only one on which we can rely for support under every event. Its inhabitants love us more I think than they do any other nation on earth. This is very much the effect of the good dispositions with which the French officers returned.

---

[23] *Ibid.*, pp. 444–446.

[24] *Ibid.*, pp. 388–390; *XIII*, pp. 362–363; William Gordon, D. D., *The History of the Rise, Progress and Establishment of the Independence of the United States of America . . .* , 4 vols. (London: 1788), *IV*, pp. 402–403.

[25] *JP, XI*, pp. 48–50, 92–97, 247–248, 338–343; Dumas Malone, *Jefferson and his Time* 3 vols. (Boston: Little, Brown, 1948–1962), *II*, pp. 112–130.

In part at least this sentiment rested on Jefferson's intimacy with Lafayette, who outdid him in hatred of England. He and Madison agreed that the marquis was a man of unlimited ambition, possessed of "a canine appetite for popularity and fame." But they were also aware that Lafayette had influence in high places, that he was "well remarked by the king and rising in popularity," though suspected of harboring republican principles. Of Louis XVI Jefferson himself had a good opinion: he had "an honest heart," and there were many enlightened men in France, including the ministers. Upon Lafayette Jefferson pinned his chief hopes for a commercial treaty; but when the Assembly of Notables met in January 1787 and the marquis' name was temporarily removed from the list, Jefferson began to have doubts. Having received his education in "our schools," Lafayette had drawn upon himself "a very jealous eye from a court whose principles are the most absolute despotism." [26]

His repeated professions of fondness for France to the contrary notwithstanding, Jefferson held to certain prejudices against Europe from which France and the French were by no means excluded. He enjoyed painting the contrast between European luxury and dissipation on the one hand and American simplicity and honesty on the other, an attitude that clearly was predetermined before he had crossed the Atlantic. His letters show that by and large he found life agreeable during his four years abroad, but he felt strongly on the subject of American youth coming to Europe before the age of thirty. In England they would learn only drinking, horse-racing and boxing; on the Continent they would contract a partiality for aristocracy and monarchy, form useless foreign friendships, or be led by "the strongest of all human passions into a spirit of female intrigue" and acquire a passion for whores. "The consequences of foreign education," he said, "are alarming to me as an American." Yet he admitted there were advantages to reading and acquiring friendships in France, a nation "to whom we are bound by the strong ties of gratitude and policy; a nation in short of the most amiable dispositions on earth, the whole mass of which is penetrated with an affection for us." [27]

[26] *JP*, *VIII*, p. 42; *XI*, pp. 48–50.
[27] *Ibid.*, *VIII*, pp. 405–408; *X*, pp. 305–309.

For the king, but not for the queen, Jefferson continued to have a high regard. Louis was "the honestest man in his kingdom, and the most regular and economical;" but rage, pride, and fear dominated Marie Antoinette, and she had no moral sense. Frederick II of Prussia irked him: a trouble-maker, Jefferson thought him, "the bull dog of tyranny to all his neighbors." But when the Empress Catherine of Russia appointed John Paul Jones a rear admiral in charge of the Russian Black Sea fleet operating against the Turks, Jefferson felt a surge of national pride. His republicanism was no proof against such attention. Sentimentally Jefferson was always a republican, capable of saying things about kings that did not square with his respect for Louis XVI, or even for his old enemy George III. Monarchies are "governments of wolves over sheep," he exclaimed to Madison. And to Washington:[28]

I was much an enemy to monarchy before I came to Europe. I am ten thousand times more so since I have seen what they are. There is scarcely an evil known in these countries which may not be traced to their king as its source, nor a good which is not derived from the small fibres of republicanism existing among them. I can further say with safety there is not a crowned head in Europe whose talents or merit would entitle him to be elected a vestryman by the people of any parish in America.

Such doctrinal aberrations drew from John Adams in London an interesting lecture on realism and social snobbery. Lessons are never wanting, declared Adams:[29]

Moral reflections, wise maxims, religious terrors, have little effect upon nations when they contradict a present passion, prejudice, imagination, enthusiasm or caprice. . . . If the Duke of Angoulême . . . or especially the Dauphin should demand one of your beautiful . . . daughters in marriage, all America from Georgia to New Hampshire would find their vanity and pride so agreeably flattered by it, that all their sage maxims would give way. . . . I have long been settled in my own opinion, that neither philosophy, nor religion, nor morality, nor wisdom, nor interest, will ever govern nations or parties, against their vanity, their

---

[28] *Ibid., XI,* pp. 92–97; *XIII,* pp. 124–129, 538.
[29] *Ibid., XII,* pp. 220–221.

pride, their resentment or revenge, or their avarice or ambition, nothing but force and power and strength can restrain them. . . .

To this pitiless diagnosis of human nature Jefferson had no ready answer. From his friend Madison and from John Jay he got much the same view. "A mere government of reason and persuasion is little adapted to the actual state of human nature in any age or country," was Jay's terse comment; and while Jefferson was slow to admit it, his faith in reason was less firm than he pretended. When off guard, he could go to the point of saying that "the unreasonable is the largest part of mankind." Moreover, his professions of love and gratitude to France do not square with his inattention to the French internal situation and his insensitiveness to the coming Revolution. In January 1787, with the French government hovering on the brink of bankruptcy, the king summoned the Assembly of Notables in the faint hope of getting the privileged classes to face up to the necessity of a tax reform that would touch their own purses. Down to this point Jefferson had paid no attention to the French predicament; not until the following August, in fact, did he begin to appreciate the gravity of the situation. Jefferson's interest, however, centered principally on the prospect of another general war at a time when France was in no position to cope with Britain. A crisis in the Netherlands, attributed to the bullying of Frederick II of Prussia, gave Jefferson another opportunity to blow off steam against kings. But his main fear, as he confided to George Washington, was that France being incapable of acting as a check upon Britain, the United States would be more than ever at the mercy of the British. "No war," he repeated, "can be safe for us which threatens France with an unfavourable issue." Shifts in the European power structure, involving Austria and Russia, however, subsequently convinced him that Britain had overreached itself and now stood isolated. "The old system is unhinged, and no new one hung in its place." [30]

In May 1789 Louis XVI resorted to the extraordinary step of convening the States General, a body comprised of the three estates of the realm — the clergy, the noblesse, and the *tiers état,* a much

---

[30] *Ibid., VII,* p. 642; *XI,* pp. 312–314; *XII,* pp. 32–33, 124–129.

larger group representing the bourgeoisie. A revolutionary situation immediately developed: the first two orders refused to relinquish their privileges and submit to reforms demanded by the third estate. In addition popular temper in Paris, particularly in the slums of the Faubourg St. Antoine, reached the breaking point over the scarcity of bread. Food riots in France were an old story but, the wheat harvest of the preceding season having been the poorest in many years, these fresh outbreaks proved more menacing than usual. Jefferson was now sending frequent and lengthy reports on the deteriorating situation; he was in Paris when the mob stormed the Bastille (July 14) and he witnessed the serious disorders that followed. Civil war, he realized, was a real possibility, but he discounted its happening, even though he personally found it difficult to keep his own household supplied with food. "Reason," he argued, would prevail; he would "agree to be stoned as a false prophet if all does not end well in this country." In October occurred the momentous march of the six thousand women from Paris to Versailles to fetch "the baker, the baker's wife and the baker's boy" and make them "house prisoners" in the Tuileries. But by that time Jefferson was homeward bound, awaiting a ship to carry him from Le Havre.[31]

III

In July 1776, barely a week after the signing of the Declaration of Independence in Philadelphia, Captain James Cook, R.N., sailed from England on his third and final voyage of exploration of the Pacific Ocean. All three of Cook's voyages were epoch-making: many mariners had roamed the Pacific during the two and a half centuries since Magellan, but none equalled Cook. Two other English navigators, Captains Wallis and Carteret, both sailing officially under orders from the Admiralty, preceded him, and he built upon their

---

[31] For Jefferson's interesting letters describing the scenes in Paris during the summer of 1789 see *JP*, XV. *Also* Alfred Cobban, *A History of Modern France* 2 vols. (Baltimore, Md.: Penguin Books, 1961), I, pp. 133–159; and George Rudé, *The Crowd in History, 1730–1848* (New York: John Wiley & Sons, 1964), pp. 93–122.

experience. Cook was a Yorkshireman who had risen from the ranks to be commander of his own vessel, H.M.S. *Resolution*. He had been at the second siege of Louisbourg (1758), and had then carefully charted the St. Lawrence and the coasts of Newfoundland and Nova Scotia. His proven genius as a navigator and his superior skill in the handling of ships and men won him the command of the exploring expeditions, the first of which began in 1768.[32]

Cook's third voyage was of unique significance because of his charting of the northwest coast of North America and his attempt to find the northwest passage across the top of the continent from the direction of the Bering Sea. As Corporal John Ledyard, a Connecticut Yankee who shipped with Cook, pointed out, other attempts to locate the passage had been made from the Atlantic side of the continent, but Cook was the first to try it from the Pacific. When at Unalaska, Ledyard under orders from Cook took a small exploring party and brought back three Russian seamen, "well-behaved, intelligent men, and very ready to give me all the information I could desire." Russian settlers were on all the chief islands between Unalaska and Kamchatka; they had come from Okhotsk in 1776 and were there to hunt the sea beaver or otter. They knew the American continent, says Cook, to be a great land, and the part with which they were familiar they called *Alaschka*. Corporal Ledyard finished his tour of duty with the British expedition and at the end of the Revolutionary War returned to his home town, Hartford, where in 1783 a local printer published the journal he had kept while on the voyage.[33]

Cook's exploits were, of course, already famous. Both French and American warships were under orders not to regard him as an enemy, if they encountered him, but to pay him all honor and respect. In

---

[32] J. C. Beaglehole (ed.), *The Journals of Captain James Cook on his Voyages of Discovery* 3 vols. (Cambridge, Eng.: Cambridge University Press, for the Hakluyt Society, 1955–1967).

[33] *A Voyage to the Pacific Ocean . . . performed under the Direction of Captains Cook, Clerke, and Gore, in the Years 1776, 1777, 1778, 1779, and 1780 . . .* 4 vols. (London: for John Stockdale et al., 1784), *II*, pp. 494, 504; *A Journal of Captain Cook's Last Voyage. . . .* Faithfully narrated from the original manuscript of Mr. John Ledyard (Hartford: Nathaniel Patten, 1783).

Paris negotiating peace, John Adams absorbed the geographical knowledge the expedition had made available. Near Kamchatka, he observed, the passage between America and Asia was no wider than between Calais and Dover. "What should hinder the Empress of Russia," Adams wondered, "from establishing a trading city on the Sea of Kamchatka, and opening a commerce with Pekin, Nankin, and Canton, the cities of China? It is so near the islands of Japan, the Philippines, the Moluccas, that a great scene may one day be opened there." [34] Not improbably Adams had read a book which William Coxe, an English traveller in Russia, had first published in 1780, pointing out the importance of the Russian advance across Siberia. A party of Cossacks had reached Kamchatka in 1696, and soon thereafter a trade in furs had begun with the Chinese. Coxe printed a number of fine maps and charts in his volume, and showed that Cook had verified the discoveries which Bering and Chirikov, the Russian explorers, had reported.[35]

The inexhaustible wealth to be gained from this new fur trade was soon learned. It was common knowledge by 1780, Cook's men having returned to London after a profitable sale to Chinese merchants in Macao. (Captain Cook himself had suffered a tragic death on his return call in Hawaii.) Sea otter fur as described by Lieutenant John Meares, a later British explorer, is:

> the finest in the world; it possesses a jetty blackness, and is of exceeding beauty. The peculiar warmth it affords, renders it a most valuable clothing in the colder climates; but considered in an ornamental view, it has a rich and magnificent appearance and, under a certain arrangement, may vie even with the royal ermine.

While in King George's Sound in September 1787, Lieutenant Meares reported, he had met Captain Grey of the sloop *Washington*. Grey's object was to open the way for American merchants, the money

---

[34] *The Adams Papers, Diary of John Adams, III* (1782–1804), (Cambridge, Mass.: Harvard University Press, 1961), pp. 109, 139–141 (entries for Feb. 25, June 16, 1783).

[35] *William Coxe, Account of the Russian Discoveries between Asia and America,* 3rd ed. (London: T. Cadell, 1787).

earned in the fur trade providing the means for paying for the teas and many other things wanted from China. Grey, commented the British officer, was very sanguine and "big with many sprightly projects in which we understood he was protected by the American Congress." [36]

Meanwhile an American named William Coxe had engaged in the China trade, realizing a net profit of $100,000 or 126 per cent on an investment made by himself and his partners on a voyage from Philadelphia. The American Coxe's observations on the prospects for success in the China trade reached Jefferson in Paris in November 1787. He had "a national object" in view, he wrote. It was to challenge the British in the China and India trade, of which they possessed "an immoderate share." If Jefferson could persuade the French to cooperate, especially if they would admit the Americans to the use of Pondichery, their own base in India, the British could be made to feel the effects of competition. In a closing sentence Coxe stated in essence what, more than a century later, was to be called the "open door policy" of the United States: "The commerce with the East shou'd if it were possible be made common by all the powers of inconsiderable influence in that country." [37]

It was an appealing idea; but Jefferson, stalled in his negotiations with Vergennes over other commercial matters, seems not to have pursued it. More pressing from the American standpoint was to get an open door for American vessels to the French West Indies and to save the whale fishery of Nantucket Island, which lay off the Massachusetts coast, from extinction. On the West Indian trade Jefferson met with a rebuff; but Nantucket whaling was another matter. Jefferson thought of it as a "nursery for seamen," indispensable for the navy he wanted for employment in both West Indian and Mediterranean waters. Success in regaining these outlets, he agreed, was of prime importance to a commercial nation. But Nantucket families,

---

[36] John Meares, *Voyages made in the Years 1788 and 1789, from China to the N. W. Coast of America* . . . 2 vols. (London: J. Walter, 1791), *I*, p. 353, *II*, p. 23; Capt. George Dixon, *A Voyage round the World, but more particularly to the North-West Coast of America* . . . (London: Geo. Goulding, 1789).

[37] *JP, XIII*, pp. 3–4; *XVI*, pp. 329–330.

Quakers in religion and neutralists during the Revolution, chose to do their own bargaining: they could move in a body to Nova Scotia where, as British subjects, they would again have the privileges of the British Navigation Laws, or they could wring concessions from France. Jefferson feared they would strike a bargain with the British government: a migration of the whole Nantucket community to Nova Scotia would deal a double blow at the United States. But the British government refused to foot the bill for the migration, which the Nantucket envoy to London demanded, and so the latter got his product admitted to a share in the cash bounties the French were paying for whale oil. The slaughter of whales now approaching a peak in the South Seas developed from the popularity of whale oil as an illuminating fuel. But Nantucket independence continued to annoy Jefferson: some of the island people had moved to the British province, and others might follow. The possibility of losing them was taken seriously.[38]

Meanwhile a surprise visit which Captain Cook's former corporal, John Ledyard, paid Jefferson in Paris brought the latter's attention back to another possibility involving the Pacific Northwest. Jefferson harbored an almost morbid fear lest the British or the French get the start of the Americans in colonizing that region. A rumor of preparations for a British exploring expedition across the continent had first excited him in 1783. Then when the French naval officer, La Pérouse, sailed from Brest in August of 1785 on a round the world voyage, Jefferson's suspicions fell on his French friends. La Pérouse had a long and enviable record of service, almost as brilliant as Cook's for whom he had high respect. He had served in the Seven Years' War, had been with d'Estaing to America during the War for Independence, and then later on a voyage to Hudson Bay. Like Cook, he had the personal qualities to lead a long exploring expedition. La Pérouse was lost at sea, but his journals were saved and brought back to France where they were edited and published. An English edition

[38] *JP*, *XIV*, pp. 217–225, 242–254; *XVI*, pp. 397–400; and for a graphic picture of the effects of commercial exploitation by the Western nations upon marine life in the Pacific see Alan Moorehead, *Fatal Impact: An Account of the Invasion of the South Pacific, 1767–1840* (New York: Harper, 1966).

was put on sale in 1798, and shows how thoroughly La Pérouse performed his work as an explorer in the Pacific. While he was still
making preparations at Brest, Jefferson had John Paul Jones try to
ascertain whether he had any colonizing intentions. Jones sent in a
negative report, but Jefferson remained unconvinced. A year later,
after reading an account in a Paris newspaper of La Pérouse's progress, he was still fretting lest the Frenchman establish a permanent
post in the Pacific Northwest.[39]

From Ledyard in February 1786 Jefferson got a startling proposition.
Ledyard volunteered to *walk* across Russia and Siberia, find his way
down the coast of North America and thence eastward to the
United States. This hope held out of finding a direct route from
America to Asia appealed to Jefferson, whom the young man greatly
impressed. Ledyard, he observed:

> has genius, an education better than the common, and a talent
> for useful and interesting observation. I believe him to be an
> honest man, and a man of truth. To all this he adds just as much
> singularity of character, and of that particular kind too, as was
> necessary to make him undertake the journey he proposes.

Ledyard actually did make the journey across Siberia on foot, the
German seaport of Hamburg being his point of departure. But when
within only a few days from Kamchatka, he suffered arrest at the hands
of the Russians who brought him back and turned him loose at the
Polish border. What a story Ledyard might have left, if only he had
committed himself to pen and paper! But he was a lone wolf, and
we have only Jefferson's scanty allusions to him on which to build.
Jefferson saw Ledyard again, in July 1788 after Ledyard had been to
London and obtained a commission to explore the Nile to its source,
thence across the Sahara to the headwaters of the Niger and so on
down to the sea. On this occasion Ledyard promised Jefferson that,
if this venture succeeded, he would go to Kentucky and try a west-

---

[39] Jean François Galoup de la Pérouse, *A Voyage round the World in the
Years 1785, 1786, 1787, and 1788 . . .* , 3 vols. (London: for J. Johnson,
1798); *JP*, VIII, pp. 372–375, 587–588; X, pp. 220–222; R. W. Van Alstyne,
The Rising American Empire (New York: Oxford University Press, 1960), p.
124.

ward trek across America to the Pacific. But Ledyard met his death in Cairo, after writing Jefferson his poor opinion of the Egyptian capital.[40]

It was a part of Jefferson's intellectual inheritance to believe that North America belonged to the United States. North America was "our continent" in his eyes, all of it; hence his swift reaction to the slightest hint that Britain or France might have colonizing projects in mind. But his imagination was almost as easily fired by hints of revolution in Latin America. A Brazilian and a Mexican, whom he did not name but whom he saw while on his tour of the south of France, put the idea into his head. The Brazilian in particular was candid in asking for arms, ammunition, ships, sailors and soldiers from the United States, and in pointing out the advantages of Rio de Janeiro as a port. Apparently Jefferson saw this gentleman several times; and while practicing discretion and keeping in mind his own hope for close relations with Portugal, he led the Brazilian to believe that he might get some aid from the United States. A revolution could not be uninteresting to us, he told him. Prospects for private gain and appeals to American veterans to volunteer their services might well attract numbers of American citizens to Brazil. With the Mexican Jefferson was more cautious, since he was aware that Spain controlled the Mississippi and had something of value to give in negotiation. But the idea that revolutions in Latin America would benefit American national interest was now a part of his mental makeup. He was disappointed that an insurrection in Peru of which he had heard had been a failure, and he concluded:[41]

> I trouble Congress with these details, because, however distant we may be both in condition and dispositions, from taking an active part in any commotions in that country, nature has placed it too near us to make its movements altogether indifferent to our interests or to our curiosity.

---

[40] *JP, IX,* p. 273; *XII,* p. 159; *XIII,* pp. 382, 516; *XIV,* pp. 187–191; Van Alstyne, *The Rising American Empire* (New York: Oxford University Press, 1960), pp. 78–79.

[41] *JP, XI,* pp. 338–343; Van Alstyne, *The Rising American Empire* (New York: Oxford University Press, 1960), pp. 78–79.

This notion of an American special interest in Peru was given another twist later in the year 1787 when Jefferson learned that talk of cutting a canal through the Panama isthmus had been renewed. Someone whom he did not identify advised him that the Spanish government had made a survey for a canal, had concluded that the project was practicable, but had for political reasons suppressed it. Jefferson wrote immediately to his colleague in Madrid, William Carmichael, asking for details and for copies of the survey for which he would be willing to pay. The survey was to him, he said, "a vast desideratum for reasons political and philosophical." He also re-iterated his interest in Latin American revolutions. But these benefits, he concluded, were for the future. They were not for "the present moment or age." Until the United States was in a stronger position, its interests would be better served by Spain remaining in control. "The womb of time," he declared ambiguously, "is big with events to take place between us and them. . . ." [42]

A famous French savant of the eighteenth century, George Louis Leclerc, comte de Buffon, with whose works Jefferson and Madison were conversant, employed a most interesting simile to point up the meaning of the War for American Independence. Britain he depicted as the sun, France as a comet. In its eccentric political movements the French comet had collided with the British sun, and in the colli-sion a fragment had torn loose from the latter's body; then, finding an orbit of its own, the fragment began performing like a new planet in the universe. This new planet, Buffon observed, was the American Empire. [43]

Orbiting thus independently, however, required the fulfillment of two conditions. All other aspects of the imperial dream — a world commercial state, expansion of the Protestant interest on a global scale, a spreading population carrying American civic ideas through-out North America, revolution in Latin America and overthrow of alien European rule — waited upon these two, which were tied to-gether. They were: the transformation of the loose wartime confed-

---

[42] *JP, XII*, pp. 423–427; *XIII*, pp. 229–235, 358–359, 399.
[43] *JP, VI*, pp. 443–444; *VIII*, pp. 110–116.

eracy of states into a permanent union with a general government, and the incorporation into this union of the western hinterland as far as the Mississippi river. "The pride of independence," feared Jefferson, was taking

> deep and dangerous hold on the hearts of the individual states. I know no danger so dreadful and so probable as that of internal contests. And I know no remedy so likely to prevent it as the strengthening the band which connects us.

Otherwise:[44]

> The states will go to war with each other . . . : one will call in France to her assistance; another Great Britain, and so we shall have all the wars of Europe brought to our own doors . . .

Alexander Hamilton, younger than Jefferson in years but more detached in his viewpoint and more sensitive to international realities, minced no words in his forecast. Independence, as he saw it in 1783, was a fiction. "I fear we have been contending for a shadow," he told Washington.[45]

> The common danger being removed, we are receding instead of advancing. . . . The road to popularity in each state is to inspire jealousies of the power of Congress, though nothing can be more apparent than that they have no power . . . and we at this moment experience all the mischiefs of a bankrupt and ruined credit.

Other considerations weighed on Hamilton's mind. A mass flight of loyalists, victims of abuse at the hands of the populace and of flagrant discrimination at the hands of patriot-controlled state legislatures, was now in full swing. The migration was especially noticeable in New York State, the gateway to the British provinces to the north. State laws depriving loyalists of their property, disfranchising them and condemning them to imprisonment or banishment, expressed the passionate hatred of the patriots for their many fellow citizens who

---

[44] *Ibid., VI*, p. 248.
[45] Harold C. Syrett (ed.), *The Papers of Alexander Hamilton*, (New York: Columbia University Press, 1961—), *III*, pp. 292, 416. Hereafter cited as *AH Papers*.

would not collaborate with them. Even such shocking measures as bills of attainder against individuals, such as an act of the New York legislature in 1779, were not unknown. Courageously Hamilton took a stand in public against this persecution. A few heated and thoughtless persons were playing on the passions of the people, he wrote. Pretending to appeal to the spirit of Whiggism, they endeavored[46]

> to put in motion all the furious and dark passions of the human mind. . . . These men inculcate revenge, cruelty, persecution and perfidy. The spirit of Whiggism cherishes legal liberty, holds the rights of every individual sacred . . . These men are advocates for expelling a large number of their fellow-citizens unheard and untried.

Still in Paris at this time, John Jay, like Hamilton a New Yorker, registered his disgust at the reports he was receiving. "The Tories," he wrote Hamilton, "are almost as much pitied in these countries, as they are execrated in ours. An undue severity towards them would therefore be impolitic as well as unjustifiable. . . ." Drawing the historical parallel of religious bigotry and persecution, Jay added:[47]

> Victory and peace should in my opinion be followed by clemency, moderation and benevolence; & we should be careful not to sully the glory of the revolution by licentiousness and cruelty. These are my sentiments, & however unpopular they may be, I have not the least desire to conceal or disguise them.

One incident in particular stirred the French. A party of loyalist refugees in 1782 had murdered an American officer named Huddy. In reprisal a military board appointed by Washington had decided to single out by lot a British prisoner of war of the same rank. The choice fell on a very young captain named Asgill, who was thereupon fated to be hanged. The case aroused a great deal of feeling, the mother of the young man in England going so far as to appeal personally to Vergennes to intercede. Vergennes did so, and Asgill was eventually saved from being punished on the gallows for a crime

---

[46] *Ibid.*, fn., p. 479, 483–497. William H. Nelson, *The American Tory* (Oxford: Clarendon Press, 1961), *passim*.

[47] *AH Papers, III*, pp. 459–460.

with which he had no connection. Vergennes' intercession seems to have been the decisive factor, since only after Washington had received the French protest and had relayed it to Congress for its approval was the young man released; but meanwhile Asgill's plight had created a very painful impression in Europe.[48] It needs to be said that John Adams, who had been very angry with the Tories during the war, cooled off rapidly and shared Jay's feeling of repugnance toward the injustices done them; but Benjamin Franklin was indifferent, while Thomas Jefferson, the future author of the Bill of Rights, had not a word of criticism.

By 1786 a serious question was developing over the future of the new settlements in Kentucky. Would they remain with the United States, or would they secede from the confederacy? Both Jefferson and Madison were alarmed lest they choose the second alternative; hearing of the possibility while in Paris, Jefferson admitted that it would be a "most calamitous event." Situated in the heartland of Ohio, Kentucky was in a position to determine the future of the United States. If it withdrew, the United States would be effectively barred from the trans-Allegheny west; the Union would then remain a loose confederacy of thirteen states strung out along the seaboard and having little in common among themselves. In other words, the whole nation-building process begun by the Revolution would be checked and the thirteen states revert to their former status as colonial dependencies. Much of the migration to Kentucky had occurred during the Revolution. Obviously these emigrants had been unresponsive to the call of the patriots; nor were the large numbers who followed them immediately after the war concerned with the future of the union. Actually, as is well known, several plans for separating and concluding a bargain with the Spanish for use of the Mississippi were laid by Western adventurers in the early 1780's; but these conspiracies were not known at the time. Jefferson's fears were better founded than he knew, but the fact that he aired them shows his grasp on the geopolitics of the situation.[49]

---

[48] Douglas Southall Freeman, *George Washington, A Biography* (New York: Scribner's, 1948–1957), V, pp. 412–414, 419, 425.

[49] *JP, VIII*, p. 112; *IX*, p. 218; Thomas Anbury, *Travels through the Interior Parts of America* . . . (a new edition, 2 vols., London: for William Lane,

For a while Madison and Jefferson hoped to find common ground with Spain, Madison in particular reasoning that it would be good policy for Spain to be liberal and open up the Mississippi. Madison relied on Lafayette to bring influence to bear on Madrid, either through Vergennes or through personal contact with the Spanish government. Lafayette could always be counted on to jump to the American side, but he had the Frenchman's traditional dislike of Spaniards and he seems not to have shared Madison's optimism. At any rate he accomplished nothing, and the Mississippi remained closed. Jefferson on his part refrained from asking Vergennes' help on this or any other issue affecting American relations with other countries. The French might "love us," but he did not care to test their friendship in the realm of practical politics.[50]

In August 1786 Madison sent word to Jefferson that John Jay was winding up a negotiation in New York with the Spanish envoy, Don Diego de Gardoqui, whereby in return for commercial concessions the United States would shelve its claims to the navigation of the Mississippi for at least the next twenty-five years. Madison felt sure the western people would consider themselves betrayed and would accordingly cut loose from the Union and tie up with some other power. He guessed, wrongly, that their choice would fall on Great Britain; western separatists were banking on an agreement with the Spanish governor in New Orleans. Jefferson concurred that the issue was crucial, replying that:

> the act which abandons . . . the Mississippi is an act of separa-
> tion between the Eastern and Western country . . . an abandon-
> ment of the fairest subject for the paiment of our public debts,
> and the chaining those debts on our necks in perpetuum. . . .
> If they [the Westerners] declare themselves a separate people,
> we are incapable of a single effort to retain them . . .

1791), *II*, p. 361; Arthur P. Whitaker, *The Spanish-American Frontier, 1783–1795; the Westward Movement and the Spanish Retreat in the Mississippi Valley* (Boston: Houghton Mifflin, 1927), *passim*. But there is in addition a considerable bibliography on these separatist plots. See Richard W. Van Alstyne, *American Diplomacy in Action* (Gloucester, Mass.: Peter Smith, 1967), pp. 65–73, 776–777.

[50] *JP, VII*, pp. 401–408, 416–417; *VIII*, pp. 110–116.

Aware that the population of Louisiana, including the town of New Orleans, was predominantly French, Jefferson thought it likely that the westerners would combine with the Louisiana French to oust the Spaniards. But, the Federal Constitution having been written and submitted to the states for ratification, Jefferson grew more hopeful: the first step would be the admission of Kentucky to the Union, then it would become the duty of the maritime states to push the Mississippi question to the limit. In the meantime, however, Jefferson hoped for a European war with its promise of a bloodless victory for America over both Spain and Britain.[51]

Jefferson, we must keep in mind, consistently sidestepped any relations with France that might entail a political commitment. Although the wartime alliance of 1778 with its reciprocal guarantees and obligations remained in force — on paper — he studiously avoided asking favors of Vergennes with respect either to the Mississippi question or to the trading posts in the northwest which the British had promised to evacuate "with all convenient speed." At one point during a long conference with the French foreign minister he did broach the latter subject, but dropped it lest he be asked for a guarantee of the French West Indies against Great Britain. Independence, more legal than real as established in 1783, had led to the maxim of nonentanglement in European affairs, and with this Jefferson was in complete sympathy. But he believed in following European affairs with the closest attention. The Turks too practiced this maxim, he observed, but to the point of keeping totally ignorant of European combinations and movements. Their ignorance, he argued, exposed them to possible annihilation. "While there are powers in Europe which fear our views, or have views on us," he held, "we should keep an eye on them, their connections and oppositions, that in a moment of need we may avail ourselves of their weakness . . . and calculate their designs and movements on all the circumstances under which they exist."[52]

But first it was necessary to master the dangers of internal weakness. The states must be "firmly hooped together" in Jefferson's

---

[51] *Ibid.*, X, pp. 229–236; *XI*, pp. 92–97, 219–223; *XIII*, pp. 211–213.
[52] *Ibid.*, IX, pp. 567–569; *XII*, pp. 445–447.

phrase. A civil war which would suck in the European powers could arise from more than one cause. Hamilton, observing the mass migration of displaced persons to Canada and Nova Scotia, thought it likely that these British provinces would be strong and well governed; and, as all the wars of the eighteenth century had demonstrated, New York was always vulnerable to attack both by sea and by land. Hamilton remarked in October 1783,

> It is true our situation secures us from conquest, if internal dissensions do not open the way; but when Nations now make war upon each other the object seldom is total conquest — partial acquisitions, the jealousy of power, the rivalship of dominion or of commerce, sometimes national emulation and antipathy are the motives. Nothing shelters us from the operation of either of these causes. The fisheries, the fur trade, the navigation of the lakes and of the Mississippi — the Western territory — the Islands in the West Indies with reference to traffic, *in short the passions of human nature* are abundant sources of contention and hostility.

With added emphasis, Hamilton reiterated these ideas in 1787 both at the Constitutional Convention and outside of it. Remarking again that the "causes of hostilities among nations are innumerable," he wrote in *The Federalist*:[53]

> America, if not connected at all, or only by the feeble tie of a simple league offensive and defensive, would by the operation of such opposite and jarring alliances be gradually entangled in all the pernicious labyrinths of European politics and wars. . . .

But there were positive as well as negative advantages of a union. Jefferson was delighted when he learned in 1786 that Virginia had taken the first step by resigning to Congress its right to regulate its external commerce. A general European war, such as he was looking for, would enrich the United States if it could stand aside. Prudent conduct, Washington agreed, would yield benefits. A one-time Pennsylvania loyalist, Tench Coxe, who showed personal prudence by turning patriot in 1778 when the British Army evacuated Philadelphia, explained the opportunities most comprehensively in a paper

---

[53] *AH Papers, III,* pp. 464–469; *IV,* pp. 325–326.

he read before a group meeting in Franklin's house just as the Constitutional Convention was about to open. It was sound policy to promote foreign trade. Disengagement from European wars, made practicable by geography, would bring profits from the carrying trade and the supply business; foreign seamen would be tempted into the American service; enactment of navigation laws, modeled on the British, would benefit shipping and facilitate capture of distant markets, even as remote as China and India. On the other hand, European belligerents would find it worth their while to keep the United States neutral. Aligned with one side, it would be a troublesome enemy to the other, especially in the West Indies. "The foundations of national wealth and consequence are so firmly laid in the United States, that no *foreign* power can undermine or destroy them." But a federal system was the prerequisite. With it accomplished, and a small navy in operation, the country would be ready to exert an influence, decisive at least in its own sphere. With all these ideas there was general assent. Washington said as much; Jefferson, we recall, had been urging a navy; Alexander Hamilton in *The Federalist* summed up the whole matter most succinctly:[54]

> . . . Let Americans disdain to be the instruments of European greatness! Let the thirteen States, bound together in a strict and indissoluble union, concur in erecting one great American system, superior to the controul of all trans-atlantic force or influence, and able to dictate the terms of the connection between the old and the new world!

V

"How do you like our new constitution?" asked Jefferson of John Adams in November 1787. "I confess there are things in it which stagger all my dispositions to subscribe to what such an assembly has proposed." With the example of Poland and its elective kingship in mind, Jefferson chiefly doubted the President — "a bad edition of a

---

[54] *JP, IX,* pp. 264, 488–491; Tench Coxe, *An Enquiry into the Principles on which a Commercial System . . . should be founded . . .* (Philadelphia: Robert Aitken, 1787), pp. 33, 45; *AH Papers, IV,* p. 345.

Polish king" was his verdict. Like Poland, the United States was vulnerable to foreign influence and the President would be either a Galloman or an Angloman. Then:

> Once in office, and possessing the military force of the union, without either the aid or check of a council, he would not be easily dethroned, even if the people could be induced to withdraw their votes from him. . . .

Jefferson was so impressed by the possibility that he developed it at some length in a letter to Madison. Once elected and finding himself opposed by one or two votes, the President would pretend false votes and foul play, and be aided by one European nation while the majority were helped by another:

> Reflect on all the instances in history antient and modern, of elective monarchies, and say if they do not give foundation for my fears, the Roman emperors, the popes, while they were of any importance, the German emperors till they became hereditary in practice, the kings of Poland, the deys of the Ottoman dependancies. Experience shows the only way to prevent disorder is to render the elections uninteresting by frequent changes.

The king of Poland could be removed at any time by vote of the assembly, yet was never removed; so it could be with the American President, who could develop gradually into an hereditary monarch. The one remedy was to make him ineligible a *second* time.[55]

Adams had his doubts too, but they were of a different order. There was a recurrent danger of foreign influence, but not in the case of a President "chosen again and again as long as he lives." The danger would arise from frequent elections:[56]

> Elections, my dear sir, elections to offices which are great objects of ambition, I look at with terror. Experiments of this kind have been so often tryed, and so universally found productive of horrors, that there is great reason to dread them.

With fine inconsistency, meanwhile, Jefferson set great store by the new minister, Eléonore F. Moustier, whom the French sent to

---

[55] *JP, XII,* pp. 349–351, 438–442.
[56] *Ibid.,* p. 396.

Philadelphia. Moustier had orders to discourage the movement in America for a strong central government, lest it get too powerful for France to handle; but after observing the American political scene, he decided to gamble on one strong government rather than on thirteen weak ones. Jefferson, to be sure, did not know the purpose of Moustier's mission, though he might have guessed it from the influence exerted by French envoys on Congress during the war. While in Philadelphia, Moustier made an exhaustive investigation of the potential wealth of the Mississippi valley; and his 300-page report, received in Paris after the outbreak of the French Revolution, led eventually to the reactivation of French policy for control of the valley through New Orleans. To Jefferson, Moustier was "a great enemy to formality," going "with the best dispositions to cultivate society without poisoning it by ill example. . . . An intimacy with him will on this account be politically valuable." And his companion, Mme. de Brehan, was "goodness itself, going for the sake of her feeble health and to remove her son from the seductions of this country." So Jefferson must have felt crestfallen a year later on learning from Madison of this "most unlucky appointment." The Frenchman was "unsocial, proud, niggardly and betrays a sort of fastidiousness toward this country." Worse still, his relations with Mme. de Brehan were illicit, "universally known and offensive to American manners. . . . On their journeys it is said they often neglect the most obvious precautions for veiling their intimacy." [57]

Next to the astonishment he frankly admitted he felt over the nature of the presidency, Jefferson was critical of the omission of a bill of rights now that the abuse of the loyalist refugees was over. Madison had well-founded doubts on this matter. Experience, he replied, demonstrated that a bill of rights was most ineffective at times when it was most needed. The allusion is unmistakable: "Repeated violations of these parchment barriers have been committed by overbearing majorities in every State." In Virginia individuals had been oppressed whenever popular feeling had been

---

[57] *Ibid.*, p. 213; *XIII*, p. 409n.; *XIV*, pp. 339–342. R. W. Van Alstyne, *The Rising American Empire* (New York: Oxford University Press, 1960), pp. 74–75, 84.

aroused against them. Madison's reflections on the subject are best set forth in his own words:

> Wherever the real power in a Government lies, there is the danger of oppression. In our Governments the real power lies in the majority of the Community, and the invasion of private rights is *chiefly* to be apprehended . . . from acts in which the Government is the mere instrument of the major number of the constituents. This is a truth of great importance, but not yet sufficiently attended to. . . . Wherever there is an interest and power to do wrong, wrong will generally be done, and not less readily by a powerful and interested party than by a powerful and interested prince. . . . in a popular Government the political and physical power may be considered as vested in the same hands, that is in a majority of the people, and consequently the tyrannical will of the sovereign is not to be controuled by the dread of an appeal to any force within the community. . . .

So what is the utility value of a bill of rights, Madison queried. Only insofar as "abstract political truths tend to counteract the impulses of interest and passion," and their impotence whenever such a clash occurred was thoroughly demonstrated in history, as Madison observed.[58]

VI

Meanwhile Ezra Stiles's lengthy discourse of 1783 on the American world mission met with an answering echo from other orators. Boston patriots exerted themselves to implant the idea that in 1770 they had been victims of an indiscriminate massacre. Actually five persons — of dubious character — had met death when a detachment of British soldiers, provoked by a hostile mob, opened fire. Each year thereafter the patriots set aside the fifth of March as "Massacre Day," and orators worked themselves into a frenzy over "the bloody Fifth of March," planned by the "ministerial harpies" and carried out by "the treacherous knaves" of "the tyrant of Britain." Patriots were told to remember "the shocking scene of that

---

[58] *JP, XII,* p. 558; *XIV,* pp. 16–21.

dreadful night, the fatal effects of which we are now still weeping over." It was "a night of horror and of the blackness of darkness!" exclaimed the Reverend John Gardiner in 1785. "The innocent, unarmed inhabitants of this peaceful though much injured town then fell victims to the brutal violence of the mercenary slaves of George the III." The minister then drew a lurid picture of "the terrors of that night": how the streets were "contaminated with murder"; how the "base, savage ruffians" drove "the remorseless steel through the warm brain-pan of the lovely hapless youth"; how he heard "quick, shrill shrieks of matrons and of maids." So by constant repetition and picturesque rhetoric local zealots built up the legend of the "Boston Massacre," which was eventually absorbed into the mythology of the Revolution.[59]

Beginning with Gardiner in 1785 the Fourth of July tended to supersede "Massacre Day" in public attention. It provided a broader stage and furnished orators with greater opportunities for developing an ideology. Independence was the "Sabbath of our freedom," "one of the greatest events that has occurred in the history of mankind." "Freed from the shackles of encroaching monarchy," America was now ready for utopia, an "empire of humanity" as one orator put it. "Hail, glorious age!" ejaculated another,

> when the potent rays of liberty shall burst upon the now benighted desert . . . when all parts of this immense continent shall be happy in ceaseless communications . . . when nations, who now hold the same jealous relation to each other which individuals held before society was formed, shall find some grand principle of combination, like that which rolls the heavenly bodies round a common center.

"In this country," asserted Simeon Baldwin, a Connecticut lawyer, "is completed that happy alliance of national blessings which a lively imagination must have painted for the foundation of a glorious empire." Noah Webster, the future compiler of the famous *American Dictionary*, was already embarked on his life mission: the education of American youth in the literature, geography, history and politics of their country. Having come of age during the Revolutionary War, Webster was an ardent admirer of George Washington. "Begin with

---

[59] See note 19 *supra.*

the cradle," he admonished his readers, "let the first word [the child] lisps be Washington." [60]

The extraordinary year 1789 — extraordinary because of the beginning of the federal union in America and of the outbreak of the French Revolution in Europe — saw the publication of two exceptional books by American authors. The first of these was Jedidiah Morse's *American Geography,* which we have already discussed; the second was David Ramsay's *The History of the American Revolution.* Each of these books was in its own way a masterpiece, the result of long and careful preparation, the product of conscientious work and clear thinking. Between them these two books bear out most completely the ideology of the Revolution.[61]

Ramsay, a South Carolina physician, accepted at the start Morse's idea of a rising empire whose population, British in origin, would spread over the continent and force European powers to evacuate. It was, to be sure, no novel idea; Sir Walter Raleigh and his fellow adventurers, we remember, had planted it fully two centuries earlier, and the British-American mind was saturated with it. Well before the eighteenth century was half over, however, men like Franklin and young John Adams were behaving as though the continent was really more their empire than it was Britain's. To their way of thinking, that is, sooner or later America not Britain would be the seat of empire. This idea took a firm hold during the Great War for the Empire, which ended with the French pushed out of the continent

---

[60] Joel Barlow, *An Oration, July 4, 1787* Hartford; John Brooks, *An Oration,* and Thomas Dawes, Jr., *An Oration, July 4, 1787,* Boston; James Campbell, *An Oration, July 4, 1787,* Philadelphia; Enos Hitchcock, *An Oration, July 4, 1788,* Providence, R. I.; Jonathan Sewall, *An Oration at Portsmouth, N. H., July 4, 1788;* Simeon Baldwin, *An Oration in New Haven, July 4, 1788;* the Rev. William Rogers, *An Oration, July 4, 1789,* Philadelphia; Samuel Stillman, *An Oration, July 4, 1789,* Boston; Theodore Dwight, *An Oration, July 4, 1792,* Hartford; Noah Webster, *An American Selection of Lessons in Reading and Speaking . . . ,* (6th. ed., Newport, R. I.: Peter Edes, 1789). The admonition appears on the title page. Webster got it from Mirabeau, the French liberal, who wrote a rhapsody on America as an agrarian utopia. From the dates of the orations herein cited we may infer that the orators got their inspiration from the new federal constitution. See also notes 8 and 9 *supra.*

[61] On Morse see note 10 *supra;* David Ramsay, M.D., *The History of the American Revolution* (a new edition in 2 vols., London: for John Stockdale, 1793).

and the Spanish barred from the land east of the Mississippi. In 1763 the whole of the eastern half of North America was British in terms of the color on the map but the psychology of future growth and the plans for shaping it up were more American than British.

Paradoxically, however, British armies and British sea power won this war. The several American Colonies gave only limited support; some of them virtually stood aside while British regulars did the fighting; others, even those like Virginia and Massachusetts which had the highest stakes in victory, were uneven in the amount of help they gave. At the very best none of the American Colonies acted more than as auxiliaries in the conflict. But with the war decisively won, the sense of dependence upon Britain diminished noticeably. Franklin, an ardent advocate of all-out war with France who had been indefatigable in asking for British help, now traded on this new feeling of independence. The Americans, he blandly told the House of Commons in 1765, had always lived "in perfect peace with both French and Indians" until Braddock came to spoil it. Americans were "chiefly farmers and planters" who did not need British troops to defend them. The troops had come "for the profit of British merchants and manufacturers," and the war, begun "for the defence of a trade purely British, was really a British war." Luckily for Franklin, nobody reminded him of his own words and actions just ten years previously. When Braddock arrived with his regiments in Philadelphia in June 1755, none of the three colonies immediately concerned — Pennsylvania, Virginia, Maryland — had made a move to supply him with the provisions needed for the expedition. But Franklin turned to and in a fortnight had assembled the necessary supplies, an accomplishment which earned the general's praise.[62]

---

[62] Lawrence Henry Gipson, *The British Empire before the American Revolution; VII: The Great War for the Empire. The Victorious Years, 1758–1760* (New York: Knopf, 1949), Chapters II-X; Richard W. Van Alstyne, *Empire and Independence. The International History of the American Revolution* (New York: John Wiley & Sons, 1965), p. 30; *Franklin Papers, VI,* pp. 13 ff. But compare the *Autobiography* (Huntington Library ed., Berkeley and Los Angeles, 1949), pp. 165 ff. Writing his *Autobiography* in the post-Revolution years, Franklin gives a version which cannot be squared with the actual record as found in his own *Papers,* except that he ostentatiously praises his own accomplishment.

Franklin's specious argument before the House of Commons in 1765 was his device for inducing Parliament to repeal the Stamp Act, but the myth took hold easily — it suited the postwar atmosphere of resentment against the British whose support was no longer needed. Superficially, moreover, appearances favored the myth; the British had taken the initiative in fighting the war; it was directed and financed from London, and therefore it took on the coloration of a British war; obviously war feeling did not permeate the masses in America, otherwise the elected assemblies would have come forward with help far more earnestly than they actually did. This war was the central episode of the eighteenth century at least in North America, for on its outcome rested the political future of the entire continent. Yet it passed into history as merely "the French and Indian War." This was the phrase applied to it by the postwar generation of revolution-minded Americans whose resentments crowded out the memory of the conflict and made them indifferent to the security it had given them. It was a misleading term, but it was efficacious in breaking the link with the past and therefore in preparing the ground for the central myth of the Revolution — the belief that America was separate from Europe, that Britain had preyed upon its Colonies for its own benefit, and that the "tyranny" avowed by king and Parliament through the enactment of the Stamp Act aimed at reducing the Colonists to "slavery."

As with Jefferson, so with Ramsay it was gospel that "God made all mankind originally equal." And with this idea of equality went the idea of independence; they were one and the same. Then Ramsay repeated the argument, already familiar, that the English colonists were from their first settlement devoted to liberty according to English ideas and English principles. With the patriots it was a maxim that they were defending the British Constitution against Britain itself. Then Ramsay adopts the familiar agrarian ideal, the characteristic that distinguishes America from Europe. With all the vacant country, every colonist is, or can be, a freeholder. Distance protects him from the "contagion of ministerial influence"; the "enervating opulence" of Europe is yet too far away to have an effect; the country has no gold and silver, but it abounds in natural riches. And with some exaggeration Ramsay depicted it as free of domination by powerful families. Repeating Franklin, he asserted that the people were farmers or planters; not one-fifteenth were merchants, manufacturers or mechanics. In such circumstances the Colonies had advanced almost to the magnitude of a nation, which Europe in its ignorance did not comprehend. The unfortunate Major General Braddock, who lost his army (and his life) in an ambush by French and Indians in 1755, was a symbol in American eyes of European haughtiness, which in its turn was a product of ignorance.

Ramsay understood that the British Empire, in consequence of its immense annexations in 1763 at French and Spanish expense, had grown too large. Britain had destroyed the balance which European sovereigns had long tried to preserve, and so had excited their envy and fear. Enlightened British politicians and writers, especially men conversant with Franklin's ideas, had foreseen this and had begun to have misgivings over the results of the war. They comprehended the position of advantage the Colonies now held in relation to the parent state and understood the weaknesses inherent in an overextended empire. Thomas Anbury, a perceptive army officer serving with Burgoyne in 1777, observed that had the Americans

> but reserved their ideas of independency for half a century longer, from their increase of population and wealth, they would have fixed it without much difficulty, or even the assistance of any other power, and thus become the first nation in the world.

But now, he added with a side glance at France,[63]

> if they attain their boasted end, it must be by the arm of some nation to whom, for want of resources to defray the expences of their alliance, she [America] will be in continual broils and disputes, which may perhaps finally terminate in a total subjection, and that abject slavery they so ridiculously pretend to dread from us. . . .

"Power, like all things human," remarked Ramsay in his book,[64]

---

[63] *Travels through the Interior Parts of America; in a series of letters,* by an Officer, a new edition, 2 vols. (London: for William Lane, 1791). The excerpt is from Letter XXV of June 14, 1777.

[64] Ramsay, *The History of the American Revolution,* I, p. 41.

has its limits, and there is a point beyond which the longest and sharpest sword fails of doing execution. To combine in one uniform system of government the extensive territory then subjected to the British sway appeared to men of reflection a work of doubtful practicability.

Coincidentally, with the removal of hostile neighbors "high notions" of liberty and independence emerged among the Americans.

This train of thought brought Ramsay to Tom Paine and his unforgettable pamphlet, *Common Sense*. An unhappy misfit at home in England, Paine bearing a letter of introduction from Franklin had made his way to Philadelphia late in 1774. There he wrote his impassioned tract which sold out three editions in the single month of January 1776. *Common Sense* suited perfectly the charged atmosphere of the time. Himself a Whig and a patriot and writing not much more than a dozen years after the event, Ramsay wrote a criticism of it that no commentator since has equalled. Paine's pamphlet, declared Ramsay:[65]

> held the most distinguished rank. The style, manner, and language of this performance were calculated to interest the passions, and to rouse all the active powers of human nature. With a view of operating on the sentiments of a religious people, Scripture was pressed into his service, and the powers, and even the name of the king was rendered odious in the eyes of the numerous Colonists who had read and studied the history of the Jews as recorded in the Old Testament. The folly of that people in revolting from a government instituted by Heaven itself, and the oppressions to which they were subjected in consequence of their lusting after kings to rule over them afforded an excellent handle for prepossessing the Colonists in favour of republican institutions, and prejudicing them against kingly government. Hereditary succession was turned into ridicule. The absurdity of subjecting a great continent to a small island on the other side of the globe was represented in such striking language as to interest the honour and pride of the Colonists in renouncing the government of Great Britain. The necessity, the advantage, and practicability of independence were forcibly demonstrated. Nothing could be better timed

---

[65] *Ibid.*, pp. 336–338.

than this performance; it was addressed to free-men, who had just received convincing proof that Great Britain had thrown them out of her protection. . . . It found the Colonists most thoroughly alarmed for their liberties and disposed to do and suffer anything that promised their establishment. In union with the feelings and sentiments of the people, it produced surprising effects. . . . The multitude was hurried down the stream. . . . Some respectable individuals . . . shrunk back . . . but the great bulk of the people, and especially of the spirited and independent part of the community came with surprising unanimity into the project of independence.

The eagerness for independence resulted more from feeling than reasoning. The advantages of an unfettered trade, the prospect of honours and emoluments in administering a new government, were of themselves insufficient motives for adopting this bold measure. . . . The revolution was not forced on the people by ambitious leaders grasping at supreme power, *but every measure* of it was forced on Congress by the necessity of the case. . . . The change of the public mind of America respecting a connection with Great Britain is without a parallel. In the short space of two years, nearly three millions of people passed over from the love . . . of loyal subjects to the hatred and resentment of enemies.

As Ramsay so carefully pointed out, Paine did play on the passions, and designed his tract "to rouse all the active powers of human nature." Therein, of course, lay the secret of his success. Kings, to his inflamed mind, were the root of all evil. Because of them the world was bedevilled by war. Monarchy was the device of "heathens" — idolaters or pagans, and therefore repugnant to all good Christians. (A contemporary critic observed that both of the ancient poets, Homer and Virgil, were "heathens"; but, while Homer and Virgil were much admired by the intellectuals of the Revolution, *Common Sense* was not keyed to them, hence the criticism made no impression.)

Then upon the original evil had been piled the sin of hereditary succession, which was equivalent to usurpation. This asseveration gave Paine his opening for a special attack on the English monarchy, whose origins would not bear the light of day. William the Conqueror was: "A French bastard landing with an armed banditti, and establishing himself king of England against the consent of the natives"; in plain terms he was "a very paltry, rascally original." And:

"In England a king hath little more to do than to make war and give away places. . . . Of more worth is one honest man to society and in the sight of God, than all the crowned ruffians that ever lived." George III was the "hardened, sullen-tempered Pharaoh," "the royal brute of Great Britain" who had made havoc of mankind; and his ministers were a "detestable junto." To accept reconciliation with them would be to "shake hands with murderers."

From these purple passages Paine turned to the question of independence, which he interpreted as meaning "a continental form of government" by a congress of twenty-six men, and which he declared would alone shield the country from involvement in wars such as the kings of England had brought on it in the past. Republics, he sentimentalized, were always at peace; monarchies were hardly ever so, since they were the victims of "enterprising ruffians." Better grounded in the facts than these epithets was the argument, already apparent to the leaders of the Revolution, that no country on the globe was so happily situated or so internally capable of raising a fleet as America. "We need go abroad for nothing," declared Paine. "Building a navy is the best money we can lay out." Then with fine inconsistency, he admitted the need for aid from France and Spain, Britain's monarchical enemies. It was "unreasonable" to expect any kind of help from them, if we mean only to use their assistance to repair the breach and strengthen the connection with Britain. We should publish a manifesto, *addressed to foreign courts,* setting forth our miseries and our desire to be freed from "the cruel disposition of the British court. . . . The custom of all courts is against us and will be so until, by an independence, we take rank with other nations." Finally, concluded Paine, "the Continental Belt is too loosely buckled." [66]

Paradoxical to the dislike of kings, which Ramsay associated with the name of Paine, was the popularity of the French monarchy, especially after the announcement of the alliance of 1778. " 'Long live the King of France,' poured forth from the breath of every private in the Army," wrote Ramsay. And Paine in *The Crisis,* a series of tracts which he started publishing in December 1776, compared the

---

[66] *The Writings of Thomas Paine, secretary for foreign affairs to the Congress . . . in the late war,* (Albany, N. Y.: by Charles R. and George Webster, 1792).

"fraudulent meanness" of England with the "open, noble and generous" conduct of France, in whom "we have found an affectionate
friend, a faithful ally." Then working up to a climactic attack on
British politics as "originally conceived in idiotism, and acted in
madness," Paine sounds the imperial note of the Revolution: Canada
and Nova Scotia will revolt and become part of the United States of
America. Both Halifax and Gibraltar were useless, he insisted; the
French and the Spanish could conquer the British West Indies and
reduce the British Navy to a cipher. For these tracts Paine accepted
money from the French minister in Philadelphia. But by this time
(August 1782) he was really a pathetic figure: French and Spanish
attempts to take Gibraltar had been repulsed, and a resounding
British naval victory in West Indian waters in April had reversed the
balance of power in that theater.[67]

Paine's romantic version of the Franco-American wartime alliance
belongs to the mythology of the Revolution. Idealizing this alliance
and clothing it with a warmth and affection rare, if not unknown, in
the history of international relations stands the name of Lafayette.
The success story of this adventurous youth — not turned twenty
when he joined the Americans in June 1777 — boggles the imagination. Numerous other Frenchmen had preceded him and many
followed, seeking commissions as he did in Washington's army. Some
of them came equipped with substantial experience in the French
army; Lafayette had had virtually none, and at home he was regarded
simply as "the boy" who had just married into the wealthy and influential Noailles family. His father-in-law, the duc d'Ayen, thought
him a madcap; naturally so, since he had run off to America flouting
the king's orders and failing even to say goodbye to his bride, whom
he had made pregnant. Having inherited large landed estates scattered through three provinces, Lafayette enjoyed a handsome income
from rents collected for him by his efficient agent from the tenant
farmers and serfs who actually worked the land. Thus the young
marquis had no need of a sense of responsibility for the things at
home that directly affected him: the business affairs of his estates

---

[67] *Ibid.*, p. 63. Van Alstyne, *Empire and Independence*, p. 202.

and the condition of the French peasants whose labors made freedom, in his case, a reality.[68]

Consumed with ambition for a military career and possessing exceptional personal charm and a capacity to please and impress men who were in a position to grant him the favors he craved, Lafayette boldly demanded and got from the politicians in Philadelphia a major-general's commission. The feat is nothing short of astounding: Congress voted him his rank within less than six weeks after his arrival, putting him ahead of native American officers, not to mention the several Frenchmen whose pleas for rank it continued to ignore. The word, moreover, was passed to Washington to whom he was introduced on the last day of July; and forthwith the young man found himself seated as a regular guest at the commander-in-chief's dinner table. Before the year was over he was given his own division to command, and from that time on was active in the inner councils of war.

The calculations of practical politicians no doubt facilitated this series of personal triumphs: Lafayette's privileged status as a member of the court nobility and the size of his purse, which he always held open, could not fail to impress. The Americans credited him with an influence in French court circles that he did not actually possess. Even the canny Franklin urged upon Washington the wisdom of letting the restless young man have his way. But Lafayette's undisguised admiration for the austere American leader and the age gap between them — he was young enough to be the son of a man who had no son of his own — were compelling factors in his favor. Already in December he could write of his feeling for Washington:[69]

> Our general is a man really made for this revolution, which could not succeed without him. I see him at closer range than any other man in the world and I see him worthy of his coun-

---

[68] These paragraphs on Lafayette are based on the works of Louis Gottschalk: *Lafayette joins the American Army* (Chicago: University of Chicago Press, 1937); *Lafayette and the Close of the American Revolution* (Chicago, 1942); *Lafayette between the American and the French Revolution, 1783–1789* (Chicago, 1950).

[69] L. Gottschalk, *Lafayette Joins the American Army,* p. 62.

try's adoration. . . . Every day my admiration for the beauty of his character and his soul grows greater. . . . His name will be revered in all ages by every lover of liberty and of mankind.

Such adulation, reinforced by incessant activity and single-minded devotion to the American cause, won the affection of a man who was not demonstrative in his affections, and even the ordinary soldiers noticed the intimacy between the father and his would-be son. Lafayette possessed no real military talents, but he managed to make himself conspicuous at opportune times, as at Yorktown; and a wound which he received at Brandywine, not long after his arrival, helped to make him a hero in the eyes of the people.

Quixotic schemes grandiose past the point of absurdity flitted through Lafayette's brain. One was to join with General Thomas Conway and other discontented French officers in America and go on a marauding expedition against the British West Indies. This accomplished, they would follow it up with an attack on the distant British outposts in India. The young man seems to have believed that Versailles would back him up in these projects. But his pet plan, which was never long absent from his mind, was to put himself at the head of an invasion force that would win Canada for America and arouse the enthusiasm of the Canadian French. In fancy he gave himself the title of "the mighty commander-in-chief of the irruption into Canada," "irruption" being the euphemism chosen by advocates of the scheme as a substitute for invasion. The attempt on Canada made in 1775 and 1776 had been a dismal failure, yet it seems to have been widely believed in America that the Canadians were still awaiting "liberation" from their British "oppressors." The significance of the Quebec Act of 1774 in reassuring the Canadian French and in laying the foundations of an autonomous Canadian nation was completely lost upon the Americans.

In his ardor for the American cause Lafayette went deeply into debt. By 1780 he was out of pocket a hundred thousand livres and, in spite of his agent's warning that "he was buying his glory at the expense of his fortune," he incurred a new and even larger debt so that he could carry on in America. Having returned to France in 1779 and recovered the favor of the court, he agitated for the sending of an expeditionary force. The "blessed words of independency and the Rights of Mankind" and other such expressions that he had picked up in America now dropped easily from his lips, though it seems not to have dawned upon him that these phrases might apply to his own peasants. An expeditionary force did leave France in May of 1780, not under the twenty-two-year-old marquis but under the comte de Rochambeau, who was a brigadier general before Lafayette was born. But in American folklore Lafayette is one of the immortals, in stature second only to Washington himself. In a sense he was the embodiment of France itself; and though his contribution to the winning of the war was negligible, his name cast a spell over the American mentality. His closeness to Washington, his largesse, his enthusiasm and ability to attract attention to himself served toward making him a legendary figure.

Other French officers did not share Lafayette's romantic views, but neither did they enjoy Lafayette's successes. Thomas Conway, an Irish soldier of fortune, nursed a private ambition to supersede Washington, and Lafayette for a short time tied his own fortunes to Conway's. Kalb, a Bavarian in the French service who accompanied Lafayette to America, had a low opinion of Washington's military ability. D'Estaing, army trained but put in command of a naval squadron, quarreled bitterly with the Americans, especially with General Sullivan who expected him to collaborate in an attack on the British on Rhode Island; and d'Estaing's men got into brawls with the Americans, especially in Boston where they were forced to stay for some months before sailing for the West Indies.

These realistic experiences got an airing from a sober French historian writing in the postwar years when the wartime alliance was beginning to crack. This author, François Soulés, used documents in preparation for his four-volume work which focused principally upon the military aspects of the war. Well aware of the historic enmity between the Americans and the French prior to the Revolution, Soulés made no effort to gloss over the resentment of the American populace when, beginning with the arrival of d'Estaing's squadron in 1778, they confronted French sailors and soldiers on their soil. Soulés is mindful of the differences in customs, dress, religion and language between the two peoples; and in matter-of-fact style he describes major outbreaks, leading to violence and bloodshed, which took place in Boston, Newport, and Charleston. In each of these cases the American authorities, conscious of the importance of keeping the French in good humor, suppressed intelligence regarding the troubles and offered rewards for apprehension of the instigators. The rewards went unclaimed, however.[70]

Lafayette escaped involvement in all these unpleasantries. Neither was he ever a party to the designs of French diplomacy, nor to the practical problems relative to the wartime connection between France and America. The Sieur Alexandre Gérard and his successor, the Chevalier de la Luzerne, managed these matters with great skill, but in so doing kept themselves out of the limelight. Back of them, of course, stood the figure of the reticent foreign minister at Versailles, the comte de Vergennes. But, for all the careful direction he gave to French diplomacy and the caution with which he approached the touchy problem of American independence, Vergennes found himself ensnared in a web which he himself had helped to spin. The kind of a permanent knot between the two countries for which Vergennes had gambled, and which Gérard and Luzerne succeeded temporarily in tying, failed to hold; it began to slip in the early stages of the peace negotiations in 1782, and the wartime alliance officially laid down as perpetual imperceptibly faded away thereafter.[71]

Both during and after the war, however, Lafayette played the gallant role of Don Quixote to the Americans. Professional French diplomats were his Sancho Panza, but he had no need of them. Nor they of him. A court noble with unusual gifts, Lafayette so captured American popular fancy with his boundless enthusiasm and his constant avowals of affection for his "beloved general" that the realism of the alliance was lost in the magic of his name. In American eyes

---

[70] Francois Soulés, *Histoire des Troubles de l'Amérique Anglaise* . . . , 4 vols. (Paris: chez Buisson, 1787), *III*, pp. 61–62; Charles Stedman, *The History of the Origin, Progress, and Termination of the American War*, 2 vols. (London: printed for the author; and sold by J. Murray, J. Debrett, & J. Kirby, 1794); Louis Gottschalk, *Lafayette Joins the American Army* (Chicago: Chicago University Press, 1937), *passim*; Van Alstyne, *Empire and Independence* (New York: John Wiley & Sons, 1965), pp. 156–158, 164.

[71] See Van Alstyne, *Ibid.*, pp. 191–232.

he was not merely a hero, he became "a kind of national patron saint."[72]

This attribute of sainthood Lafayette acquired while he was making a grand tour of all but the three southernmost of the American states during the second half of 1784. It was his third trip to America, this time a mission of goodwill only, but it yielded rich rewards in terms of popular acclaim, civic celebrations, and special honors bestowed upon him by various cities and states. Maryland's legislature made him a citizen of that state and the Continental Congress, faced with a possible demise now that the Confederation was beginning to pull apart, listened to him plead for a stronger federal union and a continuation of intimate friendship with France. Of course a week's visit with Washington at Mount Vernon formed an important part of the still young marquis's itinerary. It was Lafayette's last chance for comradeship with the man whom he deeply reverenced. Anecdotes and legends arose out of this visit to embroider it with sentiment; and, while carefully protecting his popular reputation for modesty, Lafayette took steps to coach contemporary writers, including Brissot de Warville and the Whig historian, William Gordon, to write of his exploits during the Revolution as he himself viewed them. From this pilgrimage too arose the long-lived tradition of American gratitude to France.[73]

Lafayette made one more trip to America — in 1824, forty years later — to share in the celebration of the fiftieth anniversary of the Revolution. Honors and attentions were again heaped upon him, and an "authentic biography" of the marquis appeared opportunely in Philadelphia. It was the kind of a biography that could not fail to please the man who was now close to his seventieth birthday. Wrote the author:[74]

> Amid the enjoyments of wealth and rank and domestic happiness, the voice of suffering freedom and oppressed humanity

---

[72] Louis Gottschalk, *Lafayette between the American and the French Revolution, 1783–1789* (Chicago: University of Chicago Press, 1950), p. 144.

[73] *Ibid.*, pp. 83–95, 109–150, 431–432, 437.

[74] *An Authentic Biography of General La Fayette* (Philadelphia: A. Sherman, 1824).

reached his ears and penetrated his heart, and he relinquished the earthly paradise around him, to come and share the perils and hardships and privations of our arduous conflict determined to live a hero or die a martyr in the cause of American independence.

Who could deny it? It was a most effective myth *because it was true.* And Lafayette's ears may even have burned as he listened to Edward Everett, the orator, declaim before a Phi Beta Kappa audience in Cambridge, Massachusetts on the Revolution as "that most important era in human history" and then remind his hearers of the glorious part their honored guest had played in it.[75] So Lafayette lived to see his youthful ambition realized to the full: he was elected to the American hall of fame.

VII

John Adams mingled distrust with admiration for Lafayette. While in Paris during the war he inquired about the famous Noailles family, connection with whom gave Lafayette much of his reputation, and arrived somewhat extravagantly at the conclusion that they were "more powerful than the House of Bourbon, at least they had more influence in the army. . . ." But later Adams began having unpleasant doubts about the marquis, emphasizing his unlimited ambition. Lafayette, he observed, "grasps at all civil, political and military [power], and would be thought the *unum necessarium* in everything." Still, concluded Adams, "he has so much real merit, such family supports, and so much favor at court, that he need not recur to artifice." [76] Adams's young son John Quincy held the marquis almost in contempt, characterizing him as of "the soliciting and intriguing kind," branding him as a fanatic on "the rights of man," and criticizing him for his "ungovernable ambition in disguise." [77]

---

[75] Edward Everett, *An Oration at Cambridge . . . before Phi Beta Kappa,* August 27, 1824.

[76] *The Adams Papers, III,* p. 71; *IV,* pp. 83–84.

[77] To Wm. Vans Murray, Mar. 26 and 29, 1799. *The Writings of John Quincy Adams,* Worthington C. Ford (ed.), 7 vols. (New York: Macmillan, 1913), *II,* pp. 396, 399.

Tom Paine irked both of the Adamses even more. The demagoguery of *Common Sense* disgusted the elder Adams when the pamphlet first appeared in 1776: Paine's epithets against monarchy and against George III he regarded as in very bad taste.[78] Subsequently, we remember, John Adams argued the advantages of the Constitution of 1787 because it met his idea of an elective monarchy. Meanwhile Paine left America and in due course plunged into the affairs of the French Revolution, publishing a new tract on *The Rights of Man*. The belief that all men are created equal, which Paine and Jefferson propounded in 1776, received a further ideological advance in the egalitarian atmosphere of revolutionary France. Jefferson, having made this doctrine the cornerstone of the American Revolution, praised the French version of 1791 and came out heartily in Paine's defense. But in contrast to the appearances of general acquiescence in 1776 (the sentiments of the loyalist and neutralist portions of the population being ignored), the doctrine now aroused heated argument in America. Tom Paine was no longer in favor and John Quincy Adams, now twenty-five years of age, could hardly restrain himself. Was Paine's tract, he demanded, "the canonical book of political scripture? As containing the true doctrine of popular infallibility, from which it would be heretical to depart in one single point?" And was Paine "the holy father of our political faith," the pamphlet "his Papal bull of infallible virtue?" [79]

John Quincy, however, could be as demagogic as Paine when he became excited, and his several patriotic orations supplied completeness to the myth of the Revolution. As with his father, it was an article of faith with him that the American Revolution was without precedent. It stood alone in history, and was too sacred to stand comparison with any other revolution. Its origin, he declaimed in his first Fourth of July oration (1793), "bears a character different from that of any other civil contest that had ever arisen amongst men." It was "the deliberate though energetic effort of freemen to repel the insidious approaches of tyranny." This affirmation, echoing

---

[78] *The Adams Papers, III*, pp. 330–334.
[79] *Observations on Paine's Rights of Man, . . .* by Publicola (Glasgow: A. Duncan & R. Chapman, 1792).

the cries of 1775, is then supported with allusions to "the holy temple of American Liberty," and to the "tomb of departed tyranny."

Then with ponderous rhetoric Adams reiterates the guilt thesis of Jefferson and Paine. The British nation "were divided between ignorance and terror . . . [and] indulged their vanity with preposterous opinions of insulting superiority." As for the king, he depended

> upon the prostituted valor of his mercenary legions, he was deaf to complaints, he was inexorable to the remonstrances of violated freedom . . . and ready to believe what the courtly tribe about his throne did not fail to assure him . . . Seven years of ineffectual hostility at length taught the dreadful lesson of wisdom. . . . With sullen impotence, she [Britain] yielded to the pressure of accumulated calamity.

By this time the French had guillotined their king and set up a republic; and, disregarding the historical record of the revolutionary Americans importuning the French monarchy for aid and leaning heavily upon it to see them through to independence, young Adams pictured the "French nation" fighting the battles of freedom for the Americans and then in consequence moving on to revolution themselves. He declared:[80]

> By a natural and easy application to themselves of the principles upon which the Americans asserted the justice of their warfare, they were led to inquire into the nature of the obligation which prescribed their submission to their own sovereign; and when they discovered that the consent of the people is the only legitimate source of authority, they necessarily drew the conclusion that their own obedience was no more than the compulsive acquiescence of servitude . . . the magic talisman of despotism was broken, the spell of prescriptive tyranny was dissolved, and the pompous pageant of their monarchy instantaneously crumbled to atoms. . . .

Next an oration at Plymouth in honor of the landing of the Pilgrims gave Adams the chance to advance the cause of ancestor worship. Other nations, he told his audience, were forced to trace a lawless

---

[80] *An Oration pronounced July 4, 1793, at the request of the inhabitants of the town of Boston, in commemoration of the anniversary of American Independence* (Boston: Benjamin Edes & Son, 1793).

ancestry into the "caverns of ravishers and robbers," but ours were "men upon whose virtues you can dwell with honest exultation." Unlike the Romans, whose father was "the suckling of a wolf, you are not descended from a nauseous compound of fanaticism and sensuality, whose only paradise was a brothel." No "bastard Norman tyrant" landed on the rock; on the contrary, the first settlers endeavored to found a perfect republic. And, concluded the orator:[81]

> The destinies of this empire, as they appear in prospect before us, disdain the powers of human calculation . . . the glory and greatness of all our descendants is in our hands. . . .

His full creed Adams set forth in a lengthy Fourth of July oration which he delivered in Washington, D. C., in 1821. England, he asserted, had only partially escaped from "that portentous system of despotism and of superstition," of which the Crown and the Mitre were symbols. The English "held their title to liberty, like their title to lands, from the bounty of a man; and in their moral and political chronology, the great charter of Runny Mead was the beginning of the world." Not so America, nurtured by its position and education in the more comprehensive and original doctrines of human rights which the Protestant reformers had taught, but which the Church in its sophistry and rapacity had tried to obliterate. "In the heat of this war of moral elements, our forefathers sought refuge from its fury in the then wilderness of this Western world." They were exiles of liberty and conscience. Then, just as they were attaining the maturity of political manhood, a British Parliament,

> on the naked unblushing allegation of absolute and uncontrollable power, undertook . . . to levy . . . taxes upon the people of America for the benefit of the people of Britain. This enormous project of public robbery . . . excited throughout the Colonies one general burst of indignant resistance.

Your fathers, Adams assured his audience, "went forth with a sling and a stone to encounter the massive vigor of this Goliath."

The religious reformation, Adams argued, had supplied the inspiration for this rebellion. It had weakened the crippling effects and

---

[81] *An Oration at Plymouth* . . . (Boston: Russell & Cutler, 1802).

double cords of "ecclesiastical imposture and political oppression." It had brought "an improvement in the science of mind; an improvement in the intercourse of man with his Creator, and in his acquaintance with himself. It was . . . a step in the progress of man in comparison with which" all other steps were "but the paces of a pigmy to the stride of a giant." It led to the social compact on which the exiles to New England rested. In the compact conquest and servitude had no part; there was no brute force; all was voluntary, unbiassed consent.

With this blend of Puritan piety and faith in a virtuous republic founded upon Reason, which was dogma according to the teachings of eighteenth-century rationalism, John Quincy was able to pronounce the Declaration of Independence (which he read aloud as part of his oration) a sacred text. The Declaration, he declaimed:[82]

> proved that the social compact was no figment of the imagination; but a real, solid, and sacred bond of the social union. . . . It stands, and must forever stand alone, a beacon on the summit of the mountain.

So the Revolution had risen into a sacred memory, and the Declaration of Independence was its bible. Every word of the Declaration was gospel, and Adams was a fundamentalist in his worship of it. As one of "the most detested tyrants," King George III had sinned; but, as a Christian Adams felt, his sins should be forgiven. No prayer for forgiveness occurs in the oration, however; nor could we know that Adams himself was so inclined, had he not said so in a letter to a friend who, being a liberal Catholic of Baltimore, was disposed to be critical of Adams's eloquence.[83]

---

[82] *An Address* (Washington: July 4, 1821).
[83] *Writings, VII*, pp. 113–123, 127–136.

A Rising American Nationalism

3

In contrast to this patriotic religiosity, John Quincy Adams had clear-sighted views relating to vital, though controversial issues confronting his generation. Philosophically he shared his father's ideas, though perhaps he was a shade less skeptical of human nature; and of his extensive diplomatic service in Europe, which began early in life, he took full advantage. He held a firm grip on the realities of international affairs, was fully aware of the limitations imposed upon the United States by the changing situation in Europe, and reached conclusions on specific issues eminently sensible relative to what was possible. He began his diplomatic career at The Hague in 1794, when he was still under thirty years of age and at a time when The Netherlands was facing the imminent prospect of becoming a client state of the French Republic; three years later his father, by that time President, advanced him to the post at Berlin, which had advantages over The Hague as a center for observation; in 1801 he resigned this position and returned to the United States, where he was elected to the Senate; but in 1809 President Madison sent him to St. Petersburg. He was still in Russia when Napoleon invaded that country; and the latter's disastrous retreat from Moscow, which began on October 28, 1812, gave him the impression that Russia would become the dominant power in Europe. In 1814 he was ordered to Ghent in Belgium where, in company with Henry Clay, Thomas F. Bayard and Jonathan Russell, he negotiated the peace with Great Britain which terminated the War of 1812.

Like his father, young John Quincy pinned all his hopes and fears to the permanency of the United States, whose weakness as a sovereign state posed many questions during these years. America was "like a large inn," as his father's friend Benjamin Rush picturesquely put it. "It has accommodated strangers at the expense of the landlord and his children, who have been driven by them from the bar and their bedrooms and compelled at times to seek a retreat in their garret and cellar." It had no national character, "and however much we boast of it, there are very few true Americans in the United States." [1]

With the discontent over the Alien and Sedition laws in mind, John Quincy recoiled from the danger of the Union falling apart. "A separation," he felt, would be "the greatest calamity that can befall us. . . . Nothing could make it excusable, and we can never be safe so long as any attempt for it shall not be considered as treason." Living in Berlin and observing the perennial quarrels of European states, he looked to

> the *Union* of our country as to the sheet anchor of our hopes, and to its dissolution as to the most dreadful of our dangers. . . . If once we divide, our exposure to foreign assault will at once be multiplied in proportion to the number of states into which we shall be split, and aggravated in proportion to the weakness of every single part compared with the strength of the whole. . . . Each of the separate states will from the moment of disunion become with regard to the others a foreign power. . . . Wars will soon ensue. These must end either in the conquest of one party by the other, or in frail, precarious, jealous compromises . . . leaving on both sides the burden of its army as the only guarantee for its security.

Standing armies, intolerable taxes, forced levies, contributions, conscriptions, and requisitions were, in his mind, "the unavoidable and fatal chain of which disunion is but the first link." [2]

---

[1] To John Adams, Aug. 14, 1805. *The Spur of Fame. Dialogues of John Adams and Benjamin Rush, 1805–1813,* John A. Schutz and Douglas Adair (eds.) (San Marino, Calif.: The Huntington Library, 1966), p. 31. Hereafter cited as Schutz and Adair.

[2] To his mother, Abigail Adams, July 3, 1799 and to his brother T. B. Adams, Feb. 14, 1801. Worthington C. Ford (ed.), *The Writings of John Quincy*

Prospects for "national felicity and glory" took first place among John Quincy's hopes. With the Union preserved, he was certain America would "proceed with gigantic strides to honor and consideration, and national greatness"; but once broken, "we shall soon divide into a parcel of petty tribes at perpetual war with one another, swayed by rival European powers . . . who will [at] the same time govern and despise the party they may respectively protect."[3] The good example set by the late King Frederick II of Prussia was not lost upon John Quincy, nor was the parallel between America and Prussia, both of which had arrived on the international stage at about the same time. Frederick always answered with his own hand every dispatch from every one of his ministers abroad; and he was cautious and vigilant in counteracting the intrigues of other powers and thereby escaping involvement in their rival ambitions. France, Adams observed, considered the United States as forming a weight in the balance of Europe, and Britain would necessarily pursue the same supposition. Between the two, however, Adams was much more apprehensive of France. It was *natural* policy for the government of a great state like France to ally itself with the opposition party in a small nation like America. This policy "is founded deep in the human character, and all history is full of it."[4]

Pursuing this line of thought, Adams poured scorn on James Monroe for publishing a tract based on the notion that "free people seldom intrigue together." Monroe had taken sides in the French Revolution, like Jefferson displaying his dislike of kings and assuming that only monarchs stooped to intrigue. For proof Monroe appealed to Greek history

> at a period when the only power that could have any influence over the people . . . was a king. But if Mr. Monroe had chosen another period when the Greek Republics received a nominal restoration of their liberty by a Roman consul, or had he chosen

---

Adams, II (New York: Macmillan, 1913), pp. 427, 501–502. Hereafter cited as JQA, *Writings.*

[3] To Charles Adams from The Hague, June 9, 1796, *Ibid., JQA Writings, I,* pp. 493–494.

[4] To John Adams, Jan. 20, 1797, and to Abigail, June 27, 1798. *JQA Writings, II,* pp. 88, 323–324.

to recollect any part of the Roman history, he would have found that the government of a Republic was as capable of intriguing with the leaders of a free people as neighboring monarchs.

More convincing, however, than Monroe's "lessons from history" were the contemporary experiences of Holland, Italy and Switzerland wherein the French, by intriguing with subversive elements, had obtained the upper hand and reduced these republics to subjection.[5]

Both the elder Adams and his son read with approval Edmund Burke's *Reflections on the Revolution in France,* first published in November 1790. The *Reflections* were a model expression of conservative philosophy and a blunt condemnation of the French National Assembly for usurping power and for tearing out by the roots all the historic institutions of France. "The present ruling authority in France," wrote Burke, "affects to be a pure democracy, though I think it in a direct train of becoming shortly a mischievous and ignoble oligarchy. . . . Here end all the deceitful dreams and visions of the equality and rights of men." [6] The basic political principle in France, observed John Quincy seven years later, was still "the sovereign people"; but in their name the guillotine had mowed its thousands and the grapeshot had swept off their tens of thousands. Soon a single military government would take over and make itself supreme in Europe.[7]

Like his father, John Quincy held that passion, not reason, controlled human conduct, and that fear was one of the passions. "The influence of fear is merely instinctive, and never founded on argument," he wrote his friend William Vans Murray from Berlin. "It seldom survives the pressure of actual danger, and therefore seldom interferes with the operation of active violent passions." Intelligence of the outbreak of a savage negro insurrection in Haiti evoked this sentiment, accompanied by fear lest the movement spread to the mainland of America. In such case the eastern states would be obliged to go to the aid of the southern.

---

[5] To Abigail, *Ibid.,* pp. 324–328.

[6] The Works of the Right Honorable Edmund Burke, 3rd. ed., *III* (Boston: Little, Brown, 1869), pp. 396, 492; JQA, *Writings, III,* p. 227.

[7] To John Adams from London, Sept. 19 and 21, 1797. JQA, *Writings, II,* 207–216.

"Unlimited democracy" Adams regarded as absurd, "the most extraordinary of all infatuations," [8] and out of keeping with the inherited New England notion of a virtuous republic. The Bible, roundly declared the elder Adams, was "the most republican book in the world." It furnished "the only system that ever did or ever will preserve a republic in the world." And apparently without tongue in cheek, he added: [9]

> I say then that national morality never was and never can be preserved without the utmost purity and chastity in women. . . . Therefore, my dear Fellow Citizens of America, you must ask leave of your wives and daughters to preserve your republic.

John Quincy's rejection of the French Revolution and of the war-like course it was taking, especially in 1798 when hostilities had broken out between the French and the Americans on the sea, made him feel that Europe was doomed and convinced him that the United States too must become warlike. Force and force alone was required for the government of mankind, and the United States must build a navy and seek mastery over the Caribbean. It must have the British as well as the French West India islands, the "natural connection" of those islands being with the American and not with the European continent. [10] The idea was not original with John Quincy — it dated back to American Revolutionary days — but it was he who, as secretary of state, put the official stamp of approval upon it in 1823, a quarter of a century later.

"A nation of fanatical atheists," "the terrible Republic" — these were the phrases on the tip of John Quincy's pen whenever, during the 1790's, he mentioned the French. Robespierre and the Terror were fresh in his mind. In the six years since 1789, he pessimistically wrote his father from the relatively safe haven of The Hague, the French "have contributed more to the restoration of Vandalic ignorance than whole centuries can retrieve." They had given alarming proof of a "frantic delirium" in which the arts and sciences, genius

---

[8] To T. B. Adams, Berlin, Dec. 3, 1800. *Ibid.,* p. 485.
[9] To Rush, Feb. 2, 1807. Schutz and Adair, p. 76.
[10] To Wm. Vans Murray, July 14 and 22, 1798, JQA, *Writings, II,* pp. 336–337, 343–344.

and learning might succumb to political fanaticism. And: "if the principle is finally to prevail, which puts the scepter of sovereignty into the hands of the European Sans Culottes,[11] they will soon reduce everything to the level of their own ignorance."[12] With France under a military government, "by turns anarchical and despotic, and perhaps with all the democratical forms." and with Europe enjoying scarcely any liberties worth fighting for, America must somehow be "rescued from all the disgraceful fetters of foreign influence."[13]

The French, argued John Quincy, were bent on sucking the United States into another war with Great Britain; and he readily comprehended that this had been their purpose in sending Citizen Genet to America in 1793. Genet had paid his respects to the populace rather than to the government, had played on the latent sense of enmity toward Britain, had fed the appetite for adventure, plunder and conquest. Unperceived by themselves, the Americans would make war on the British independently of France but in so doing would serve French interests just as effectively as though they were in open alliance. With difficulty Washington had checkmated Genet; but now in 1795 with the dispatch of a second and more experienced envoy, M. Adet, the French Republic was in the mood for a second try. It was important to head off the pending rapprochement with Britain which John Jay had prepared with Lord Grenville in London the year previous; and Adet was just the man for the job. The French had used him to subvert the Swiss in Geneva.[14]

Having personally conferred with Jay in London, Adams appreciated the value of the latter's diplomacy. It meant an honorable peace with Britain; but should it fail and war ensue, inevitably the

---

[11] *Sans-Culotte* was the epithet adopted by opponents of the Revolution to express their contempt. The *culotte* was the garment worn by gentlemen to cover the body from the waist to the knees. The Revolutionaries, or *patriotes* as they called themselves, discarded it in favor of the *pantalon* (trousers).

[12] From The Hague, July 27, 1795. *Ibid., I,* p. 389.

[13] From London, Sept. 21, 1797. *Ibid., II,* pp. 215–216.

[14] *Ibid., I,* pp. 148–176; and to John Adams, May 22, 1795. *Ibid.,* pp. 353–363. On Citizen Genet in America and on Jay's treaty see R. W. Van Alstyne, *American Diplomacy in Action* (Gloucester, Mass.: Peter Smith, 1968), pp. 687–688, 707–714, and other entries in the index.

American Union would break up — it could not survive the shock of another conflict with the mother country. But England itself was under a strain; its deficiency in manpower for the navy was prodigious and its resources limited. France held ten thousand British seamen prisoners of war. Britain would be annihilated if it lost control of the sea. "In short, Sir," he confided to his father, "the situation of this country, external and internal, appears to be perilous, and its prospects gloomy in the extreme." [15]

In The Hague John Quincy kept himself informed on the controversy raging in America over Jay's treaty. Not so much the treaty itself but the men who were sponsoring it — they were the real objects of attack. A combination of personal envy toward Jay, factious enmity within the government, and subversive French influence working secretly operated against the treaty to make it appear thoroughly unpatriotic. It was too much to expect that any treaty with Great Britain would ever be acclaimed. The two nations were too much in competition with each other to make this practicable. Young Adams took account of the damage that popular emotions, feeding on prejudice, could inflict upon a beneficial international agreement. He noted[16] that in all ages and in all countries

> instability has been the most essential characteristic of popular opinion. It is so in America, and will infallibly become so more and more in proportion as the increase of population shall multiply the quantity of opinions. The revolutions of popular opinion are to be considered as things of course. . . . We are . . . all much alike in this respect, and the man who has never been at different periods strenuously attached to opposite opinions, would be one of the rarest phenomena in creation.

In Adams's mind Jay's treaty was confirmation of the soundness of Washington's system of neutrality. It would resolve the doubt of peace or war with Great Britain, and, while the French might be expected to intensify their intrigue in America, it would be contrary to their interests to begin a war. But if the treaty failed of ratification,

---

[15] Oct. 23, 1794; Aug. 31 and Sept. 12, 1795. JQA, *Writings, I*, pp. 201–209, 400–417.

[16] To his brother Charles, Sept. 15, 1795. *Ibid.*, pp. 417–418.

they would have a fresh incentive for pushing the United States into hostilities with their great enemy. Washington alone could head this off. Only the weight of his character and reputation, his firmness and intrepidity, could stem the torrent still tumbling with fury and so loud that it could be heard in Europe. But if Washington's system prevailed, Adams believed that within ten years the United States would be ranked among the most powerful and opulent nations. It was already wealthy, and he was perplexed by the success partisanship was having at such a time in generating animosity against the President.[17] Foremost to his way of thinking was the British agreement to turn over the historic lake posts in the northwest; and he feared that factionalism and intrigue in America would ruin the treaty and sacrifice this very practical gain. Moreover, historically, he knew, these posts had been of vital importance to Canada; and their evacuation demonstrated that Britain was prepared eventually to sacrifice that country.

The posts were duly relinquished as per agreement on June 1, 1796, but seven weeks later John Quincy in The Hague was still in suspense. "I now think almost day and night upon the delivery of the Western posts," he wrote his father, July 21. "I now hope for the event as anxiously as it is dreaded by all the Gallo-Americans." [18] The French were at fault in thinking they could maneuver Washington from office and change American policy in their favor. Having at last learned of the treaty's success, Adams was certain that Washington now "stands fixed as the foundations of the world." The French could not "root out that man's merits and services from the memory" of Americans; and should Jefferson, who had opposed the treaty, follow Washington as President, he would pursue the same general system of policy.[19]

Adams attributed persistent French illusions about American friendship to the intrigues and false notions inculcated in French minds by Americans living in Paris who were enemies of Washington. "The greatest enemies of America in France are Americans them-

---

[17] To Sylvania Bourne, Dec. 24, 1795. *Ibid.,* 466–468.
[18] *Ibid., II,* pp. 3–14; and to Timothy Pickering, Nov. 4, 1795. *Ibid.,* pp. 35–40.
[19] To Jos. Pitcairn, Nov. 13, 1796. *Ibid.,* pp. 40–43.

selves," he told his father. "Our treaty with Britain is a stalking horse, the use of which they were taught from our side of the water." [20] And though unable to say why, the newspapers of Paris evinced a strong dislike for the treaty; nor had they anything good to say about Washington's Farewell Address, which the rest of Europe greatly admired. James Monroe was particularly culpable: as Washington's minister to France, he had virtually betrayed his chief and poisoned the minds of his French friends. He had also fed and housed that "filthy beast," Tom Paine, until Mrs. Monroe had turned him out. Paine had written a libellous attack on Washington while enjoying Monroe's hospitality; and this and Paine's facetious remarks on the Christian religion aroused all of Adams's instincts against him.[21]

By this time the Directory had seized power in France and Bonaparte was beginning to appear on the horizon — "the comet of the day," John Quincy described him. "He is certainly not an ordinary man. It is not easy to see what the French Republic will do with him." The French were now experts at picking a quarrel: they had ruined Geneva, and would do the same to all the Italian states. In America, the Directory hoped to overturn the federal government and had replaced M. Adet with another seasoned diplomat, Joseph Fauchet, who had had close contact with Monroe. By promoting a southern or a western republic and thus isolating the eastern states they could best accomplish their ends; but, thought Adams, they were more likely to dirve the United States even closer to Britain.[22] "There is not one *nation* in Europe, but what mixes a little envy and a little fear in their sentiments and opinions concerning us and our present affairs," he told his friend Joseph Pitcairn. "All of them have that sort of feeling with which under the ancient regime an old nobleman looked upon a *parvenu*."[23]

---

[20] May 20, June 7, July 2, 1797. *Ibid.,* pp. 167–170, 177, 181.

[21] To Abigail, Feb. 8, 1797; and to John Adams, Jan. 14, Mar. 30, Apr. 30, May 11, 1797. *Ibid.,* pp. 77–89, 109–111, 148, 161–162, 166–167.

[22] To John Adams, Apr. 3 and May 20, 1797, and to Pitcairn, Jan. 13, 1797. *Ibid.,* pp. 74–77, 155–157, 167–170.

[23] To Pitcairn, Mar. 31, 1797. *Ibid.,* pp. 154–155.

From his new post in Berlin John Quincy awaited intelligence of the outcome of Napoleon's invasion of Egypt. Its failure, for which he hoped, would benefit America; but if it succeeded, France would be the ruler of all Europe; or if it resulted only in a draw with Great Britain, all the old dangers would remain alive. But in the long run, Adams had faith, America would overcome the risks of separatist conspiracies, thickly sown though they were. Nature, he was confident, "has given us the most effectual security against any permanent French domination." America was out of reach, and could not be treated like the European satellites. Meanwhile, alluding again to the idea, which he had borrowed from Turgot, Louis XVI's one-time finance minister, that Europe would ultimately lose its West Indian colonies, he suggested that it was almost time to conquer and annex these islands. The conquest would feed the martial spirit, which Adams regarded as essential for the preservation of the country.[24]

Seeing the world through the eyes of the Adamses, father and son, the influential Reverend Jedidiah Morse, whose book, *An American Geography,* had long since given him his fame, took to his pulpit to warn his congregation, and beyond it the country at large, against the "atheistical, demoralizing and detestable principles" which the agents of that "corrupt and corrupting nation," France, were spreading among the citizenry. Having learned of the British naval victory over Napoleon at the mouth of the Nile, for which John Quincy had been hoping, Morse in his Thanksgiving sermon for 1798 rejoiced in the breathing spell it would give both the United States and Europe, but cautioned nevertheless against further French attempts at subversion such as had been successfully tried out in Switzerland. The Directory, he charged, was plotting to send an expedition of blacks from Haiti to foment a rebellion of the Southern negroes.

To make his case complete the clergyman in a fifty-page appendix to his sermon printed diplomatic documents to show how cunning French diplomacy had been ever since 1778 when, taking advantage of the wartime alliance against Britain, it set out to draw America into the French orbit. John Adams must have supplied Morse with these

---

[24] To Murray, Jan. 27 and Mar. 20, 1798. *Ibid.,* pp. 240–247, 270–273.

documents: they reflected his point of view and made him the central hero in thwarting what Morse called the perfidy and "shameless effrontery" of France. But, like Adams, Morse recognized that France was only doing what her "national interest" dictated. "For my part," he declared, "I look first for the *interest* of a nation; having found where that lies, I always expect them to pursue it, let the appearances be as they may." Having said that, he was ready to echo Washington; *"Our true interest,"* he wanted his readers to know, *"consists in avoiding too close a connexion with any nation, and by a just and pacific policy to derive commercial benefits from all."* Then, borrowing his text from Psalms 11:3 — "If the foundation be destroyed, what can the righteous do?" — Morse pointed at religion and government as the foundations and painted the contrast between America with its Christian rulers and France, whose revolutionary assembly had abolished the Sabbath and profaned the churches with the worship of infamous prostitutes.[25]

Variations upon these themes by Morse, accompanied by a liberal sprinkling of copybook phrases useful today by orators who enjoy denouncing "Godless Russia," dropped from the pens of other New England clergymen. Europe exhibited "a disgustful scene of Gothic barbarity and blood," and the French were "cannibals" out to plunder the world. There have always been individuals who denied God; "but never, till very lately, did we hear or read of the rulers of a whole nation espousing the cause of atheism." From "the workshops of Satan" these demoralizing principles could spread, and within a few years America, "this happy Christian country," would become the theatre of French anarchy and immorality.[26]

---

[25] Jedidiah Morse, A Sermon Thanksgiving, Nov. 29, 1798, 2d. ed. (Boston: Samuel Hall, 1799); and *Ibid., A Sermon, exhibiting the present dangers and consequent duties of the citizens of the U. S. A.* (Charlestown, Fast Day, Apr. 25, 1799: Samuel Etheridge.)

[26] Theodore Dwight, *An Oration . . . on . . . American Independence,* July 4, 1798. (Hartford: Hudson & Goodwin, 1798); Abiel Holmes, *Sermon on Fast Day, April 25, 1799.* (Boston: Young & Minns); Samuel Stillman, *Sermon, April 25, 1799* (Boston: Manning & Loring); Amos Stoddard, *An Oration,* July 4, 1799 (Portland: E. A. Jenks); Edward St. Loe Livermore, *An Oration in commemoration of the dissolution of the political union between the U. S. A.*

II

Two seasoned European observers, one English the other French, spent upwards of two years in America, 1795 to 1797, and subsequently published informative and provocative books on the impressions they had gained.[27] The Englishman was Isaac Weld, twenty-five years of age and a writer on geography; the Frenchman was the duc de la Rochefoucault Liancourt who, after the manner of his famed seventeenth-century ancestor, wrote with verve and dry wit. An exile from the French Revolution, La Rochefoucault was nevertheless thoroughly French in outlook, but translations of his book into English and German showed that both the author and his subject had a wide appeal. John Quincy Adams read him attentively while in Berlin, and Jefferson was familiar with the book. Weld was only half the age of the Frenchman, but he also possessed a well-developed critical sense; and while each one wrote from his own standpoint, they concurred in many of the judgments on what they saw and heard in America.

Jay's treaty was, as La Rochefoucault put it, the universal topic of conversation and the principal subject of discussion in the newspapers. Naturally the Frenchman viewed the treaty with distaste, and he criticized it several times in the course of his two volumes. It was "a monument to the weakness of America," temporarily profitable to the merchants but productive of evil consequences in the long run. It violated previous engagements with France and:[28]

---

and France, July 17, 1799 (Portsmouth, N. H.: Charles Peirce); Thomas White Thompson, *An Oration, July 4, 1799*, at Salisbury, N. H. (Concord: Geo. Hough.); and for a more objective speech see Alexander Addison, *An Oration on the rise and progress of the U. S. A. to the present crisis.* . . . (Philadelphia: John Ormond, 1798).

[27] Isaac Weld, Jr., *Travels through the States of North America and the Provinces of . . . Canada during the years 1795, 1796, and 1797.* (London: John Stockdale, 1799). Hereafter cited as *Travels;* the duke de la Rochefoucault, *Travels through the United States of North America, the Country of the Iroquois, and Upper Canada, in the years 1795, 1796, and 1797,* 2 vols. (London: R. Phillips, 1799). Hereafter cited as La Rochefoucault.

[28] La Rochefoucault, *I*, pp. 381–382, 408.

it evidently clashes with the repeated professions of friendship which America has so loudly and repeatedly made to France. . . . America cannot but be aware of the unfriendly sentiments, nay hatred and ill-will, which the English government entertains toward the Union. . . . England will ever consider the inhabitants of the United States as revolted subjects . . . ; and though Great Britain condescends at present to enter into temporary negotiations with America, it is because . . . she hopes to derive signal advantages from a treaty, which cannot but considerably increase the sale of her manufactures, displease France, alienate her from America, and injure her trade. She hopes, by means of this rupture, to render America dependent on the English government, and in this state of dependence to force her to conclude another alliance. . . . To conclude a treaty of amity on such a foundation is to deceive America; as it clearly presumes that she must break off the former connexion with France, *her true and natural ally* who, as soon as she shall have obtained a regular settled government . . . will become more powerful than ever.

But La Rochefoucault found consolation in the exasperation against England that spread through all ranks of American society, and in the spell-binding power that the memory of Lafayette exerted over popular sentiment. "My new acquaintances," he wrote while traveling through western New York, "were people of uncouth manners, and without the least education; but their opinions were just and sensible, and their judgments extremely correct."

They manifested a strong attachment to France, and most earnestly wished her[29]

success. They hate England, confide in their President, and speak of Lafayette with tears in their eyes. This universal attachment to Lafayette, and the grateful sentiments of him expressed *by all,* refute in a forcible manner the charge of levity and ingratitude preferred against the Americans. 'May he come,' said a man to us this morning, 'may he come, we will make him rich. It is through him that France made us free . . . .

Vexed though he was over the ratification of Jay's treaty, La Rochefoucault nevertheless understood why this document survived the resentments that it aroused. It precipitated violent debates in the

---

[29] *Ibid.,* p. 366.

senate, but the majority in that body were "previously determined to accept it, even without knowing the articles it contained." Confidence in Washington tempered the popular feeling; and[30]

the dread of involving the United States in a war with England at length gained a majority . . . ; in the same manner as that motive had influenced not only the president, but the majority of the individuals in the states, who finally adhered to the treaty, to the latter of whom all alliance with England of whatever kind was extremely obnoxious.

In substance John Quincy Adams agreed with this analysis; and Isaac Weld, who refrained from expressing himself directly on the treaty, inferred the same causes behind its acceptance. A description he wrote of a scene which he witnessed at an inn in Pennsylvania bears a touch of humor:

It is scarcely possible for a dozen Americans to sit together without quarrelling about politics, and the British treaty, which had just been ratified, now gave rise to a long and acrimonious debate. The farmers were of one opinion, and gabbled away for a long time; the lawyers and the Supreme Court judge were of another, and in turns they rose to answer their opponents with all the power of rhetoric which they possessed. Neither party could say anything to change the sentiments of the other one. . . .

Weld has an impressive paragraph on George Washington:[31]

Few persons find themselves for the first time in the presence of G — l W — , a man so renowned in the present day for his wisdom and moderation, and whose name will be transmitted with such honour to posterity, without being impressed with a certain degree of veneration and awe; nor do these emotions subside on a closer acquaintance; on the contrary, his person and deportment are such as rather tend to augment them. There is something very austere in his countenance, and in his manners he is uncommonly reserved. I have heard some officers that served immediately under his command . . . say that they never saw him smile during all the time that they were with him. No man has ever yet been connected with him by the reciprocal and uncon-

---

[30] *Ibid., II,* p. 517.

[31] Weld, *Travels,* pp. 59–60.

strained ties of friendship; and but a few can boast even of having been on an easy and familiar footing with him.

But Weld was surprised at the lack of enthusiasm he found for the Fourth of July celebration, "Some people," he remarked, "call the anniversary day the day of American Repentance." This attitude was not uncommon, he thought, especially among the phlegmatic people of upstate New York and among the Virginia planters, who in their private lives no longer experienced the quiet happiness that had been theirs before the Revolution.[32]

On certain fundamentals Weld and La Rochefoucault were in agreement, the Frenchman being characteristically the more candid of the two. It is an "indubitable and well-known truth," he observed, "that interest and the passions are the spectacles through which men view the greatest events." In New England the national spirit was stronger than elsewhere, but the "universal and predominating passion is the desire of gain, openly avowed; and under an appearance of frank bluntness, much shrewdness and cunning. The saying in other states is that 'the Yankees are honest according to the letter of the law.'" Sentimentally New England clung to the memory of France in the Revolution, but it was too hard-headed to ignore the benefits of a commercial agreement with England. Moreover, the significance of the British punctually transferring the western posts did not escape the Frenchman's notice: he was obliged finally to admit that Jay's treaty had conformed to American national interest, though he felt that on both sides jealousies and resentments were so strong as to bring on a war between the two nations at some time in the future.[33]

Both of these writers were unsparing in condemning the Americans for their ruthless treatment of the Indians. In place of fairness and kindness, Weld wrote, and instead of practicing restraint, the whites regarded the Indians

merely as wild beasts . . . ; and actuated by that insatiable spirit of avarice, and that restless and dissatisfied turn of mind, . . . instead of keeping within their territories where millions of acres

---

[32] *Ibid.*, p. 157.
[33] La Rochefoucault, *II*, pp. 149–151, 202, 214, 308.

remain unoccupied, . . . they crossed their boundary lines and fixed themselves in the territory of the Indians, without ever previously gaining the consent of these people. . . .

They shot the Indians with as much unconcern as they would a wolf or a bear, he noted.[34] The Americans living on the frontiers, concluded La Rochefoucault, "are greater robbers and more cruel than the Indians, against whom it is alleged as a crime, that they exercise the right of retaliation." The storekeepers take advantage of the half-savage sort of people who inhabit the back settlements, and the latter in turn abuse the poor Indians. "In fact the conduct of mankind at large is in general nothing more than a chain of frauds and impositions, only somewhat less barefaced than those of the storekeepers in the new American dominions."[35]

Meanwhile "all of the old spirit of 1776" was rekindling — Thomas Jefferson so observed — and John Jay's treaty with England rubbed salt on the wounds. La Rochefoucault seems to have been right in his analysis: *any* agreement with England aroused passion and precipitated fears of a monarchical tendency in the government. Without knowing the content of the treaty Jefferson confessed his own prejudice. Writing to a friend he made an interesting admission:[36]

. . . . I have always found that rogues would be uppermost, and I do not know that the proportion is too strong for the higher orders and for those who, rising above the swinish multitude always contrive to nestle themselves into the places of power &

---

[34] Weld, *Travels,* pp. 362–363.

[35] La Rochefoucault, *I,* pp. 45, 162–163. Invaluable in understanding American attitudes and policy toward the Indians are the following articles by Reginald Horsman: "British Indian Policy in the Northwest, 1807–1812," *Miss. Valley Hist. Rev.,* XLV (June 1958), pp. 51–66; "American Indian Policy in the Old Northwest, 1783–1812," *William and Mary Quarterly,* XVIII (Jan. 1961), pp. 35–53; "The British Indian Department and the Resistance to General Anthony Wayne, 1793–1795," *Miss. Valley Hist. Rev.,* XLIX (Sept. 1962), pp. 269–290; "American Indian Policy and the Origins of Manifest Destiny," *University of Birmingham Hist. Journal,* XI (1968), pp. 128–140. Also Jack Ericson Eblen, *The First and Second United States Empires* (Pittsburgh, Pa.: University of Pittsburgh Press, 1968), pp. 237–270.

[36] To Thomas Mann Page, Aug. 30, 1795. Paul Leicester Ford (ed.), *The Writings of Thomas Jefferson* (New York: G. P. Putnam, 1896), VII, pp. 24–25. Hereafter cited as Ford, *Jefferson.*

profit. . . . Our part of the country is in considerable fermenta-
tion, on what they suspect to be a recent roguery of this kind.
They say that while all hands were below deck mending sails,
splicing ropes, and every one at his own business, & the captain
in his cabin attending to his log book & chart, a rogue of a pilot
has run them into an enemy's port. But metaphor apart, there
is much dissatisfaction with Mr. Jay and his treaty. . . .

Alexander Hamilton shared with Jay a prominent place in Jefferson's black books. Hamilton was "really a colossus to the anti-republican party." He, "Jay, &c in the boldest act they ever ventured on to
undermine the government, have the address to screen themselves,
& direct the hue and cry against those who wish to drag them into
light. . . ." [37] Hamilton and Jay had the President's ear, to so much
of the discomfiture of Jefferson that he had resigned and gone home
to Monticello. "I have laid up my Rosinante in his stall, before his
unfitness for the road shall expose him faltering to the world," he
wrote ruefully to his friend Mann Page.[38] But Jay's treaty remained
"an execrable thing . . . really nothing more that a treaty of alliance
between England and the Anglomen of this country, against the
Legislature and people of the United States. . . ."[39]

In his eagerness to outdo the "Anglomen" Jefferson persuaded a
Philadelphia publisher to reissue a book by a radical Scotsman, James
Callender, who was working for the overthrow of the British government. The book purported to be "an impartial history of abuses in
the government of the British Empire" and described graphically the
loss of life and property other nations had suffered as a result of
"British quarrels" over the past century. Every other nation, declared
Callender, "must be entitled to wish that an earthquake or a volcano
should first bury the whole British islands in the centre of the globe,"

---

[37] To Madison, Sept, 21, 1795. *Ibid.*, pp. 32–33.

[38] Jefferson's frequent literary allusions show how well read he was in the
great works of European authors; and in spite of his doctrinaire denials, he
absorbed some of the satirical attitudes of writers like Cervantes, La Rochefoucault and Montaigne. See for example his letter to Madison, Jan. 1, 1797
Paul Leicester Ford (ed.), *VII, The Writings of Thomas Jefferson* (New York:
G. P. Putnam, 1896), pp. 98–100.
The allusion above is to Don Quixote's famous horse, Rosinante.

[39] To Rutledge, Nov. 30, 1795. *Ibid.*, p. 40.

and Jefferson was quoted as saying that the book contained an account of an "astonishing concentration of abuses." [40] David Ramsay, the South Carolina physician who we remember had scolded Tom Paine for playing on popular passions against George III in 1776, now borrowed a leaf from Paine's tract in depicting America, in consequence of Jay's treaty, again a mere appendage of Great Britain summoned by its "foreign master" to make war on France. Ramsay was affected by the thought of France, a great and mighty nation, imitating the American example; and so "we may hope that revolutions will follow revolutions till despotism is banished from our globe." But in the meantime kings and nobles were waging cruel war against the rights of man.[41] Mathew Carey, the Irishman who had come to America and with Franklin's help become a successful Philadelphia printer, joined in flaying the treaty before the House of Representatives. The treaty was "that badge of American dishonour and disgrace — that sacrifice of American prosperity and independence — that memento of executive and senatorial usurpation"; and Carey aspired to rescue "your devoted country from the impending ruin prepared for it by the wily, the machiavellian politics of a British minister whose craft and intrigues have, in a few weeks, acquired more for his haughty, his insolent, his piratical nation" than when "she was assisted by murderous bands of hireling Hessians." [42]

Most unrestrained of the many diatribes which lumped Jay's treaty, England, George Washington and the cause of kings together was Tom Paine's *Letter to George Washington*, written in the home of James Monroe in Paris and published by Benjamin Franklin Bache, editor of the *Aurora* of Philadelphia, well known for its radical republican views. Monroe himself was not far behind Paine in attacking Washington and the treaty in a tract that Bache also published; and to support his case Monroe added four hundred pages

---

[40] James Thomson Callender, *The Political Progress of Britain: or an impartial history . . . from the Revolution of 1688 to the present time . . .* (Philadelphia: Richard Folwell, 1795).

[41] David Ramsay, M. D., *An Oration . . . July 4, 1794 . . .* (London: W. Winterbotham, 1795).

[42] Mathew Carey, *Address to the House of Representatives . . . on Lord Grenville's Treaty* (Philadelphia: Mathew Carey, 1796).

of diplomatic documents demonstrating the value of keeping close to France.[43] Levelling at Washington adjectives like "deceitful," "perfidious," and "hypocritical," Paine recalled his own superior contribution to the Revolution and charged that Jay had rendered the United States an object of contempt in Europe. Monroe on his part accused Washington of throwing away all the advantages of the alliance with France and of plunging "us into a war with our ancient ally, and on the side of the kings of Europe contending against her for the subversion of liberty." "Free people seldom intrigue together," sentimentalized Monroe, "because there is no motive for it"; but now "we are made fast by treaty and by the spirit of those at the helm to a nation bankrupt in its resources, and rapidly verging either to anarchy or despotism." Between them, we recall, Monroe and Paine drew the wrath of John Quincy in Berlin.

The best road to an understanding of these extraordinary outbursts against "the fatal British treaty" and against the Washington administration, which was to blame for it, lies through the mind of Thomas Jefferson. Jefferson "groaned" under the bondage which still held the United States to Great Britain. Britain was "the workshop to which we go for all we want"; "the labors of our hands and lands" all go to it; to it "belongs either openly or secretly the great mass of our navigation," or as Monroe and other tract writers put it, "we have been kicked, cuffed and plundered all over the ocean." The British "are advancing fast to a monopoly of our banks & public funds; . . . they have in their alliance the most influential characters in & out of office." And so "it is impossible for us to say we stand on independent ground, impossible for a free mind not to see & to groan under the bondage in which it is bound." The British even "possess our printing presses, a powerful engine in their government of us." [44]

---

[43] Thomas Paine, *Letter to George Washington . . . on affairs public and private* (Philadelphia: 1796); James Monroe, *A View of the Conduct of the Executive in the Foreign Affairs of the United States, connected with the mission to the French Republic during the years 1794, 5, & 6* (Philadelphia: B. F. Bache, 1797).

[44] To Elbridge Gerry, May 13, 1797. Ford, *Jefferson, VII, pp. 119–124.*

With these facts or, more accurately, alleged facts which Jefferson in his excitement greatly exaggerated, Jay's treaty had little if any connection. It did relinquish the abstract principle, free ships make free goods (except contraband of war), meaning that a belligerent may not lawfully interfere with a neutral vessel on the high seas. But the exception made of contraband was flexible, and the principle was unworkable unless it were accompanied by command of the sea, which Great Britain at this time possessed to an unusual degree. John Quincy Adams, son of the man who initiated the principle in the American commercial treaty with France in 1778, understood this and adopted a calm and practical attitude accordingly. The thing reduced itself, as he said, "to a mere question of force, in which the belligerent, being ready armed, naturally enjoys the best advantage."[45]

But "free ships" had been wedded to the American Revolutionary tradition, and so when ignored as was the case in all wars there was an emotional reaction of which Jefferson's was typical. Jay's treaty was a surrender to what today would be dubbed "colonialism," hence the feelings of rage and frustration aroused against it. In anger Jefferson made a wish for "an ocean of fire between us & the old world." Considering the commercial ambitions he had long harbored, he would certainly have been the first to register shock if the United States had suddenly found itself cut off from its foreign trade by some means more practical than his extravagant metaphor.

With Washington out of office, however, Jefferson could indulge in a little optimism, as expressed in a letter to Aaron Burr in June 1797:[46]

I had always hoped, that the popularity of the late President being once withdrawn from active effect, the natural feelings of the people towards liberty would restore the equilibrium between the executive and legislative departments, which had been destroyed by the superior weight and effect of that popularity; and that their natural feelings of moral obligation would

---

[45] To Pickering, Oct. 31, 1797, May 17, 25, 1798. JQA, *Writings, II*, pp. 218–221, 285, 288–294.

[46] *Ibid., VII*, pp. 145–149.

discountenance the ungrateful predilection of the executive in favor of Great Britain. . . .

III

To the American patriot, the Revolution was a sacred memory and George Washington its immortal hero. The winning of independence was like the performance of a miracle and the British surrender at Yorktown a testimonial to Washington's godlike leadership. Exclaimed the Reverend Ezra Stiles in his famous sermon:

> O Washington! How do I love thy name! how have I often adored and blessed thy God, for creating and forming thee the great ornament of human kind! upheld and protected by the Omnipotent, by the Lord of Hosts, thou hast been sustained and carried through one of the most arduous and important wars in all history.

Since the days of Joshua the son of Nun there had been nothing to equal it.

Busts and portraits of the great man made him a familiar figure in one form or another to the postwar generation. While in Paris in 1785 Jefferson managed to induce the celebrated French sculptor Jean Houdon to go to Virginia to execute a marble statue. Houdon had already done busts of Voltaire, Franklin, Lafayette and others; and while in Virginia he made a plaster mould of Washington's features, but returned to France to work on the statue. Houdon created a marble figure of Washington's exact height (six feet, two inches), but using an unknown model in France, he sculptured a body resembling a French gentleman of the period. Not an artistic success, the Houdon statue, probably owing to the sculptor's fame, is still accepted and praised as a satisfactory representation. An Italian sculptor, coming a few years after, modelled a bust in the style of a Roman general. Beginning with Charles Willson Peale in 1772, Washington was honored with a long list of painters, each of whom created his own image. The classic portrait — the one universally familiar throughout America — was the work of Gilbert Stuart, done over a period of approximately a year, September 1795 to September 1796, when Washington was the elder statesman in his sixty-fourth year. The leading art student of Washington portraits, Gustavus A. Eisen, credits Stuart with a genius for portraying the inner character of the man, and with a remarkable memory which enabled him to paint many of the faces at later times. Stuart in 1796 gave to Isaac Weld his own personal impressions of the man. Washington, he said, had "features totally different from what he had observed in any other human." They were "indicative of the strongest and most ungovernable passions, and had he been born in the forests, it was his opinion that he would have been the fiercest man amongst the savage tribes." [47]

While Washington was sitting for Gilbert Stuart, he shared in the execrations showered upon the Federalists, or "English party," by their heated republican opponents. La Rochefoucault commented upon the mutual bitterness between these parties, the one striving to give the Constitution a monarchical tendency by strengthening the executive, the other aspiring for a stronger legislative branch which it denominated republican. Monroe accused Washington's administration of plunging "us into a war with our ancient ally, and on the side of the kings of Europe contending against her for the subversion of liberty!" While keeping in the background and refraining from any direct criticism of Washington, Jefferson nevertheless feared and distrusted the President and voiced his relief when the latter gave way to John Adams, a less popular figure who would accordingly be a safer President. Privately Jefferson lauded Monroe's book as "masterly" and "unanswerable," and interested himself in getting it into circulation. He also gave his tacit endorsement to Tom Paine's scurrilous *Letter;* and in his final opinion "it was the irresistible influence and popularity of General Washington played off by the cunning of Hamilton, which turned the government over to anti-republican hands." [48]

But there was one thing on which Jefferson and the republicans saw eye to eye with their opponents: the preservation of the Union.

---

[47] Gustavus A. Eisen, *Portraits of Washington.* 3 vols. (New York, 1932); Rembrandt Peale, *Portrait of Washington* (1820); Weld, *Travels,* p. 60.

[48] Monroe, *A View of the Conduct . . . ,* p. lxv; Ford, *Jefferson, VII,* pp. 180, 190, 195, 263

There was attachment to it on both sides, as La Rochefoucault testi-
fied; but the attachment was to no small degree a matter of necessity.
Conspiracies to separate the West, or part of it, from the United
States were common knowledge; and the alternative to Union was
disaster. Rivalries among the states, with France and Britain entering
the arena, were a certainty. Independence was impossible without
Union, and a divorce — Jefferson's word — from both France and
Britain was the sole means of escape from a return to colonial status.

With Washington's death in December 1799 partisan doubts about
him vanished forever. He was now one of the Immortals, thrust by
his admirers ahead of other great men of the past. Alexander of
Macedon, Caesar, Cromwell, Frederick of Prussia, to whom he was
compared — none was his equal. Napoleon too was mentioned, but
rejected as unworthy. As First Consul taking office the same year as
Washington's death, Bonaparte was now at the head of the procession
in republican France. The event, ominous in Jefferson's eyes as a
proof of the danger of standing armies, brought a fresh outburst
of indignation from John Quincy Adams. Bonaparte, "the Corsican
ruffian," was "that hideous monster of democracy, begotten by
madness upon corruption which produced such infinite mischief in
Europe." By contrast, Washington's was "one of the greatest names
that ever appeared upon earth for the pride and consolation of the
human race. . . . His character will remain to *all* ages a model of
human virtue, untarnished with a single vice." Subconsciously, it
seems, fear of Napoleon and uneasy feeling about the future con-
duced to the spontaneous deification of the American general.[49]

Two paintings, dated approximately 1800, depict the Washington
cult. One, "the Apotheosis of Washington," shows the hero being
carried aloft by an angel assisted by the virtues, while Columbia and
the orphaned states of the Union weep below; in the other, the
"Commemoration of Washington," the general is shown rising from
the dead with two angels hovering immediately above in readiness
to bear him upward. Washington's "fame was a sea without a
shore." He was "the victorious leader in our American Israel," the

---

[49] J. Q. Adams to Murray, Feb. 11, 1800. JQA, *Writings, II,* pp. 451, 453, 514.

illustrious chief with whom the heroes of antiquity could not compete. "Over his talents virtue and religion cast their sacred lustre." These and many other expressions of adoration came from the lips of preachers and other orators. Even the hard-headed Chief Justice John Marshall, writing his ponderous five-volume biography some five years later and taking as sardonic a view of human nature as John Adams, conceded that "the superintending care of Providence" had watched over his hero.[50]

Neither at the time nor later did Marshall receive appropriate recognition for this masterly work, written with all the clarity, sanity and intellectual acumen characteristic of his famous decisions as chief justice. His five volumes are really history in its broader sense, their author comprehending the nature of historical forces, setting forth the geopolitics of the American Colonies, and analyzing realistically and unemotionally the interests of the several parties involved. Marshall understood the complex background of the War for Independence and depicted it as an international conflict engrossing the rival interests of the major powers, France and Britain. Nor does he overlook American ambitions in the conflict, taking note particularly of the futile efforts to subjugate Canada and making no effort to gloss over George Washington's fears lest British peace offers win back a war-weary public and bring the war to a premature end. In Marshall's pages the Revolution is neither sacred nor romantic nor does Washington, even though guided by "Providence," seem more than the fortunate leader possessing qualities demanded of a general conducting a defensive war against British regulars. But this stubborn refusal on Marshall's part to substitute the mythology of the Revolution for history defeated him. Patriotism preferred myth to reality, and the Revolution and its hero had to be romanticized. This feat the famous Parson Weems, Marshall's contemporary, accomplished superlatively.

---

[50] John Marshall, *Life of George Washington,* 5 vols. (London: Richard Phillips, 1804–1807). Lithographs of the paintings are in the Henry E. Huntington Library and Art Gallery, and are reproduced in Schutz and Adair. The library has a collection of sermons and eulogies, from which these excerpts are drawn.

Mason L. Weems was a canny Scot, born and raised in Maryland and just past forty years when in 1800 he had his great and lasting success: *A History of the Life and Death, Virtues, and Exploits of General George Washington.* Then follows on the title page a picturesque elaboration telling the reader what to expect: "a great many curious and valuable anecdotes, tending to throw much light on the *private* as well as *public* life and character of *that very extraordinary man:* the whole happily calculated to furnish a feast of true Washingtonian entertainment and improvement, both to ourselves and our children." With this as a starter, the author emphasizes his intention to promote the love of virtue among the citizens and his conviction that "our Washington" is the supreme exponent of all the virtues. "May we become a nation of Washingtons," prayed Weems. "Then and not till then may we expect the true millenium of American glory to commence." Next to piety comes patriotism, "this first of Republican virtues." Washington's was "not the patriotism of a Caesar, or an Alexander. Human devils! who could rob and murder millions of mankind to enrich their own states." His was the patriotism "that raised the republics of ancient Greece and Rome to be the mistresses of the world." [51]

Two other editions followed the first in quick order during the same year, the fortunate author doing considerable rewriting and adding each time to his list of anecdotes. To his original story of young Washington giving sage advice to Major General Braddock who "swelled and reddened with most unmanly rage" (Weems was probably unaware that Braddock recommended the young Virginia militiaman for a commission in the British Army), he added the story of a handsome Indian warrior, after vainly trying to pick off Washington from ambush, swearing that Washington was not born to be killed by a bullet. This of course strengthened the belief that Washington was no mere mortal; and God having so raised him up, perhaps He[52] "may be about to establish here a mighty empire for the reception of a happiness unknown on earth, since the days of blissful Eden.

---

[51] The excerpts are from the very rare first edition, "printed for the Rev. M. L. Weems, of Lodge No. 50, Dumfries, by Green & English, George-Town."
[52] *Ibid.,* from the second edition, which is also very rare.

An Empire where religion shall continue, through immemorial time, to unfold aloft her sacred banner . . . an empire that shall afford a welcome retreat to all the uncorrupted sons of freedom . . . an Empire that shall open a vast theatre for the display of the grand transactions of providential wisdom."

Weems himself has an interesting story to tell, though he could hardly embellish it with the two prime virtues which he stresses so heavily. He never identified himself with the patriot side in America, and he had no personal contacts with Washington. Most of the war years he spent in Britain studying for the ministry, and subsequently he was ordained in the American Episcopal Church; but book selling and the writing of short biographies made a stronger appeal to him, and in 1794 he formed an association with Mathew Carey that lasted for thirty years. His success in selling at twenty-five cents per copy little pamphlets, each with a moral to it, gave him the idea for a book on Washington; and six months prior to the general's death Weems had nearly completed his first version. He told Carey about it in June 1799, adding his assurance that "I cou'd make you a world of pence and popularity by it." Then again, within a month after Washington's demise, Weems pressed his case hard, telling Carey:

> Washington, you know is gone! Millions are gaping to read something about him. I am very nearly primed and cocked for 'em. 6 months ago I set myself to collect anecdotes of him. My plan! I give his history, sufficiently minute — I accompany him from his start. . . . to the President's chair, to the throne in the hearts of 5,000,000 of People. I then go on to show that his unparalleled rise & elevation were due to his Great Virtues.

The secret to Weems' success lay in his genius for thinking up human interest stories and presenting them, however implausible, in a perfectly serious and convincing style. New ancedotes appeared in each successive edition, so that each new edition was like a new book. Most enduring, as well as delightful, of them all is the famous cherry tree story, in which "little George" confesses to his "Pa" that he had cut down the tree with his little "hatchet." The story, averred Weems, came from "an aged lady" who had told it to him twenty years before; but Weems did not remember it until he was getting out his fifth edition in 1806! In this edition, too, Weems billed himself "formerly rector of Mount-Vernon Parish," though no such parish ever existed.

By this time Napoleon Bonaparte was cutting quite a figure in the world, so our author begins his book with an account of an alleged meeting between some youthful Americans and "the mighty Corsican" who was eager to know "how fares your countryman, the great Washington?" To the reply "he was very well" Napoleon rejoined: "Ah, gentlemen! Washington can never be otherwise than well: — The measure of his fame is full — Posterity shall talk of him with reverence as the founder of a great empire, when my name shall be lost in the vortex of Revolutions!" [53]

Originally a pamphlet of less than eighty pages, the book had grown in eight years to exceed two hundred, after which time, much to Weems' own disgust, it remained about the same. Ill-advisedly the author had sold the copyright to the publisher, who could not be budged. The work was "not *half finished*, not *half finished*," he complained. Several most valuable chapters . . . ought still to be added." But Weems nevertheless had good cause to be satisfied: his book kept on selling, and by 1825, the year of his death, it had entered its twenty-ninth edition.

Meanwhile, ever careful to remind his readers of his own identity as a minister of the church, Weems drew on his oratorical talents to sanctify the republic and its hero. Quoting Cicero and invoking the ancient Roman republic as his model, with Brutus, Scipio and Cato as its great defenders, Weems delivered an oration "on the beauties and beatitudes of a republic, and the abominations and desolations of despotism." Rome's heroes were great because they held the barrier against the encroachments of ambitious men like Caesar, but "the tear of sentiment unutterable starts into our eyes, when we hear the great name of Washington." Other preachers descanted upon "the immaculate Washington" and "the undaunted Washington" and depicted Independence Day as "the political jubilee of our American Israel"; and John Corry, another biographer of Washington but more

---

[53] For the facts about Weems and his book I am indebted to Marcus Cunliffe's introduction to a new edition published by the Belknap Press of Harvard University Press, 1962.

inclined than Weems to stick to facts, nevertheless assumed that his hero was "above all Greek, above all Roman fame." [54]

Piety, Christian zeal, primitive simplicity of manners — these were the qualities pronounced indispensable for the safety of republics; if they were weakened, despotic government would follow. Survivors of the Revolution, notably John Adams and his close friend, Dr. Benjamin Rush, who had been among its leaders, agreed with the principles readily enough, but did not regard them as real or permanent. Paradoxically they admitted to each other, in their intimate correspondence, the necessity of preserving the myth of the Revolution centered around "the Great Character," but they disliked "the idolatrous worship" of Washington. His companions in arms and contemporaries in the Revolution did not believe in his divine talents and virtues. But, concluded Adams, it was "expressly agreed to blow the trumpet of panegyric in concert . . . to make that Character popular and fashionable with all parties and with all persons, as a center of union, as the central stone in the geometrical arch. There you have the revelation of the whole mystery," he added. "Something of the same kind has occurred in France and has produced a Napoleon and his empire." [55]

IV

Samuel Blodgett, a septuagenarian who as a young man of twenty-one had been with the Massachusetts expedition against Louisbourg in 1745, published in 1801 a book that he called *Thoughts on the Increasing Wealth and National Economy of the United States of America*. A statistical table, previously published in European and American periodicals and demonstrating the economic progress the country had made, impelled Blodgett to write the book. The table

---

[54] Rev. M. L. Weems, *The True Patriot* . . . (Philadelphia: for the author, by Wm. W. Woodward); John Corry, *The Life of George Washington* (London: B. Crosby & Co., 1802); Stephen Longfellow, Jr., *An Oration July 4, 1804* (Portland: Jenks & Shirley); Abiel Holmes, *A Discourse at Plymouth,* Dec. 22, 1806; James Mittemore, *An Oration* July 4, 1806.

[55] Schutz and Adair, pp. 93, 206–215, 229.

he declared, was fair proof that America had been *"selected by an indulgent providence to become hereafter the greatest and most powerful nation of the universe."* An increase in population, an extension of commerce, a complete system of public finance, and an inflow of private capital from Europe were the means to this end. Reminding his readers that all the enlightened men familiar with America from Walter Raleigh to Benjamin Franklin were convinced of this, Blodgett proceeded to describe the prospects for profitable investment on the part of European capitalists. Like John Adams, Blodgett conceived of the United States as "another Europe" — rich and varied in natural resources and diversified in heathful climates. But it must attract foreign capital if it was to succeed. For his knowledge of American geography Blodgett paid his respects to the "ingenious and indefatigable Dr. Morse"; and for the relationship between population, land values and public credit he drew on the writings of Adam Smith, Arthur Young and Alexander Hamilton.[56] Omitting consideration of annexing the Louisiana country west of the Mississippi, he pointed to the immense acreage of vacant land still within the United States that had not been settled. Out of a total of 640 million acres, only 38 million or less had been improved.

Blodgett influenced another writer two years later who preferred to be known only by his pen name, Sylvestris, but who published a thoughtful volume entitled *Reflections on the Cession of Louisiana to the United States.* The cession was a windfall, the kind of an event that the most optimistic politican would not dare to anticipate. Sylvestris comprehended the geopolitics of the Louisiana cession. It gave the United States the advantage of having no neighbor to the west. Louisiana was a strong, impassable barrier against invasion or even annoyance from the west or the south. "For now the United States are, as it were, insulated from the rest of the world"; there was no power to lure the western states from the Union or to offer competition in the sale of public lands. The French, had they not decided upon withdrawal, might have been dangerous

---

[56] Samuel Blodgett, *Thoughts on the increasing wealth and national economy of the United States of America,* (Washington: Way & Graff, 1801), pp. 20–23, 30–31.

rivals in the development of the interior: an offer of free lands by them might have induced a mass migration from the east to the west bank of the river.

Louisiana, argued Sylvestris, should be treated as *a treasure in bank:* territory to be left idle until the country to the east of the river had been satisfactorily settled. Colonies, he pointed out, are always expensive to the parent state in their first settlement; and as soon as they grow strong, they are unwilling to continue in subjection as our own recent conduct shows. Moreover, as we advance toward Mexico, we shall view its mines with the same cupidity that the Spanish first beheld them: "and this will no doubt lead to the nefarious project of conquering the Spanish dominions, first on this side and then beyond the streights of Darien [Panama]." Such a conquest would make a strong popular appeal. But:

> when we are willing to exchange our present constitutions and government, and our present enviable state of liberty, with all its attendant blessings for the riches and the wretchedness of Spain, we shall deserve all the miseries which such an achievement would entail upon us, and our posterity, forever.

Then the author restates the old ideal of an agrarian republic, realizable only if the United States abstained from exploiting Louisiana and left it to the Indian nations. In this case:[57]

> Our whole country . . . will consist of an extensive and numerous agricultural people, detached from all the other civilized nations of the globe, forming one general and powerful confederacy of republican states, nursed in the lap of liberty, sprung from one common stock, cherishing the same fraternal sentiments towards each other. . . . The demon of discord is the only enemy. . . , and he might be chained for centuries beyond the Mississippi if the policy which is here recommended be adopted.

Between these two authors the paradox central to American ideology becomes clear: on the one hand the ambition to become the most powerful nation in the universe, on the other the dream

---

[57] Sylvestris (St. George Tucker), *Reflections on the Cession of Louisiana to the United States* (Washington: Samuel Harrison Smith, 1803), pp. 9, 23.

of an agrarian paradise. The first author was a pragmatist: perceiving the direction historical currents had been taking since they had started flowing two centuries earlier, he stipulated the conditions requisite to sustain the flow. The second author composed an epic in prose: with Louisiana in hand, America could march onward to the promised land. But only by avoiding temptation and by practicing heroic self-restraint: ambitions must be resolutely thrust aside, a program of disciplined, systematic colonization pursued relentlessly.

In fancy the American west, suddenly doubled in size in consequence of the cession, was "the garden of the world." The phrase itself began to circulate at the time of the cession.[58] But as an equivalent of the Hebrew Garden of Eden or of the Homeric paradise, it was only a metaphor. Thomas Jefferson, the deity of American agrarianism, conceived of an altogether different type of utopia: an empire, or a very large state coming out of embryo as he expressed it in 1801.[59] Napoleon's decision to put Louisiana into his hands gave him opportunities that few, if any, nationalist statesmen have ever experienced.

Jefferson lost little time initiating a series of moves. His first — one that had been on his mind since 1783 — was to send Lewis and Clark on their way up the Missouri river in search of a route to the Pacific. Meriwether Lewis was Jefferson's friend and neighbor in Charlottesville, Virginia, and enjoyed the privilege of choosing his partner, William Clark, younger brother to the better known George Rogers. The party was actually on its way *before* Jefferson had received from Paris intelligence of the cession, but the President protected the party against trouble with the French and also the British by securing passports from the ministers of those two countries respectively. Lewis was told to explore the interior generally, especially the rivers draining south and southwest toward the Gulf of Mexico and the Pacific, and to report on the possibilities of divert-

---

[58] It occurs in an oration given by David A. Leonard at Raynham, Mass., May 11, 1804 (Newport: Oliver Farnsworth). See Henry Nash Smith, *Virgin Land. The American West as Symbol and Myth* (Cambridge: Harvard University Press, 1950) for an extended analysis of this metaphor.

[59] To W. C. Claiborne, July 13, 1801. Ford, *Jefferson*, VIII, p. 71.

ing the transcontinental fur trade from British into American hands. Obviously Jefferson intended to push to the very limit whatever advantage came his way. Then a French friend, who was aware that the British were ahead in the far northwest, reminded him that it might be possible to establish an all-American route to Asia via the mouth of the Columbia; and Jefferson immediately dispatched a messenger to overtake Captain Lewis with a copy of the Frenchman's letter. So the idea of the "North American road to India," as Thomas Hart Benton was later to describe it, began to take root. If successful, it would lead to the United States becoming the medium between Europe and Asia. It would mean a revolution in the world's trade routes to the enormous advantage of the United States. Jefferson may not have grasped all of the implications of this idea, but there is no doubt of the importance which he attached to the Lewis and Clark expedition. In his mind it was a long step toward the United States becoming a world power.[60]

Within a year after returning from his journey Meriwether Lewis committed suicide, but in the meantime he wrote a two-volume account of his experiences which was subsequently published in book form in Philadelphia. In his book Lewis was as unsparing in his criticism of his fellow-countrymen for hypocrisy and injustice toward the Indians as the English and French commentators, Weld and La Rochefoucault, had been. American pressure on the Indians to give up hunting in favor of farming, and thus become "civilized," failed to impress when the Americans themselves were bending every effort to exploit the fur trade.[61] To Jefferson's way of thinking, as to Franklin's in former days, a monopoly over the fur trade was a sure road to empire. Both of these statesmen were typically American in their Indian policies: dispossession of the tribes and forced migra-

---

[60] Ford, *Jefferson*, VIII, pp. 193–199; R. W. Van Alstyne, *The Rising American Empire* (New York: Oxford University Press, 1960).

[61] Meriwether Lewis, *History of the Expedition under the Command of Captains Lewis and Clark, to the sources of the Missouri River, thence across the Rocky Mountains and down the River Columbia to the Pacific Ocean . . . during the years 1804–5–6.* 2 vols. (Philadelphia: Bradford & Innskeep, 1814). Nathan Schachner, *Thomas Jefferson. A Biography.* 2 vols. (New York: Appleton-Century-Crofts, 1951), II, pp. 731–734, 785–786, 795–796.

tion at the least possible inconvenience and expense to the United States and its nationals.

For the time being, however, the satisfaction of acquiring the port of New Orleans took first place. There had been last-minute uncertainties regarding the future of this small French-inhabited town on the lower river; strategically it was so valuable. In taking it back from Spain in 1800, France took the first step toward resuming its former dominance over the interior. Then a sudden closing of the port late in 1802 showed how the future of the United States could be affected. New Orleans was the outlet for the western states, whose protests convinced Jefferson of the Union breaking up unless his envoys in Paris could reach an accord with Napoleon. Meanwhile costly setbacks shook French plans too, and showed that effective recovery of Louisiana was not so obvious as it had seemed on paper; and then a new war with Great Britain made it clear that the plan was hopeless. Napoleon had no real alternative in April 1803 but to yield Louisiana to the United States under the guise of a "purchase," and Jefferson got the credit for a prodigious diplomatic victory.

The peculiar location of New Orleans made it a natural center for intrigue and for schemes of aggrandizement on the part of any nation that held it. A senate debate in February 1803, when the outcome was still uncertain, brought this out clearly. With New Orleans in American hands, the next step would take in the Floridas. Spain was no match and there being no other neighbor, the United States would have no serious problem of defending its own territory. On the contrary the road to further expansion would lie open and the opportunity must not be lost. Louisiana was "a natural and necessary part of our empire." [62] Jefferson did make an attempt to follow through: he initiated several measures aimed at maneuvering the Spanish into relinquishing the Floridas to the east and the whole of the coast to the southwest as far as the Rio Grande. To do this he realized he needed either a British or a French alliance; but a tenta-

---

[62] *Mississippi Question. Report of a Debate in the Senate . . . on the 23rd, 24th, and 25th February 1803. . . .* (Philadelphia: W. Duane, 1803), p. 126. Jefferson to John Dickinson, Aug. 9, 1803, Ford, *Jefferson, VIII,* pp. 261–263.

tive approach to Napoleon met with a rebuff, and although he thought seriously of making advances to the British government on the supposition that it would welcome American aid in its war with France, he made no actual move in this direction. He also conceived of a military colony on the Roman model, settlers to be given lands west of the Mississippi in return for performing military duty when called upon, but this too fell through.[63]

Visits and personal talks with Alexander von Humboldt, the German explorer who came to see him in 1804 after spending more than a year in Mexico, fired Jefferson's imagination with respect to that country. But there were other men, notably General James Wilkinson and the former vice president, Aaron Burr, who harbored schemes of their own for organizing private armies for the conquest of Mexico; and indirectly at least these adventurers learned much from von Humboldt. A splendid map of Mexico drawn by the German got into their hands, and plans took shape for an invasion with New Orleans as the starting point. Said Jefferson of this conspiracy:[64]

> Burr's enterprise is the most extraordinary since the days of Don Quixote. It is so extravagant that those who know his understanding would not believe it if the proofs admitted doubt. He has meant to place himself on the throne of Montezuma and extend his empire to the Allegheny, seizing N. Orleans as the instrument of compulsion for our Western states.

But Jefferson took the conspiracy seriously, knowing that Burr was having success in assembling boats and supplies on the Ohio river and that he had the ear of important men in the west, notably of the senator from Kentucky. In New Orleans discontent among the local population generated by the American annexation provided the proper atmosphere for a coup d'état; and from a reliable agent who made two trips to Vera Cruz Burr learned of what resistance he might expect from the Spanish if he attempted an invasion.

---

[63] To Madison, Aug. 27 and Oct. 11, 1805; to Claiborne, Apr. 27, 1806. Ford, *Jefferson, VIII*, pp. 377–379, 380, 442. Van Alstyne, *American Diplomacy in Action* (Gloucester, Mass.: Peter Smith, 1968), pp. 533–537.

[64] To Charles Clay, Jan. 11, 1807. Ford, *Jefferson, IX*, p. 7. Don Quixote was one of Jefferson's favorite literary figures. Also *ibid.*, pp. 354–356 *et passim*.

Burr's plans collapsed and he was arrested for conspiring against the Union, not for plotting war against Spain. He seems to have whetted the appetite for conquest. If Jefferson, rather than Burr, had given the order, Andrew Jackson for one would have gladly complied. "I would delight to see Mexico reduced," Jackson declared, "but I will die in the last ditch before I . . . see the Union disunited." And Jefferson himself was impressed. "We ask but one month to be in possession of the city of Mexico," he wrote. And if Burr had not tried to break up the Union and had been satisfied with Mexico, "so popular is an enterprise on that country in this, that we had only to be still, & he could have had followers enough to have been in the city of Mexico in 6 weeks." [65]

Thinking that the territory to the west of the Mississippi would not really be colonized for many a year, Jefferson nevertheless wanted all of it at least as far as the Rio Grande whenever an opportunity arose to take it away from Spain. In 1805 an expedition led by Lieutenant Zebulon Montgomery Pike set out from New Orleans for Santa Fé, the old capital of the province of New Mexico. Pike, it was hoped, could persuade the Indian tribes to come over to the American side, thus diverting their trade from Mexico and paving the way for incorporation into the United States. With the Indians he had poor success, and the Spanish don at Santa Fé easily saw through the scheme. A prisoner, though a lavishly treated one, Pike was ordered to report to the captain general in Chihuahua. This meant a journey down the Rio Grande to El Paso and two hundred miles beyond before reaching his destination. Eventually Pike returned to the United States none the worse for wear, but on the contrary with a great stock of knowledge about conditions in the Mexican provinces. The captain general entertained him during the month of his detention and sent him on his way under escort, with provisions and even money to insure a comfortable journey.[66]

For the benefit of the American government Pike wrote a full account of his experiences, concluding that the Mexicans were ripe

---

[65] To James Bowdoin, Apr. 2, 1807. Ford, *Jefferson, IX,* p. 41. Thomas Perkins Abernethy, *The Burr Conspiracy* (New York: Oxford University Press, 1954), p. 111.

[66] Abernethy, *The Burr Conspiracy,* pp. 119–137.

for rebellion and painting a glittering picture of the advantages the United States would derive from it. The Americans would get "the almost exclusive trade of the richest country in the world for centuries," including the carrying trade:

> For Mexico, like China, will never become a nation of mariners, but must receive the ships of all the world into her ports, and give her bullion in exchange for the productions of their different countries. . . . Our numerous vessels would fill every port, and from our vicinity enable us to carry off at least nine-tenths of her commerce. Even on the coast of the Pacific no European nation could vie with us: there would also be a brisk inland trade carried on with the southern provinces via Red River, . . . we should become their factors, agents, guardians, and in short, their tutelar genius. . . .

Napoleon, the lieutenant conceded, might spoil these prospects if he got control of Spain; but twenty thousand men under good officers from the United States would be enough to effectuate a revolution in Mexico and thus "to emancipate another portion of the western hemisphere from the bonds of European tyranny and oppression." [67]

Jefferson himself was thinking along the same lines, the language he used in private sounding much like the language Daniel Defoe had used in his anti-Spanish tracts published in London nearly a century previously. Currently relations between the United States and Great Britain were at the dangerous stage, a serious crisis having arisen at the end of June 1807 over the *Chesapeake* affair. Avowing his "contempt" for the Spanish government, Jefferson propounded his ideas for the benefit of Madison, saying:[68]

> I had rather have war against Spain than not, if we go to war with England. Our southern defensive force can take the Floridas, volunteers for a Mexican army will flock to our standard, and rich pabulum will be offered to our privateers in the plunder of their commerce and coasts. Probably Cuba would add itself to our confederation. . . .

---

[67] Zebulon Montgomery Pike, *Exploratory Travels through the Western Territories of North America* . . . (London: Longman, 1811), pp. 389–390.

[68] Aug. 16, 1807. Ford, *Jefferson*, IX, pp. 124–125.

"The grossest outrage which one nation can commit against another." This was the way the editor of *The American Register*, a seven-volume work, felt about the British attack on the frigate *Chesapeake* two years after the event had occurred. A British admiral, infuriated at learning of the desertion of some of his seamen from a squadron anchored in Chesapeake Bay and especially perhaps when four of them signed on for duty on the American warship, ordered his officers, in the event of their encountering the *Chesapeake* at sea, to hail the vessel and search her for the deserters. On June 22, 1807, the captain of the *Leopard* carried out this assignment, opening a broadside on the *Chesapeake* when the latter refused the demand, forcing the American frigate to strike her colors and then removing the four men. In Jefferson's opinion the episode aroused such a state of excitement as had not been felt since the battle of Lexington. British armed vessels operating in Chesapeake Bay and its neighborhood were committing atrocious acts, as he saw it; and the President was satisfied that the public, among whom there was sharp dissent over other aspects of his foreign policy, would have united behind a demand for war over this incident. But, aware that the United States had no means of waging effective war and believing that the British government, when apprised of the matter, would disavow it, Jefferson confined himself to a proclamation ordering British warships out of American ports and harbors.[69]

The other aspects of his policy, for which he could not get support outside of his party, involved experiments in economic warfare which the President hoped would bring concessions from both Britain and France freeing American seagoing commerce from various restrictions imposed upon it by the belligerents in their warfare against each other. From nonimportation, which struck principally at British goods, Jefferson moved by 1809 into a complete legislative program of nonintercourse, aimed at cutting off all foreign trade and shipping. But this program met with powerful opposition from the commercial

---

[69] *The American Register, or general repository of history, politics and science, for 1806–07.* 7 vols., *III*, Chapt. 3; Ford, *Jefferson, IX*, pp. 86–101, 105–106, 115–119; Reginald Horsman, *The Causes of the War of 1812* (Philadelphia: University of Pennsylvania Press, 1962), p. 102.

and shipping interests of the northeast; and merchants and ship-owners of New England devised ways and means of evading the law which enabled them in a measure to continue benefitting from the abnormal European, particularly British, demand for their services. The British carrying trade was much too lucrative to be ignored.

John Quincy Adams put his finger on the unique characteristic of the impressment issue. It was the kind of a question that could arise only between the United States and Great Britain, that is, only after the one had gained independence of the other. Impressment was the eighteenth-century equivalent of the draft, invoked by the British in their successive wars with the French and reaching the peak of its development in the prolonged wars with Napoleon. The keenest kind of competition between the British and the Americans for seamen underlay the issue: on the British side a defensive attitude arising from the Navy's difficulties in keeping its warships at full strength; on the American side an affluent merchant marine bidding high for services and so offering constant temptation to British seamen to desert.

Rage and feelings of frustration prevailed on both sides, the British viewing impressment as necessary for the prosecution of the war, the Americans looking on it as "a relic of colonial servitude." The *Chesapeake* affair occasioned a small flood of hostile pamphlets on the subject; and John Quincy Adams's views, expounded in a lengthy letter to a Massachusetts senator, received the benefit of a separate publication of which a hundred thousand copies were reportedly printed. Father John Adams also appeared in print, letters critical of British impressment which he had originally written when President being now reissued in book form. John Adams denounced impressment as kidnapping, denied that it had any validity under English law, concluded that pride in the Navy had got the better of the English sense of justice, and warned that if not given up it would lead to continual warfare at sea.[70]

---

[70] J. Q. Adams to Harrison Gray Otis, March 31, 1808, JQA, *Writings, III*, pp. 189–223; *The Correspondence of John Adams . . . concerning the British doctrine of impressment . . .* (Baltimore: the *Evening Post*, by H. Niles, Sept. 15, 1809); Tench Coxe, *An Examination of the Conduct of Great Britain*

Such incidents as the *Chesapeake* affair did not recur, and impressment involving American seamen actually lessened thereafter. But the rigors of British naval warfare against Napoleon increased, and the American government under Madison made no headway against "the tyrant of the ocean," the phrase which Jefferson adopted to express his indignation. American policy under Jefferson and his successor aimed at securing "neutral rights," meaning in the broadest sense not merely a British surrender on impressment but a grant to America, the only neutral, of the right to trade freely with the Continental nations of Europe which, with the exception of Russia, were now subject to the decrees of Napoleon. In perhaps an unguarded moment, when he was hoping for Napoleon's help against Spain, Jefferson admitted that he depended on France and Russia for establishing neutral rights by treaty, "among which should be that of taking no person by a belligerent out of a Neutral ship, unless they be the *soldiers* of an enemy." [71]

The inability to make good on neutral rights disillusioned American leaders of their dream of independence. A Virginia pamphleteer taunted Jefferson with this and quoted the Roman historian, Livy, to drive home his point: "That State alone is free which rests upon its own strength, and depends not on the arbitrary will of another." [72] This indeed was the American dream, but the great European war exposed the fallacy. Impressment was the symbol word which brought neutral rights down to the popular level, making them something worth fighting for. It provided a rich field for human interest stories

---

respecting *Neutrals* (Philadelphia: B. Graves, 1807); James Cheetham, *Peace or War* (New York: 1807); William Coleman, *Remarks and Criticisms of the Hon. J. Q. A.'s Letter . . .* (Boston: Joshua Cushing, 1808); Van Alstyne, *American Diplomacy in Action* (Gloucester, Mass.: Peter Smith, 1968), pp. 723–728; J. T. Zimmerman, *Impressment of American Seamen* (New York: Columbia University Press, 1925).

[71] To James Bowdoin, Apr. 2, 1807, Ford, *Jefferson*, IX, p. 40; James Madison, *An Examination of the British Doctrine which subjects to capture a neutral trade not open in time of peace.* 2d. ed. (America, printed; London, reprinted for J. Johnson & W.J. & J. Richardson, 1806).

[72] John Thierry Danvers, *A Picture of a Republican Magistrate . . . being a full length likeness of . . . Jefferson . . .* (New York: E. Sargent, 1808).

and narratives of personal hardship. The lengthy title of one of these, printed in Boston in 1811, is a good case in point:[73]

> A narrative of Joshua Davis, an American citizen, who was pressed and served on board six ships of the British Navy. He was in seven engagements, once wounded, five times confined in irons, and obtained his liberty by desertion. The whole being . . . a faithful narrative of the discipline . . . of pressed seamen . . . , and containing information that never was before presented to the American people.

Remembering the intense seriousness with which John Quincy Adams took his patriotism, we look with especial interest at his attitude toward these provocative issues. He agreed that the British orders in council struck at "the root of our independence." They were "outrageous violations of our neutral rights," though impressment, which as he correctly said was separate and apart from the orders in council, was "the only ineradicable wound." But actually, to John Quincy's practical mind, "neutral rights" was nothing but an empty phrase, and even from impressment he recoiled from making a war issue of it. He did not believe that Jefferson and Madison, in their attempts at economic reprisal, would accomplish anything, nor could he sympathize with the idea of making war for the protection of commerce. For the nation to go to war in defense of a special interest was alien to his way of thinking, and "neutral rights" could hardly be divorced from the "rights" of trade. Father John Adams argued for a navy: "The navy, the navy, a navy is the grand desideratum, and the *unum necessarium.*" But the son thought otherwise: the United States was impotent at sea and should admit it. Not in half a century could it create a navy capable of challenging the British; and British jealousy was such that Britain would seize the first chance to annihilate a potential rival. Many other objections came to John Quincy's mind: financing a navy would put a strain on internal resources, and it would enhance a special interest group which, in close alliance with commercial interests, would feed

---

[73] See also *Niles Weekly Register*, Apr. 8, 1812, *II*, p. 119 and subsequent issues.

at the public trough. Here he felt he could use England as an example: "There is no department of the English government in which the nation is so outrageously plundered as in the navy. Our nation," he seemed sure, "would be plundered about twice as much as the English. . . ." [74]

John Quincy's position here was consistent with the favorable attitude he had maintained in 1795 toward Jay's treaty: to preserve "the great system of American neutrality in European wars which Washington with so much difficulty established." Jefferson-inspired legislation to defend "neutral rights" was a fatal departure from this system, an irritant which, considering the "mulish obstinacy" of Great Britain, pointed at a war which "would play the game into the hands of France, and make us both the dupes of her craft and perfidy." Under the spell of Napoleon, "this extraordinary personage," France had moved "from unbounded democracy to despotism." Like Alexander of Macedon, Napoleon would get himself deified, for he has "the idea that heroes like himself are a species susceptible of being propagated, and that he only wants a suitable wife to produce a Napoleon the second, whom he can train up in his own principles for the benefit of mankind."

John Quincy's overriding passion was for the preservation of the Union, which he equated with the social compact. The alternative to the federation of the states was the appearance of a Caesar, a Cromwell, "or some such ferocious animal"; or perhaps a state of perpetual war between the different sections with an indefinite number of monarchies, oligarchies and democracies arising as in ancient Greece. His fear became an obsession:

> It enters into most of my meditations upon history, upon government, and even upon the poetry that I read. Marmion, . . . the Lady of the Lake, have no moral to me but to show the consequences of dividing states which nature admits of being united. The picture of border wars is a memento to me of what awaits us, if we ever yield to that senseless and stupid call for division, which I have so long heard muttered in my own neighborhood.

[74] To H. G. Otis, March 31, 1808, *Writings, III,* pp. 189–223; to John Adams from St. Petersburg, Oct. 14, 1811, *ibid. IV,* pp. 240–243.

The social compact, however, was something more sacred than a mere political union. The phrase came from the eighteenth-century philosophers, but for its inner meaning John Quincy resorted to his bible. To him the social compact was the covenant with the Lord, which the Pilgrims had faithfully invoked on the *Mayflower* in 1620. Bible-reading was the one key to perfection, for it unlocked "the history of one peculiar nation, certainly the most extraordinary nation that has ever appeared upon earth." [75]

Integrity, piety, Christian zeal, primitive simplicity of manners — these were the qualities which distinguished the virtuous American republic from Europe, where the Evil Spirit of delirium and stubbornness had spread darkness and gloom, blood and desolation. Recognizing the signs of the coming war with Britain, and fearing it, John Quincy nevertheless kept his faith. To his father he again wrote:

> The whole continent of North America appears to be destined by Divine Providence to be peopled by one *nation*, speaking one language, professing one general system of religious and political principles, and accustomed to one general tenor of social usages and customs. . . . I believe it indispensable that they should be associated in one federal Union. . . . [76]

Thoughts like these filled John Quincy's mind while he was serving the Madison administration very ably as its minister to Russia. Rather to his own surprise, he had found himself in congenial company at

---

[75] To Orchard Cook, Aug. 22, 1808; to Wm. Eustis, Feb. 28, 1810 and Aug. 24, 1811; to John Adams, Apr. 30, 1810 and Oct. 31, 1811; and to his son whom he named after George Washington, Sept. 8, 1811. *Writings, III*, pp. 241, 403, 426–427; *IV*, pp. 189, 211–217, 266–267.

[76] To John Adams, Aug. 31, 1811, and to Wm. Plumer, Sept. 8, 1811, *Writings, IV*, pp. 204–211. Abiel Holmes, D. D., *A Discourse at Plymouth on . . . the fathers* (Cambridge, Mass.: 1806); Tristam Burges, *Liberty, Glory and Union, or American Independence: an oration at Providence, July 4, 1810,* begins "Our independence has given a new era to the world"; Peyton Randolph Freeman, *An oration,* Portsmouth, New Hampshire, July 4, 1810; Benjamin Trumbull, D. D., *A General History of the United States of America . . . 1492 to 1792: or Sketches of the Divine Agency, in their Settlement, Growth and Protection; and especially in the late Memorable Revolution.* 3 vols. (Boston: Farrand, Malloy & Co., 1810). *Also* Walter La Feber, *John Quincy Adams and American Continental Empire* (Chicago: Quadrangle Books, 1965) for an excellent synthesis of Adams's ideas.

St. Petersburg. Needing British support against France, the tsar's ministers shared his regret that the United States had gone to war with Great Britain over issues that were beyond its control, and they began proposing themselves as mediators in the conflict. The Russian response to Napoleon's invasion, which began and ended in 1812, aroused John Quincy's admiration: "The spirit of patriotism has burst with the purest and most vivid flame in every class of the community," he reported. "The exertions of the nation have been almost unparalleled, the greatest sacrifices have been made cheerfully and spontaneously."

But beyond that Adams appreciated the new position of strength that Napoleon's defeat would bring to Russia: under the tsar Russia would become the arbiter of Europe; and since Adams had little faith in American ability to impose its will upon Great Britain at sea, he was anxious for the tsar to pave the way for a peace. But Napoleon's defeat also had the effect of freeing Great Britain in Europe and of giving it the opportunity to take the offensive against America. Subscribing to the English newspapers, John Quincy observed the rise of war feeling in England and feared that now the war would be long and hard on both sides. "John Bull among his whimsies has taken it into his head that his trident is at stake," he told his mother. Bull's real object in the present war is the dismemberment of the American Union, his professed object the press gang. American independence was at stake, but so was freedom in Britain itself. Impressment was a bad cause, branding England "with the mark of the most odious despotism." The odds were heavily against the United States, so Adams in his prayers fell back upon "the divine goodness" to open up a rational prospect for peace.[77]

Meanwhile he could not reconcile his religious belief in the American Republic spreading over the whole of North America with the abortive invasion of Canada, about which he learned in November 1812. A comparison with Napoleon's experience in Russia was inevitable. The American attempt on Canada, he prophesied, would

---

[77] These paragraphs are a distillation of Adams's ideas as expressed in his several letters between Nov. 24, 1812 and Feb. 18, 1813. *Writings, IV,* pp. 406–437.

end "in total and most disgraceful defeat," would leave behind it "a deep mortgage of reputation to redeem." Perhaps he was unaware of the clamor of the War Hawks for the British provinces. "I sicken at the name of Canada," he told his mother in the following April. "Will bitter experience teach us wisdom?" Even if the invasion succeeded, it would not outlast the war: Britain was still too powerful and would require the return of its colonies. But in the long fight with Napoleon Britain had overstrained; its power "must soon decline," and then:[78]

It is in the stage of weakness which must inevitably follow that of overplied and exhausted strength that Canada and all her other possessions would have fallen into our hands, without the need of any effort on our part, and in a manner more congenial to our principles and to justice than by conquest.

By contrast Jefferson was impatient for conquest, sharing eagerly the aggressive attitudes struck by the western War Hawks. This is how Jefferson wanted the war to end:

The acquisition of Canada this year, as far as the neighborhood of Quebec, will be a mere matter of marching, and will give us experience for the attack of Halifax the next, and the final expulsion of England from the American continent. Halifax once taken, every cock-boat of hers must return to England for repairs.

And he was in a vengeful mood:[79]

Their fleet will annihilate our public force on the water, but our privateers will eat out the vitals of their commerce. Perhaps they will burn New York or Boston. If they do, we must burn the city of London, not by expensive fleets . . . , but by employing an hundred or two Jack-the-painters, whom nakedness, famine, desperation and hardened vice, will abundantly furnish from among themselves.

The failure of the invasion stunned him: only the "detestable treason" of the commanding general, William Hull, could cause such a miscarriage. (Hull was outsmarted by his Canadian opponent, General

---

[78] To T. B. Adams, Nov. 24, 1812, *ibid.*, pp. 406–407.
[79] To Duane, Aug. 4, 1812. Ford, *Jefferson, IX,* p. 366.

Brock, but he was not guilty of "treason." Jefferson chose to remain credulous, however, for he was still deceiving himself three years later.)

Jefferson was a confirmed believer in "our hemisphere," a preconception which his talks with the baron von Humboldt had helped to strengthen. Even though Mexico and the Spanish provinces farther south might be priest-ridden and fated to sink into military despotisms, still "in whatever governments they end they will be *American* governments, no longer to be involved in the never-ceasing broils of Europe. . . . America has a hemisphere to itself." Presumably he still hugged his prejudice against kings, the curse of Europe, but the tsar Alexander of Russia stood apart — a virtuous man interested in promoting "neutral rights," and under whose reign Russia is "the most cordially friendly to us of any power on earth." Toward Napoleon he felt no fear. With a large army at his back the Emperor of the French was failing in Spain, so how could he threaten America across an ocean held by England, his bitter enemy, "whose peace, like the repose of a dog, is never more than temporary?" But because England was controlled by commercial interests fattening on war, and because as tyrant of the ocean it levied tribute on every flag traversing the ocean, it must be opposed.[80]

Lieutenant Francis Hall, an English traveller visiting Jefferson at Monticello shortly after the war, wrote a pleasing pen picture of the elder statesman offering a more personal side to his character. Hall found Jefferson:[81]

> tall in person, but stooping and lean with old age, thus exhibiting that fortunate mode of bodily decay which strips the frame of its most cumbersome parts, leaving it still strength of muscle and activity of limb. His deportment was exactly such as the Marquis de Chastellux describes it, above thirty years ago: 'at first serious, nay even cold, but in a very short time relaxing into a most

---

[80] To Lafayette, Feb. 4, 1815; to von Humboldt, Dec. 6, 1813; to Duane, July 20, 1807, to Dr. James Brown, Oct. 27, 1808; to Thomas Law, Jan. 15, 1811. Ford, *Jefferson, IX,* pp. 507, 431, 120–121, 210–212, 292–293.

[81] Francis Hall, *Travels in Canada and the United States in 1816 and 1817,* (London: Longman, 1818), pp. 377–379.

agreeable amenity, with an unabated flow of conversation on the most interesting topics, discussed in the most gentlemanly and philosophical manner. . . .

It must be interesting to recall and preserve the political sentiments of a man who has held so distinguished a station in public life as Mr. Jefferson. He seemed to consider much of the freedom and happiness of America to arise from local circumstances. 'Our population,' he observed, 'has an elasticity by which it would fly off from oppressive taxation.' He instanced the beneficial effects of a free government, in the case of New Orleans, where many proprietors who were in a state of indigence under the dominion of Spain, have risen to sudden wealth, solely by the rise in the value of land, which followed a change of government. . . . Mr. Jefferson has not the reputation of being very friendly to England, but we should, however, be aware that a partiality in this respect, is not absolutely the duty of an American citizen; neither is it to be expected that the policy of our government should be regarded in foreign countries with the same complacency with which it is looked upon by ourselves: but whatever may be his sentiments in this respect, politeness naturally repressed any offensive expression of them. . . . His repugnance was strongly marked to the despotic principles of Bonaparte, and he seemed to consider France under Louis XVIII as scarcely capable of a republican form of government.

Meanwhile the approach of hostilities with Great Britain stimulated new versions of the Revolution and encouraged orators to ask what "our Washington" would do in the present emergency. Parson Weems was in his eighth edition, "greatly improved," in 1809. How could so great a man have ever been born in America, he queried rhetorically. "Why that's the very prince of reasons why he should have been born here, on the greatest continent rising from beneath the frozen pole and sustaining on her ample sides the roaring shock of half the watery globe." The authentic history of our country, declared another writer, presents to our view "a man more exalted and perfect than the poets of other nations have imagined. We must not dishonor his name by bringing it into competition with the crowd of kings, warriors, and politicians whom vanity or ignorance have called great."

Federalist-minded orators, like Daniel Webster in Massachusetts, who opposed another war with Britain, painted the contrast between

Washington's careful policy of neutrality and the Jefferson-Madison program of getting entangled with the monster Napoleon, "the most fierce, sanguinary and relentless that has hitherto ravaged the earth." But two histories published in Boston played on "British despotism," reminded New Englanders of how their loyalty and zeal in capturing Louisbourg in 1745 had been "abused" by the British government's return of the fortress to France, and pointed to Washington as the popular deliverer in 1776. Richard Rush, son of John Adams's doctor friend, depicted the Revolution as "the most brilliant political anniversary of the world," and hoped that this new war "may produce, auspiciously and forever, the effect of throwing us at a safer distance from so contaminating an intimacy, making our liberty thrive more securely and ourselves more independent." And another Fourth of July orator, in Charleston, South Carolina, took up the same theme. "The early inhabitants of America heard not the name of king," he insisted, "felt not the arm of tyranny until they were cursed with the ferocious civilization of Europe. . . . We abhor — we deprecate — we detest the idea that any freeman would renew the chains of colonial dependency and sink into the vassal of Britain," or of Napoleon, "that sanguinary monster." But the war against Britain must be prosecuted: "So shall our empire flourish with the rival glory of arts and arms." [82]

The most penetrating remarks came from the pen of that shrewdest of French observers, Charles Maurice de Talleyrand, who had previously visited America. Talleyrand understood the peculiar legacy that England had left to America and showed how it was strengthened by the devotion to the memory of Washington, "a Nation's Joy," as a new biographer put it in 1813: "To no purpose," he wrote, "do the names of republic and monarchy appear to place between the two governments distinctions which it is not allowable to confound: it is

---

[82] Robert Goodloe Harper, *An Oration on the Birth of Washington* (Alexandria, Va.); Daniel Webster, *An Address at Portsmouth, N. H.,* July 4, 1812; Benj. Trumbull, *A General History of the United States of America.* 3 vols. (Boston: Farrand, Malloy & Co., 1810), *I*, pp. 295–338; John Landrum, *A Concise and Impartial History of the American Revolution* . . . 2 vols. (Boston, Trenton: James Oram, 1795); Richard Rush, *An Oration, July 4, 1812, in the Capital, Washington;* William Crofts, Jr. (Charleston: W. P. Young).

clear to every man who reaches to the bottom of ideas, that in the representative constitution of England there is something republican, as there is something monarchical in the executive power of the Americans." The worship of Washington confirmed this latter characteristic, "for the force of opinion attached to his person throughout the whole of America readily represents *that kind of magical power which political writers attribute to monarchies.*" [83]

Using the pen name of Hector Bullus, James Kirke Paulding, a newcomer in the field of American letters, turned out a rollicking good satire on *The Diverting History of John Bull and Brother Jonathan:*[84]

Squire Bull, a choleric old fellow who held a good manor in the middle of a great mill pond . . . fell into madness at times, and fancied himself master of the whole mill-pond. . . . With a most ludicrous solemnity Bull notified his neighbours that if he caught any of them trying to get over to his enemy Beau Napperty, he would use them worse than dogs. This Beau Napperty was lord of the manor of Frogmore, just over against Bullock Island, and was hated by Squire Bull worse than either the Pope, or the D—I, who had formerly been the prime objects of John's indignation. . . . Beau Napperty was called beau, from the singular disposition he always showed for dressing himself smartly, . . . and if his back was well covered, he did not much care what became of his belly. . . . As he grew up his pride outgrew his body at such a rate that people often wondered how the latter could hold it all . . . he was the most troublesome, pernicious, quarrelsome little rascal in the world, and kept the whole neighbourhood in a complete uproar for many years, by breaking down fences, questioning boundaries, seizing boats, and even sometimes burning barns and houses . . . Beau Napperty ordered his neighbours not to carry on any business with John. This order came to nothing at all with respect to Brother Jonathan, one of Bull's best customers. . . . Yet did Squire Bull, like a great blockhead as he was, just do for Beau Napperty what he could not do for himself . . . He decided that it was absolutely necessary to his

---

[83] John Kingston, *The Life of General George Washington* (Baltimore: the Author); Charles Maurice de Talleyrand-Périgord, *Memoir concerning the Commercial Relations of the United States with England* (Boston: Thomas B. Waite & Co., 1809), p. 6. Italics inserted.

[84] Hector Bullus, *The Diverting History of John Bull and Brother Jonathan* (New York: Innskeep & Bradford, 1812).

honour to retaliate . . . by hindering the peaceable neighbours, who had taken no part in this cursed quarrel, from having the least intercourse, or even speaking to any of Beau Napperty's tenants. . . .

Although Hezekiah Niles, the militant Quaker editor of the Baltimore *Niles Weekly Register* called for the exercise of austerity and self-sacrifice, qualities characteristic of "Roman patriotism," and argued that with them America could win the war on land (he made no allusion to the sea), wartime literature reflected no sense of optimism or confidence in victory. "The war I justify, but the conduct of it I abhor," John Adams's tersely expressed sentiment, seems to have summed up the general view. "If Canada must be invaded, not a foot should have been set on that shore till we had a decided superiority of naval force upon all the Lakes. . . . Disgrace after disgrace. Disaster on the heels of disaster, ruin upon ruin will be the course."

As American frigates successfully engaged at sea British warships like the *Guerrière*, reportedly caught unprepared and under-manned, they brought scattered words of praise. "The year 1812 will, I hope, be immortal in the history of the world for having given the first check to the overgrown power and tyranny of Britain and France," enthused Dr. Rush. "Russia and the United States may now be hailed as the deliverers of the human race." [85] But the younger, though more sophisticated John Quincy Adams in faraway St. Petersburg was more realistic. He wrote his mother:[86]

The exploits of our heroes upon the ocean have . . . saved our national character . . . but have exerted . . . a perfect frenzy of resentment in England. Hitherto we have rather gained than lost in the estimation of the world by those vicissitudes of war; but upon the water the contest is too unequal. The day of misfortunes must come. . . . Our frigate warfare must be nearly if not quite at an end. . . . If we can build and equip line of battleships and frigates in numbers sufficient to form a squadron, we may

---

[85] Adams to Rush, Sept. 4, 1812, and Rush to Adams, Apr. 10, 1813. Schutz and Adair, pp. 245, 278.
[86] June 5, 1813. JQA, *Writings, IV,* pp. 487–488.

give our Lady Macbeth mother a new demonstration of the legitimacy of our descent from herself; but years must pass before this will be practicable . . .

The exhibition of American weakness on land, coupled with the several single ship victories at sea which irked the British but were otherwise barren of result, may or may not have been the motivating cause in determining the British government to take the offensive with an expeditionary force of fifteen to twenty thousand men. Both John Quincy and Thomas Jefferson thought that something of this sort would come as retaliation. Scarcely had the first surrender of Napoleon occurred in 1814 when the British began assembling the expedition at Bordeaux; and for an interesting and authentic narrative of the expedition we turn to a book written by a young officer, Lieutenant George Gleig, who volunteered enthusiastically and kept a journal. Mathew Carey first published the book in Philadelphia, and by 1827 it had gone through three editions.

The objective of the expedition to Chesapeake Bay, according to the lieutenant, was to scatter the flotilla of American gunboats. There was no intention to capture Washington, but the rout of the Americans was so complete that, with the capital city only four miles away, the temptation to take it and levy a contribution was too strong to be resisted. The commanding officer, General Ross, took only a small body of troops with a flag of truce, but when the truce was refused and the general's horse shot from under him, all thoughts of an accommodation were laid aside and the British soldiers proceeded to burn and destroy everything in the city connected with the government. Unfortunately, writes Gleig, "a noble library . . . and all the national archives were also burned." With ill-grounded confidence President Madison had prepared a feast for his officers, and:

When the [British] detachment sent out to destroy Mr. Madison's house entered his dining parlour, they found a dinner-table spread, and covers laid for forty guests. Several kinds of wine, in handsome cut-glass decanters, were cooling on the side-board; plate-holders stood by the fire-place, filled with dishes and plates; knives, forks and spoons were arranged for immediate use; in short, everything was ready for the entertainment of a ceremonious party, . . . whilst in the kitchen . . . spits, loaded with joints of various sorts, turned before the fire . . . and all the other requisites for an elegant and substantial repast were exactly in a state which indicated that they had been lately and precipitately abandoned.

You will readily imagine that these preparations were beheld by a party of hungry soldiers with no indifferent eye. . . . They sat down to it . . . ; and having satisfied their appetites . . . and partaken pretty freely of the wines, they finished by setting fire to the house which had so liberally entertained them.

The author thought the American government had behaved with extreme folly and absurd confidence:[87]

Had the emergency been contemplated, and in a proper manner provided against, or had any skill and courage been displayed in retarding the progress of our troops, the design, if formed at all, would have been either abandoned immediately, or must have ended in the total destruction of the invaders.

The form taken by the British offensives against America in 1814 justified John Quincy's assumption that dismemberment of the Union was the object. One army entered the United States from the north; it followed the historic route of Lake Champlain, but it was repulsed and retired forthwith to its Canadian base. The Chesapeake expedition pointed at splitting the United States in the middle, but it made no attempt at a follow-through. The third expedition aimed at the lower Mississippi, the capture of New Orleans being its apparent objective. But this invasion turned into a costly defeat at the hands of Andrew Jackson.

All three of these campaigns seem to have been conceived in a spirit of reckless anger and wounded pride, having no object in view other than retaliation, and they exhibited John Bull at his worst. New Orleans dealt his military reputation a bad blow. The admiral who ordered the burning of Washington did his own country a lasting injury; an act of "Gothic barbarism" postwar American writers called it. "The conduct of the British while in possession of Washington,"

---

[87] *A Narrative of the Campaigns of the British Army at Washington, Baltimore, and New Orleans under Generals Ross, Pakenham and Lambert in the Years 1814 and 1815,* by an officer who served in the expedition. (Philadelphia: M. Carey & Son, 1821), pp. 134–135, 137.

wrote one author whose book went through three editions from 1815 to 1817,[88]

> "is without a parallel in the history of civilized nations. In the wars of modern Europe no examples of the kind . . . can be traced. In the course of the last ten or twelve years most of the capitals of the principal powers of Europe have been entered by Bonaparte . . . yet no instance of such wanton and unjustifiable destruction has been seen.

John Quincy Adams, who had consistently viewed the war with misgivings, voiced the same thought and went on to say:[89]

> no wars are so cruel and unrelenting as civil wars; and unfortunately every war between Britain and America must and will be a civil war . . . The ties of society between the two nations are far more numerous than between any two other nations upon earth . . . But whenever these ties are burst asunder by war, the conflicting passions of the parties are multiplied and exasperated in the same proportion.

Adams was not unmindful that the year previous an American invading force had treated Toronto, the capital of Upper Canada, in similar fashion; but he would not agree that the two incidents were of equal importance. Washington had a symbolic fascination for the American mind which Toronto could not achieve in the British.

From 1815 to 1816 no less than eleven American writers published histories of the war.[90] All eleven filled their pages with accounts of

---

[88] Anon., *History of the American War of 1812, from the commencement until the final termination thereof* . . . , 2nd. ed. (Philadelphia: Wm. M'Carty, 1816), p. 183.

[89] To his wife Louisa from Ghent, Oct. 7, 1814. *Writings, V,* pp. 153–155.

[90] Samuel R. Brown, *An Authentic History of the Second War for Independence,* 2 vols. (Auburn: J. G. Hathaway, 1815); Alexander James Dallas, *An Exposition of the Causes and Character of the War* . . . (Concord, N. H.: Isaac & Walter R. Hill, 1815); John Lathrop, *A Compendious History of the Late War* . . . (Boston: J. W. Burdett, 1815); Thomas O'Conor, *An Impartial and Correct History of the War* . . . (New York: John Low, 1815). This work was in its fourth edition in 1817; John Russel, Jr., *The History of the War* . . . (Hartford: B. & J. Russel, 1815); Anon., *Sketches of the War* . . . *interspersed with geographical descriptions of places and biographical notices* . . . , 2 vols. (Rutland, Vt.: Lay and Davison, 1815); James Butler, *American Bravery displayed* . . . *since the declaration of war by the President* [sic].

naval engagements and battles on land, accused the British of "the accursed practice of impressment" and other outrages and of conducting war incompatible with civilized usages, and conveyed the impression of victory. Moreover, Parson Weems scored another triumph in getting out his sixteenth and seventeenth editions in the single year 1816; he quoted an army general on his title page as congratulating him for treating his "great subject with admirable success in a new way."

The elderly Jefferson also allowed his temper against the British free rein. Their government was "totally without morality, insolent beyond bearing, inflated with vanity and ambition . . . hostile to liberty wherever it endeavors to show its head, and the eternal disturber of the peace of the world." True, Bonaparte was "very wicked," but in expelling the Bourbons he had given the world a valuable lesson. He hated America, but he was less dangerous than England. Jefferson felt satisfied with the American military performance, however, and was convinced that the war had cemented the Union. There was not now on earth a government established on so immovable a basis. Manufacturing, stimulated by the war, he was now ready to accept as necessary to independence; "and the less we have to do with the amities or enmities of Europe the better. Not in our day," he added, "but at no distant one, we may shake a rod over the heads of all, which may make the stoutest of them tremble. But I hope our wisdom will grow with our power, and teach us, that the less we use our power, the greater it will be." [91]

At somewhat greater length and with less passion, John Quincy Adams analyzed the results of the war and expressed himself on the outlook for Europe. Having negotiated the peace treaty with Great Britain, Adams was now installed in London as United States minister.

(Carlisle, Pa.: Geo. Philips, 1816); Anon., *History of the American War of 1812 . . .* , 2nd. ed. in 1816, followed by a third in 1817. (Philadelphia: by Wm. M'Carty); Robert B. McAfee, *History of the Late War . . .* (Lexington, Kentucky: Worsley & Smith, 1816); Anon., *The Naval Temple. . . .* (Boston: Barber Badger, 1816); John Lewis Thomson, *Historical Sketches of the Late War . . .* (Philadelphia: Thomas De Silver; also by M. Carey et al., 1816).

[91] To Lafayette, Feb. 14, 1815, and to Thomas Leiper, June 12, 1815. Ford, *Jefferson, IX*, pp. 504–511, 519–522.

In the meantime the Emperor Napoleon had, to Adams's astonishment, returned from Elba to make himself again the master of France only to be defeated at Waterloo and sent by his British captors into permanent exile on the island of St. Helena. This abrupt end to the many years of war since the start of the French Revolution in 1789 left Adams wondering about the future of Europe. This would depend on how France was treated, and here he feared the worst. Louis XVIII had been made king by the force of British arms, hence France was little better than a British puppet. With the partition of Poland fresh in his memory, he dreaded lest a similar fate be meted out to the French. This would be catastrophic, for France was the mainstay on the Continent against Britain.

Britain itself was in bad shape: multitudes of starving, unemployed seamen on its hands, farmers and landholders bearing a heavy tax burden in the face of falling prices for wheat and breadstuffs, a widening gulf between the landed and the business interests. Adams posed the question whether the government, though conciliatory and peacefully disposed, could resist the temptation to go to war again as a way out of its problems. If it could not, "the danger is that they will plunge the nation headlong into a war with us, because it is against us only that they will be able to stimulate the national passions to the tone of war." Old causes of war between the two countries had disappeared — impressment, for instance, seemed to Adams a dead issue; but new issues were in the making and could come to a head within seven years. An Anglo-American war was more like a civil than an international conflict. The war just past

> consisted not merely of battles won and lost, but every incident on one side or the other wounded the pride and mortified the feelings of the nation. Our naval victories sting the British nation to the quick, while the ineffable disgrace of our military discomfitures in Canada, and the shameful disaster at Washington, still grate upon every national fibre that we possess.

Jefferson's resort to embargoes and non-intercourse was a proven failure. Moreover, Adams continued, two years of war had brought the United States to the edge of bankruptcy, while Britain had survived twenty years with its public finances still unimpaired. To America peace was a vital need to Adams's way of thinking; and before exposing itself to another war, the government should make sure that the Union would stand firm, as it had not done in the war just over.[92]

Still in London and ruminating further on the meaning of the War of 1812, John Quincy conceded that its benefits outweighed its injuries.

> It has raised our national character. . . . It has demonstrated that the United States are both a military and a naval power, with capacities which may hereafter place them in both these respects on the first line among the nations of the earth . . . It has partly removed the prejudice against that best and safest of national defences, an efficient navy. And it has shown us many secrets of our own strength and weakness . . . .

But, he feared, the danger of the Union dissolving was not over; "great, anxious and unremitting care" would be required to surmount it.[93]

V

America is now "the acknowledged centre of the earth." The sentiment was Henry Brackenridge's, expressed after his return from a goodwill voyage to South America. An official mission appointed by the President made the voyage on a frigate, and Brackenridge was its secretary. Having lived for some years in Louisiana, where he familiarized himself with the literature of French and Spanish explorers, he became an enthusiast for Latin American independence and the effects it would have in raising the reputation of the United States. His first book was on Louisiana, published first in 1814 and

---

[92] To Abigail, Mar. 19, 1815, and to John Adams, Mar. 21, Apr. 24, Aug. 31, Oct. 9; and parallel letters to other correspondents, *Writings, V,* pp. 290–294, 297, 304–309, 362–364, 407–412.

[93] To Alexander H. Everett, Mar. 16, 1816, *ibid.,* 537–538. Henry Clay also thought the power of France as a counterpoise to Great Britain was gone forever; hence another war between the United States and Britain was a certainty. James F. Hopkins (ed.), *The Papers of Henry Clay,* 3 vols. (Lexington: University of Kentucky Press, 1961), *II,* p. 152. Hereafter cited as *The Papers of Henry Clay.*

again in 1817 before he left for South America, and in it he reiterated the gains from ridding this continental heartland of unwanted European neighbors, whose presence would prove fatal for the American Union. "Who would deposit the key of his house in the hands of his enemy?" he asked rhetorically. But, he admitted, only Providence had made the annexation of Louisiana possible. Henry Clay received an autographed copy of this book from the author; and when in March 1818 Brackenridge arrived in Buenos Aires, he wrote the congressman a long letter describing his travels and warmly urging the cause of republicanism in South America.[94]

Brackenridge was especially pleased with Buenos Aires, a city of freedom where only plain citizens and republican soldiers were to be seen. No one wanted a king and so, he wrote:[95]

> We have it in our power to direct and fix the destinies of a great people — Good Heaven! is it possible that our enlightened statesmen cannot lift up their minds to the magnitude of the subject . . . The simple acknowledgment of these people will be productive of consequences of which you can scarcely form an idea. . . . I do not hesitate to say, that the moment we acknowledge them, they will adopt every feature of our government and constitution, and such is the idea which they have of the justice, wisdom, and disinterestedness of our country, that they will be guided by our advice in everything . . . .

Henry Clay shared this enthusiasm for the Great Cause, as he called it, of South America; and he came forward as chief advocate of recognizing and encouraging Latin American independence. A system prevailed in the New World that did not exist in the Old, and once independent of Spain, the Spanish Americans would obey the laws of this system. Once they were successful, the United States would be raised high as the natural leader of New World republics.

---

[94] Henry Brackenridge, *Views of Louisiana; containing geographical, statistical and historical notices of that vast and important portion of America.* (Baltimore: Schaeffer & Maund, 1817).

[95] To Henry Clay, Mar. 3, 1818, *The Papers of Henry Clay, II,* pp. 443–446; H. M. Brackenridge, *Voyage to South America, performed by order of the American Government in the years 1817 and 1818* . . . , 2 vols. (Baltimore: by the author, 1819.

There were economic advantages too: Britain, our commercial rival, would again be entangled in the wars of Europe and the United States could then engross the whole of the trade of South America.[96]

Clay was vexed that the issue of slavery in the territories had arisen to thrust Latin American questions into the background. In Congress "the words, civil war and disunion, are uttered almost without emotion," he complained, though he thought the current question concerning Missouri would be settled by a compromise, as indeed it was. He was eager to get on with the recognition of the South American and Mexican patriots and with the seizure of Texas, the two steps to be taken simultaneously. Meanwhile, John Quincy Adams, now Secretary of State, had concluded with the Spanish minister, Luis de Onis, a treaty acquiring title to the Floridas and fixing the southwestern boundary of the United States at the Sabine River. In Clay's, as well as in Jefferson's eyes, this was a great mistake: Adams had lost a chance to take Texas by merely occupying it and ignoring the Spaniards. Clay and Jefferson would make the Rio Grande the southwestern boundary and not bother with Spain, helpless to cope with the wars of independence on the part of its several colonies.[97]

Adams too subscribed to the theory that the United States had a "natural dominion" over North America, but he did not want to move too fast or too aggressively. Like his British counterpart, Lord Castlereagh, whom he held in high regard, he was anxious to avoid committing provocative acts. A quarrel with Spain would breed a quarrel with Britain, especially if South America was the cause. As minister to Great Britain, Adams had grown sensitive to the general hostility there and on the Continent. America was abhorred for having aided and abetted the French in the long wars just past. In Britain the feeling was more bitter than it had ever been, and[98]

---

[96] Speech on Recognition of the Independent Provinces of the River Plata, Mar. 24–25, 1818, *The Papers of Henry Clay, II,* pp. 512–539.

[97] Clay to Adam Beatty, Jan. 22, 1820, and speech on Adams-Onís Treaty, Apr. 3, 1820, *ibid.,* pp. 766, 803–815. Jefferson to Lafayette, Dec. 26, 1820. Ford, *Jefferson, X,* pp. 179–181.

[98] To Erving, June 10, 1816; to John Adams, Aug. 1, 1816; to Plumer, Jan. 17, 1817; to Richard Rush, May 20, 1818, *Writings, VI,* pp. 45, 58–63, 139–144, 319–327.

royalists everywhere detest and despise us as Republicans. . . .
We are considered not merely as an active and enterprising, but
as a grasping and ambitious people. . . . The universal feeling
of Europe in witnessing the gigantic growth of our population
and power is that we shall, if united, become a very dangerous
member of the society of nations . . . .

Adding to this fuel was the popular propensity in Britain to emigrate
as the alternative to poverty and unemployment following in the
wake of war. Anywhere but to the United States — this was the
sentiment commonly expressed in the British newspapers. But among
the emigrants America remained the favorite, and with them the
name and writings of Morris Birkbeck carried weight. John Quincy
thought highly of Birkbeck, "well known as one of the most intelligent and respectable farmers in England and . . . distinguished in the
literary world." [99] Birkbeck moved his large family to America in
1817 and took possession of 26,400 acres of farm land in Illinois in
expectation of founding a settlement of his fellow countrymen on his
"English Prairie." He wrote two books in praise of his experiences,
and each book went through seven editions and was published on
both sides of the Atlantic. Mathew Carey published the second one,
Letters from Illinois, and John Melish drew the map. Unconsciously
Birkbeck was putting into practice the ideas propounded by Franklin
many years before that English people were to be preferred as settlers
in America. A successful farmer in England, he boasted of still greater
achievements in Illinois, and he wrote:[100]

> Republican principles are universal. . . . Here every citizen is
> part of the government, identified with it not virtually but in
> fact. I love this government; and thus a novel sensation is ex-
> cited; it is like the development of a new faculty. I am become
> a patriot in my old age; thus a new virtue will spring up in my
> bosom.

To all these men patriotism and republicanism were one and the
same thing; and comparisons with ancient Rome came naturally to

---

[99] Adams to Monroe, Oct. 12, 1816 and Oct. 9, 1817. *Ibid.,* pp. 104–109, 216.
[100] From the first edition, pp. 49–50.

them. For a brilliant description of the Roman Empire in the second century A.D., when Rome was at its best, they had but to turn to the opening chapter of Edward Gibbon's great *History*, first published interestingly enough in the year 1776 and, through fifteen successive editions, attracting admiring readers to its pages. "That public virtue," writes Gibbon, "which among the ancients was denominated patriotism, is derived from a strong sense of our own interest in the preservation and prosperity of the free government of which we are members." Moreover, "in the purer ages of the [Roman] commonwealth, the use of arms was reserved for those ranks of citizens who had a country to love, a property to defend, and some share in enacting those laws, which it was their interest, as well as duty to maintain."[101] These observations admirably fitted the climate of opinion in America after the War of 1812.

Against the criticisms of her fellow countrymen an English feminine writer sprang vigorously to the defense of the Americans, "those modern Romans." Praising the "truly grand and morally sublime" conduct of the patriots of '76, an idea which she got from reading David Ramsay, the patriot historian, she found the Continental Congress "so pure" that "not one member of that magnanimous assembly [could be] even suspected of . . . a desire of personal aggrandizement." And she insisted in her concluding pages:[102]

> no nation has perhaps ever produced, in the same term of years, more high-minded patriots and able statesmen than the American. Who laid the foundation of these republics? Not robbers and bandits, as some of our ministerial journals would persuade their readers, but the wisest citizens of the wisest country then existing on the globe.

Nursing his indignation against Britain for impressing American seamen, Henry Brackenridge drew the parallel of the Roman citizen

---

[101] Edward Gibbon, *The History of the Decline and Fall of the Roman Empire*, 3 vols. (New York: The Modern Library), *I*, p. 9.

[102] *Views of Society and Manners in America; in a series of letters from that country to a friend in England, during the years 1818, 1819, and 1820*, by an Englishwoman (London: Longman, 1821).

and the dignity and authority he carried with him wherever he went. Britain, he declared,[103]

> is not aware that an humble American citizen is a personage of more importance than an obscure British subject can be! . . . She did not know that the American seamen were, in general, of a different class from her own; more decently brought up, of better families and morals, and many of them looking forward . . . to be mates and captains of vessels . . .

Making a spirited argument before the House of Representatives for a system of national roads planned and built to make the United States militarily effective, Henry Clay too appealed to the example of Rome:

> Those great masters of the world, the Romans, how did they sustain their power so many centuries, diffusing law and liberty, and intelligence all around them? They made military roads. . . .

With his eyes particularly on a road that he wanted built from St. Louis to the Pacific Northwest, Thomas Hart Benton, the senator from Missouri, also invoked the precedent of the Roman Empire and cited Gibbon as his source. Benton concentrated on reviving Jefferson's scheme of the North American road to India, pictured the wealth and power that had always gone to the city or nation that got control of the communications with eastern Asia, and insisted that St. Louis was destined to become the Venice of the New World, the city that would draw the wealth of Asia through its gates and make the United States the commercial mistress of the globe.[104]

Viewing Jonathan Trumbull's familiar picture of the signers of the Declaration of Independence, John Quincy Adams put down on paper the feelings of piety and patriotic pride that swept over him at sight of the picture. The men whose likenesses appeared on the canvas, he told his father, were the founders of "the greatest nation

---

[103] H. M. Brackenridge, *History of the late War Between the United States and Great Britain* . . . , 3rd ed., revised and corrected (Baltimore: Cushing & Jewett, 1817), p. xiv.
[104] *The Papers of Henry Clay, II*, p. 477; Henry Nash Smith, *Virgin Land. The American West as Symbol and Myth* (Cambridge, Mass.: Harvard University Press, 1950), pp. 24–25.

this Ball of Earth has seen or ever will see." The picture represented "the sublimest scene ever acted upon the face of the earth, [but] the painter has fallen, as Raphael or Michelangelo . . . would have fallen, infinitely below the subject." The occasion was "not merely the birthday of a powerful nation. . . . It was the opening of a new era in the history of mankind. It laid a new cornerstone to the foundations of human society — deeper, loftier, more durable than the everlasting hills." The Declaration[105]

> was the first solemn proclamation to the human species of their unalienable rights. . . . Who from this view of that picture would infer that over the head of every individual who put his hand to that proclamation was even then waving in combined and terrible defiance the flaming sword of war. . . . No, it is not in canvas to exhibit the stupendous magnitude of that scene . . . .

These sentiments, upon which Adams elaborated in his Fourth of July oration three years later, registered the burning patriotism of his generation. The origins of America were divine, proven so by the ritual in the cabin of the *Mayflower* and again by the Declaration of Independence. Out of these acts had come the American Union — the social compact of John Locke, but something more than the civil society which Locke had depicted. It was more sacred than profane. Thus the birth of the United States was like the Second Coming of Christ. It was a religious miracle, performed first by the Pilgrims in 1620 and re-enacted by the signers of the Declaration a century and a half later.[106]

Other New England writers and orators rallied around this theme, vehemently repeating and embellishing the myths of the Massachusetts Puritans. Pointing out that "repetition is alike necessary to preserve truth and to give it impression," the Rev. Abiel Holmes, pastor of the First Church in Cambridge, son-in-law of Ezra Stiles and father of the subsequently distinguished Supreme Court justice, Oliver Wendell Holmes, bracketed the whole of New England with the

---

[105] Dec. 14, 1818. Reel No. 147 of the Adams Manuscripts. By permission of the Adams Manuscript Trust.

[106] *An Address*, Washington, July 4, 1821; and see JQA, *Writings, VII*, pp. 113–123, 127–136.

handful of *Mayflower* Pilgrims. "The purity of their morals and the excellence of their Christian character are attested by their contemporaries," he said; and he even gave his listeners and readers the impression that, except for the Pilgrims and other religiously motivated bands, America would never have been colonized. "Our act of celebration begins with God," asserted George Bancroft, the coming historian. "The festival which we keep is the festival of freedom itself. . . ." God had ordained the United States to be "the leader of civilization's triumphant parade to glory"; the colonists had fled from an "Egyptian bondage" to found a new nation dedicated to freedom for all. Accordingly, "the cannibal of the South Sea forgets his horrid purpose and listens to the instructions of religion . . ." [107] No other half-century period of history had "ever presented so many or so might revolutions, such grand displays of national force. . . ."

An Italian historian, Charles Botta, made a shrewd comment on how this image of the divine origin of the United States had achieved its stature. Botta was the author of a two-volume *History of the War of the Independence of the United States of America,* which was translated into English and published in Boston in 1826. The Americans, he said, "were not only Protestants, but Protestants against Protestantism itself." They refused submission to any authority in the field of religion, and this refusal they applied to other subjects, notably to government. America "abounded in lawyers . . . accustomed to the most subtle and the most captious arguments," and by them the people had been made familiar [108]

> with those sophistical discussions which appertain to the professions of theology and of law, the effect of which is often to generate obstinacy and presumption in the human mind. . . .
> The republican maxims became a common doctrine: and the memory of the Puritans . . . was immortalized. These were their apostles, their martyrs.

---

[107] Abiel Holmes, *Two Discourses on the Completion of the Second Century from the Landing . . . at Plymouth, 22 December 1620;* George Bancroft, An Oration at Northampton, Mass. July 4, 1826.

[108] Charles Botta, *History of the War of the Independence of the United States of America.* 2 vols., translated from the Italian by George Alex. Otis, 2nd. ed. (Boston: Harrison Gray, 1826), *I,* pp. 11–12.

The future educator, Horace Mann, exclaimed:[109]

> In the past evolution of that vast series of events which the Almighty has enchained together for the accomplishment of his wondrous purposes the American Revolution constitutes one of the most transcendently important and glorious, [and it is] not without reason that a great nation, extending from the Eastern even to the Western ocean . . . forms, on this day, but one vast temple."

So the young enthusiast postulated not merely American divinity but its extension to the Pacific, an assumption quite common at the time but premature by a full quarter of a century.

Timothy Dwight, a theologian and past president of Yale, who had once been a chaplain in the American Revolutionary Army, exemplifies the Italian historian's observation. In a four-volume work which he published in New Haven in 1821 he ably argued the case for New England and its history, stressed its uniqueness as a land of learning, laws, freedom, arts and the true religion, and concluded that:

> It requires little forecast to perceive that the people of the United States will in their progress fill almost the whole continent of North America; populate in the end all the extensive regions which are north of the kingdom of Mexico; and station themselves within half a century on the shores of the Pacific Ocean. This is a tract larger than the whole Russian empire . . .

This population, he continued, will be double the Russian, will consist of freemen, will profess the Protestant religion, and "will of course be intelligent, refined and, it is hoped, virtuous and happy.[110]

---

[109] Horace Mann, *Oration July 4, 1823 at Dedham, Mass.* For similar sentiments see Charles Pelham Curtis, *An Oration July 4, 1823,* Boston; Edward Everett, *An Oration at Cambridge before . . . Phi Beta Kappa August 27, 1824;* Charles Sprague, *An Oration July 4, 1825 in Boston.* 2nd edition.; Henry Colman, *Oration at Salem July 4, 1826;* Caleb Cushing, *A Eulogy on John Adams and Thomas Jefferson, Newburyport, July 15, 1826* (Cambridge: Hilliard & Metcalf). *Also* R. W. Van Alstyne, *The Rising American Empire* (New York: Oxford University Press, 1960), pp. 91–99.

[110] Timothy Dwight, *Travels in New England and New York.* 4 vols. (New Haven; published by the author, 1821), *IV,* p. 520.

"What a noble prospect is opened for the circulation of thought and sentiment in our country," exclaimed Edward Everett in his Phi Beta Kappa oration at Cambridge in August 1824. Underscoring "that most important era in human history," the Revolution that had begun fifty years earlier, this already prominent orator continued:

> Instead of that multiplicity of dialect, by which mental communication and sympathy are cut off in the old world, a continuing expanding realm is opened and opening to American intellect, in the community of our language, throughout the widespread settlements of this continent . . . an empire more extensive than the whole of Europe.
>
> If there is any faith in our country's auspices, this great continent . . . will be filled up with a homogeneous population; with the mightiest kindred people known in history; our language will require an extension which no other ever possessed; and the empire of the mind . . . will attain an expansion of which we as yet can but partly conceive. The vision is too magnificent to be fully borne; — a mass of two or three hundred millions . . . held in their several orbits of nation and state . . . .

In his Fourth of July oration of 1826, especially important as the fiftieth anniversary of the Declaration of Independence, Everett repeated these sentiments and added another one that was also gospel to the American mind: the belief that war is the sport of kings and princes, who "raise their soldiers by conscription, and drive them at bayonet point into the battles they fight for reasons of state." By contrast, republics wage only just and necessary wars. The American Republic furnishes an example to the world in fulfillment of its destiny.[111]

Aware of President Monroe's recent Doctrine, the prominent Philadelphia lawyer and congressman, Charles J. Ingersoll, took up the theme of America versus Europe in a paper he read before the American Philosophical Society. "When North America," he declared, "can say to Europe 'you shall not recolonize South America,' the matter is settled." Commemoration of independence

> will sound along the vast spine of mountains from the frozen ocean to the Straits of Magellan; will pervade the Pacific; will

---

[111] Edward Everett, *An Oration July 4, 1826 at Cambridge.*

cross the Atlantic, proclaiming independence, startling enthroned monarchs. Cordial, glorious and formidable are the free sympathies of an independent nation . . . proving that the voice of the people is the voice of God.

It was the seventeenth-century Puritan divines' picture of the New Jerusalem all over again.

"No event more noble [than the Declaration of Independence] adorns the annals of society," decided the well-known Unitarian minister and writer from Dartmouth, New Hampshire, Henry Colman:[112]

> The light of American freedom begins to be reflected from the summits of the Andes; and their luxuriant valleys are vocal with the kindred and rapturous sounds of liberty and Washington. Sister republics in a brilliant group are rising to meet us in the Southern Hemisphere. . . .

Subscribing to these ideas, an English writer, Isaac Holmes, published a volume based on four years of residence in America, a country which had risen swiftly into empire

> prodigious in extent of territory and great in importance . . . ; and as yet, it only appears as the foundation of what will hereafter become one of the greatest political superstructures that was ever raised. . . . As a power yet in its infancy, it will become a giant among the nations of the earth.

Since the fall of Rome no event was so great as the American Revolution; and its leader, George Washington, was "one of the greatest men that ever appeared in the world . . . whose name is enrolled in the archives of immortality." [113]

Such homage supplied new magic to the name of Washington and to the tradition of the Revolution. Lafayette's last visit, the deaths of John Adams and Thomas Jefferson within a month of each other, the fiftieth anniversary of the Revolution, and Monroe's announce-

---

[112] Charles J. Ingersoll, *A Communication on the Improvement of Government,* October 1, 1824 (Philadelphia: Abraham Small); Henry Colman, *Oration at Salem July 4, 1826.*

[113] Isaac Holmes, *An Account of the United States of America, derived from Actual Observation. . . .* (London: the Caxton Press, 1823), p. 400.

ment of a policy of self-assumed hegemony over the New World all provided a stage where the heroes of the Revolution could be put on dress parade and the United States itself confidently praised as the empire of the future. George Washington was "the champion of freedom, the glory of his country, the founder and father of a great empire, the pride of modern times, the ornament of the human race." The heroes held "a sort of patent of nobility, undisputed by the bitterest enemies to aristocracy," who were delighted to trace their descent to English families of rank and to boast of their pure English blood; and the Union which they created would endure for ages.[114]

There was acid on the pen of the satirist, James Kirke Paulding, when in 1825 he wrote the following ballad:[115]

Oh Johnny Bull my Joe John, I wonder what you mean,
Are you on foreign conquest bent, or what ambitious scheme!
Ah! list to Brother Jonathan, your fruitless plans forego;
Remain on your fast-anchored isle, O Johnny Bull my Joe.

Oh Johnny Bull my Joe John, don't come across the main,
Our fathers bled and suffered, John, our freedom to maintain,
And him who in the cradle, John, repell'd the ruthless foe,
Provoke not, when to manhood grown, O Johnny Bull my Joe.

Oh Johnny Bull my Joe John, you're proud and haughty grown,
The ocean is a highway which you falsely call your own,
And Columbia's sons are valiant, John, nor fear to face the foe,
And never yield to equal force, Oh Johnny Bull my Joe!

---

[114] John Royer, *The Monument of Patriotism . . . Biographical Sketches of the Lives . . . of some Men who signed the Independence . . . an eulogium on the Character of . . . Washington, compiled from the most authentic Authors,* New ed. (Pottstown, 1825), p. 44; Adam Hodgson, *Letters from North America. . . .* 2 vols. (London: Hurst, Robinson & Co., 1824), *II,* pp. 25 ff., 194–196.

[115] This ballad is to be found in an extremely rare collection of American chap books, printed in 1825. The collection is owned by the Henry E. Huntington Library & Art Gallery.

Oh Johnny Bull my Joe John, your Peacocks keep at home,
And ne'er let British seamen in a frolick hither come,
For we're hornets, and we're wasps, John, who as you
    doubtless know,
Carry stingers in their tails, Oh Johnny Bull my Joe.

INDEX

Index

Acadia, and Massachusetts, 8–9, 10, 19, 20, 29, 30
 deportation of the Acadians, 48, 50
Adams, John, 2, 14, 16, 71, 72
 on human nature, 76–77
 on future of the Pacific, 80
 on the Constitution, 92–93, 97, 110, 111, 118, 119, 124–125, 138
 on George Washington, 142, 143, 152, 154, 163, 179
Adams, John Quincy, 110
 Fourth of July orations, 111–114, 115, 116, 117, 118, 119, 120–124, 133, 134, 137, 152
 on impressment, 154; and the Union, 155–156, 157–158, 163, 164, 165, 166, 168, 169, 171–172, 174
Adet, Monsieur, minister from the French Republic, 120, 123
Aix-la-Chapelle, treaty of, 40
Alien and Sedition Laws, 116
America, and colonists, 1
 as the New Rome, 2, 18, 20, 24, 27, 28, 39, 40, 43, 44, 52
 British fear of, 54–55
 as utopia, 58–60, 62–63, 65, 66, 67, 68, 72, 73, 76, 77, 83
 and Latin America, 84–85
 and Kentucky, 88
 fear of European entanglement, 90–91, 96, 97, 99, 100, 106, 107, 111, 113, 115, 116, 117, 118, 120, 121, 122, 123, 124, 125
 European observations on, 126–130, 131, 133, 137, 143, 144, 145, 146, 147, 149, 150, 151, 152, 154, 157
 and "our hemisphere," 159, 160, 161

America, as Brother Jonathan, 162, 163, 165, 166, 167–168, 170, 171–172, 173
 alleged divine origins, 175–177, 180
American empire, 3, 4, 61, 65–66, 85, 113, 178
American Revolution, 4, 13
 and Louisbourg myth, 40
 sanctification of, 59–60, 62, 74, 79, 88, 96
 Ramsay's view of, 102, 104
 and Lafayette, 104, 105, 109, 110, 111, 114, 133, 135, 142
 later versions of, 160, 161, 177, 178–180
Anbury, Thomas, observant British officer, 100
Apotheosis of Washington, 137–138
Aristotle, 16

Bache, Benjamin Franklin, 132
Bancroft, George, 176
Bank of England, 17, 21
Barlow, Joel, and the American utopia, 64–65
Benton, Senator Thomas Hart, 146
 and the Roman Empire, 174
Berkeley, Bishop George, 1, 11
 on patriotism, 12, 13, 60
Beverley, Robert, on Virginia, 20
Birkbeck, Morris, and Illinois, 172
Blodgett, Samuel, 142–143
Board of Trade, Report of 1721, 26–27, 28
Bolingbroke, Henry St. John, Viscount, 1, 2, 14
 Idea of a Patriot King, 15, 16
Bollan, William, and New England ambitions, 36–37

Boston, 8, 9, 10, 19, 28, 29, 30
  and Louisbourg, 33, 34, 35, 36, 38, 39, 40, 41
  and Halifax, 42, 43, 50
  and anti-French feeling, 70–71, 95–96
  and French sailors, 107–108, 158, 161
Botta, Charles, and America, 176
Brackenridge, Henry, 169–170, 173
Braddock, Major General Edward, 48, 49
  prejudice against, 50, 98, 100, 139
Bradford, William, of Plymouth, 7
  and Pequots, 8, 11
Brandywine, 106
Britain, and "duty," 1
  and trading companies, 5, 6, 7, 13, 17, 19, 22, 24, 27–28, 29, 31, 33, 34
  and Cape Breton, 37, 38, 40, 43, 44
  and the Hudson's Bay Company, 47
  and problem of backing the Colonies, 49–50, 51, 53, 54, 58–59, 62, 69, 72, 73, 75, 77, 84, 85, 86, 89, 90, 97, 100
  and Tom Paine, 101–104, 113, 116, 117, 120, 121, 124, 127, 130, 131, 132
  and Jefferson, 133–134, 137, 140, 147, 150, 151, 152, 154–155, 157
  and War of 1812, 158–159, 160, 161
  as John Bull, 162, 163–164, 165, 166, 167, 168, 171, 172, 180–181
British Empire, concept of, 6, 7, 20
  and Daniel Defoe, 23–24
  and William Bollan, 37, 44, 52, 100
Buffon, George Louis Leclerc, comte de, 85
Burke, Edmund, on the French Revolution, 118
Burnet, Governor William of New York, 31
Burr, Aaron
  and Jefferson, 134, 148, 149
  president of College of New Jersey, on French History, 50

Callender, James, and Jefferson, 131
Canada, 2, 10, 19
  and Samuel Vetch, 28, 29, 30, 34, 37, 39, 41, 45, 46, 48, 53
  fall of celebrated, 54–55, 62
  and Loyalist migration, 91
  and Tom Paine, 104, 106, 122, 138
  invasion of, 157–159, 163, 166, 168
Cape Breton Isle, 30, 33, 34, 35
  strategic value of, 37, 38, 39, 40, 42, 43, 48
Carey, Mathew, Philadelphia publisher, 62, 63, 132, 140, 164, 172
Caribbean Sea, 7, 22, 31, 32, 45, 119
Cartagena, Spanish fortress, 23, 31, 32
Catholics, French, 8, 10, 36, 39
  victory over and end of Church predicted, 55, 59
Charlevoix, Pierre de, Jesuit writer on the Mississippi, 36–37, 53, 56, 64
Chauncy, Charles, warlike Boston clergyman, 50
Cherbourg, new French port, 69–70
Chesapeake Affair, 150, 151, 152, 153
China, 28, 67, 81, 91, 150
Clarke, William, Boston writer, 44
  on war and empire, 47–49, 51
Clay, Henry, 2, 115, 170–171, 174
Colbert, Jean-Baptiste, and French sea power, 37
Colden, Cadwallader, and New York interests, 31, 46
Colman, Henry, New Hampshire preacher, 179
Conway, General Thomas, 106, 107
Cook, Captain James, explorer, 66
  and his voyages, 78–80, 82
Cooper, Samuel, Boston clergyman, celebrates victory over France, 56
Corry, John, biographer of Washington, 141–142
Coxe, Daniel, pleads for British aid, 27, 28
Coxe, Tench, and ideas on national power, 92
Coxe, William, American in the China trade, 81

Coxe, William, English traveller and writer on Russia, 80
Crèvecoeur, Michel, and the American utopia, 62–63
Cromwell, Oliver, and Western Design, 6–7, 21, 58, 137, 155
Crown Point, strategic value of, 41, 48, 53
Cuba, 57, 150

Dampier, William, English explorer, 17–18
Darien Expedition, and Scottish Union with England, 18, 44
Declaration of Independence, 78
  and J. Q. Adams, 114, 174–175, 178–179
Defoe, Daniel, and commerce, 17
  and the Act of Union,(1707), 18
  and Father Hennepin, 19
  and war against Spain, 21–24, 26, 33, 150
Douglass, William, important Boston writer, 38–39, 43–44, 47
Drake, Sir Francis, and New Albion, 7
  and California, 22
  and Defoe, 24
Dummer, Jeremiah, 29, 30
Duquesne, fort at head of Ohio, 53, 54
Dwight, Timothy, theologian, 177

Edinburgh, 17, 18
Elizabethan English, and New World, 1, 4, 6
England: See Britain
Esquemeling, Alexander O., Dutch writer on piracy, 32
Estaing, Charles-Hector, comte d', 107
Europe, and Britain, 6, 11, 12, 24, 27, 44, 47, 52
  American conception of, 60–61, 66
  and Jefferson's prejudices, 75, 76, 88, 99, 115, 117, 119, 123, 124, 125, 136, 143, 157, 159, 166, 167, 171, 172, 178

Evans, Lewis, geographer, 49–50
Everett, Edward, orator, 110, 178

Floridas, 4, 147
Fort Oswego, 31
Fourth of July, 96, 111, 113–114, 129, 161, 175, 178
France, 1, 13, 18, 21, 29, 33, 36
  and sea power, 37, 38, 40
  and Santo Domingo, 45
  fears of, 48, 49, 52
  and victory over, 55, 57
  and Scioto Land Company, 65
  and Jefferson, 68, 69, 70, 72, 73, 75
  and the French Revolution, 78, 84, 85, 86, 90, 98, 100
  and Tom Paine, 103–104, 106, 111, 117, 118, 119, 122, 124, 125, 129, 133, 134, 137, 147, 148, 153, 155, 160, 168
Franklin, Benjamin, 1, 2, 11, 19, 31, 38, 44
  dislike of Pennsylvania Dutch, 46, 47, 49
  on population increase and imperial power, 51–52, 54, 59
  and Lebensraum, 60–61, 63, 88, 97
  and the myth of the French and Indian war, 98–99, 100, 101
  and Lafayette, 105, 132, 135, 143, 146, 172
Frederick II, King of Prussia, 76, 77
French and Indian War, myth of, 98–99
French Revolution, 118–119, 126, 168

Gardiner, Rev. John, and "Massacre Day," 71, 96
Genet, Edmond Charles, Citizen, 120
Gentleman's Magazine, The, influence of, 34, 35, 40
  and Franklin, 51
George III, 2, 13, 14, 76, 103, 111, 112, 114
Gérard, Alexandre, French minister in Philadelphia, 108
Gibbon, Edward, historian, 173, 174
Gilbert, Sir Humphrey, and North America, 4

Gleig, Lt. George, on capture of Washington, D.C., 164–165

Goldsmith, Oliver, 1

Gordon, William, historian of the Revolution, 74, 109

Great Lakes, 7, 28; and Niagara, 48, 53

Grey, Captain Robert, American explorer, 80–81

Grotius (Hugo de Groot), and the "just war," 9

Hakluyt, Richard, geographer, 4

Halifax, 42, 43, 158

Hall, Lt. Francis, English traveller, on Jefferson, 159–160

Halley, Edmund, and the *Atlas Maritimus,* 24, 25

Hamilton, Alexander, and Loyalist migration, 86–87, 91, 131, 136, 143

Harley, Robert, and Daniel Defoe, 21

Harrington, James, and the ideal republic, 58

Havana, 23, 31

Hayes, Edward, Liverpool merchant, 4

Hennepin, Father Louis, and exploration of the Mississippi, 19

Hobbes, Thomas, 6

Holmes, Isaac, English writer, 179

Holmes, Rev. Abiel, 175–176

Honfleur, French port, Jefferson's interest in, 70

Houdon, Jean, sculptor, 135

Houstoun, James, Scottish writer, 44, 45

Hubbard, Rev. William, New England writer, 9–10

Hudson Bay, 47, 53

Hudson River, 7

Humboldt, Alexander von, renowned German explorer, 148–159

Huske, John, M.P., and writer, 50

Hutchins, Thomas, geographer, 64, 66

Hutchinson, Thomas, and Colonial union, 49

Impressment, 153–154, 157, 167, 173

Independence, 86, 90, 96, 102
and Tom Paine, 103, 106, 108, 112, 157, 169, 170
and See Declaration of

Indians, 1, 7–8, and warfare in New England, 9, 10
and French, 26, 31, 37, 45–46, 48
the "noble savage," 61, 129–130, 139, 144, 146, 149

Jackson, Andrew, 149

Jamaica, 7, 19, 21
and slave trade, 22, 44

Jay, John, 67, 77
and discrimination against Loyalists, 87, 88, 120, 121, 131, 133

Jay's Treaty, 121–122, 127–128, 130, 131, 132, 134, 155

Jefferson, Thomas, 2, 3, 11, 14, 16
ideas and ambitions of, 67–70, 73–78, 81–85, 86
and Loyalist persecution, 88, 89
on the Constitution, 92–93
and Tom Paine, 111, 112, 117, 130, 131
and Britain, 133–134; 135, 145, 146, 147, 150, 151, 153
on conquest of Canada, 158, 159–160, 161, 167, 168, 171, 179

Jeffreys, Thomas, London geographer, 56–57

Jones, John Paul, and Russia, 76, 83

Kalb, Johann, German soldier, on George Washington, 107

Kamchatka, 80, 83

Kennedy, Archibald, New York writer, 44
on conquering Canada, 45–46

Kentucky, 61–62, 83, 88, 90

Lafayette, Marie Jean-Paul Gilbert du Motier, marquis de, 75, 89, 104–110, 127, 135, 179

Lahontan, Baron, books on America, 20

La Luzerne, Anne-César de, and Congress, 108
La Pérouse, Captain, French explorer, 82–83
La Rochefoucault Liancourt, duc de, French observer of America, 126–130, 136, 137, 146
La Salle, French explorer, 19, 25
Latin American revolutions, and Jefferson, 84–85
Law, John, and the Mississippi Company, 25
Lawson, John, North Carolina writer, 26
Ledyard, Corporal John, and Captain Cook, 79
   and Jefferson, 82–84
Lewis and Clark expedition, 145–146
Lewis, Meriwether, 145–146
Little, Otis, and Nova Scotia, 42 43
Livy, Roman historian, 2, 153
Locke, John, 175
London, 5
   and early books on empire, 7, 19, 25, 26, 31, 34, 36, 41, 42, 50, 52
   and books on the Great War, 56–57, 61, 73, 167, 169
Louis XVI, King of France, and Jefferson, 75, 76, 77–78, 124
Louisbourg, 30
   capture of, 33, 35
   as myth, 40–41, 42, 43, 44, 48, 54, 56, 79, 161
Louisiana, 25, 90, 143, 144, 147, 169, 170

Machiavelli, Niccolo, 2, 13, 15
Madison, James, 75, 76, 77, 88, 89, 93
   questions value of bill of rights, 94–95; 115, 150, 152, 156, 161
Mann, Horace, educator, 177
Marshall, John, 138
Massachusettensis, pseudonym for New England writer, 36–37, 38
Massachusetts, 7
   and French Papists, 8
   and Indian warfare, 9

Massachusetts, and appeal to England, 11, 41, 48, 50, 98, 100, 152, 160
Mather, Cotton, and the American Israel, 10, 30, 58
Mather, Increase, Boston clergyman, 10
Mayhew, Jonathan, Boston clergyman, and the Protestant interest, 55, 56
Meares, Lt. John, 80
Mexico, 29, 57, 148, 149, 150, 177
Mexico, Gulf of, 27, 53, 57
Mississippi Company, 25
Mississippi River, 27, 30, 36, 45
   and the St. Lawrence, 53, 57, 64, 66, 84
   and union, 86, 88–89, 90, 91, 98, 143, 144, 148, 149, 165
Mississippi Valley, 19, 25, 26
   as hinterland, 37
   geopolitics of, 57, 66
   and Moustier's report, 94
Mitchell, Dr. John, cartographer, 44
   his influential book, 53–54
Moll, Herman, cartographer, 20, 21–22
Monroe Doctrine, 178, 179–180
Monroe, James, 117, 123, 132, 133, 136, 178
Morse, Jedidiah, geographer, 65–66, 97, 124–125, 143
Moustier, Éléonore F., French minister to Philadelphia, 73, 93–94

Nantucket whaling, and Jefferson, 81–82
Napoleon, and retreat from Moscow, 115, 124, 137
   and Washington, 141, 142, 147, 148, 150, 152, 153, 155, 157, 158, 159, 160, 161, 162, 167, 168
Neal, Rev. Daniel, and New England, 30, 39
New England, 7
   and Indian Wars, 9–10
   the American Israel, 10–11, 18–19, 29, 30, 31, 34, 36, 38

and Acadians, 39
and Louisburg myth, 41, 42, 43, 45, 50, 55, 56
and the social compact, 114, 119, 129, 152, 161, 175
Newfoundland, and fisheries, 4, 19, 29, 37, 45, 79
New Mexico, 149
New Orleans, 25, 53, 66
and Western separatism, 89–90, 147, 148, 160
in War of 1812, 165
Newport, R. I., and fear of France, 50, 108
New World, 1, 5, 10, 21, 57, 92, 170, 174, 180
New York, 19, 26, 29, 31, 41, 45
and German immigration, 46, 48, 53
and Crèvecoeur, 62
and discrimination against Loyalists, 86–87, 91, 127, 158
Niles, Hezekiah, of Niles' Weekly Register, 163
Noailles family, and Lafayette, 104, 110
North Carolina, 4, 26
Nova Scotia, 30, 34, 39
and Chebucto Bay, 42
and Protestant immigration, 43
and Jesuits, 45
importance of, 48
and New England, 50, 53, 56, 79, 82, 91, 104

Oldmixon, John, and British Empire, 20–21, 39
Oldys, William, biographer of Raleigh, 20, 31

Pacific Northwest, 82
Pacific Ocean (South Sea), 18, 25
and Captain Cook, 66, 78–80, 83
and route to Asia, 145–146; 150, 177
Paine, Tom, and Common Sense; Ramsay's appraisal of, 101–102, 103–104, 111, 112, 123, 132, 133, 136

Papists: See Catholics
Paris, 24, 26
and Franklin, 61, 63
and Jefferson, 67, 69, 73, 78, 87, 88, 122, 145
Parliament, British, 6
cash indemnity to Massachusetts, 41, 51, 113
Paterson, William, Scottish financier, 17
Patriotism, 1, 2, 12, 13
Idea of a Patriot King, 15
and myth, 137, 154, 157, 172
Paulding, James Kirke, 162, 180–181
Payne, John, American merchant and writer, 44, 52
Pepperrell, William, and Louisbourg, 42
Peale, Charles Willson, portrait painter, 135
Penhallow, Samuel, Boston writer, 30
Pennsylvania, 26, 36, 46, 128
Pequot Indians, 7–8
Perrin, William, on French ambitions, 33
Philadelphia, 104, 109, 131, 132, 146, 164, 178
Phips, Sir William, and raid on Canada, 19, 29
Pike, Lt. Zebulon Montgomery, 149–150
Pilgrims, Plymouth, 7–8, 112
Pope, Alexander, 1
and patriotism, 12, 16
Popery, 7, 10, 35
identified with France, 36, 43, 55, 56
Portugal, and the Mediterranean trade, 69, 84
Price, Dr. Richard, on the American Revolution, 59–60
Prince, Rev. Thomas, on Cape Breton, 34, 35n, 36, 39
Protestants, 1
and world mission, 5, 10
"Protestant interest," 18, 40, 43
and victory over France, 55, 56–57

and the American Republic, 58–59, 85, 176, 177
Prussia, 117
Puritans, and the American Israel, 9, 11, 12

Quebec: *See* Canada
Quebec Act (1774), 106

Raleigh, Sir Walter, and empire, 4
and war, 5–6
biography of, 20, 23, 24, 31, 97, 143
Ramsay, David, and his history, 97, 99–100, and Tom Paine, 101–102, 103, 132, 173
Rio Grande, 147, 149, 171
Robson, Joseph, on Hudson Bay, 47
Rochambeau, Jean-Baptiste de Vimeur, comte de, 107
Rogers, Captain Woodes (1711) and Robinson Crusoe, 22
Rolt, Richard, writer, on Cape Breton, 43
Rome, and patriotism, 1, 2
as example, 5, 6, 13, 35, 113, 138, 141, 142, 163, 172–174, 179
Rush, Benjamin, 116, 142, 163
Russia, 76, 77, 80; and J. Q. Adams, 115, 125, 153, 156–157, 159, 163, 177

Santa Fé, 149
Scioto Land Company, 65
Scotland, 1, 6
and Darien Expedition, 17
and the Protestant interest, 18
and Union with England, 21, 44
Selden, John, seventeenth century publicist, 6
Shirley, Governor William, and plans for conquest, 33–34, 36, 39, 41, 48, 50; and Franklin, 51
Smith, Adam, and Anglo-French commercial treaty of 1786, 71–72; 143
Smith, Rev. William, Philadelphia, and Protestant interest, 56

Soulés, Francois, French historian of American Revolution, 107
South Carolina, 20
and rice trade, 70, 132, 161
South Sea Bubble (1720), 12, 23, 26
South Sea Company, 21–22, 25
Spain, 1, 5
and Cromwell, 7, 13
and the Pacific, 17–18, 21, 22
and sea power, 23, 27, 29, 31, 32, 33, 38
and Gibraltar, 40, 45, 57, 69, 84, 90, 147, 149, 150, 153, 170
Stiles, Ezra, of Yale, on the American Israel, 58–59, 60, 65, 95
and Washington, 135, 175
St. Lawrence River, 4, 7, 10, 20, 27, 30, 37, 43, 45
"prodigious water-carriage," 53, 54, 57, 79
Stockdale, John, London publisher, 60–61, 66n., 79n., 97n.
St. Petersburg, 115, 163
Stuart, Gilbert, portrait painter, 135, 136
Swift, Jonathan, 1, 14–15

Talleyrand, Charles Maurice de, 161–162
Tory Party, 13
Trenchard, John, and *Cato's Letters*, 13–14, 15, 34, 35n.
Trumbull, Jonathan, portrait painter, 174

United States: *See* America
Utrecht, Peace of (1713), 12, 15, 26–27, 29, 37
viewed as an "infamous" treaty, 39, 45, 50

Vans Murray, William, and J. Q. Adams, 118
Vera Cruz, 148
Vergennes, Charles Gravier, comte de, French foreign minister, and Jefferson, 73, 81
intercedes for Captain Asgill, 87–88; 89, 90

Vernon, Admiral Edward, and war in the Caribbean, 32

Versailles, and the Jacobites, 40; and Lafayette, 106

Vetch, Samuel, Scottish adventurer, 28–29
and Nova Scotia, 30, 46

Vinal, William, and anti-French feeling in Rhode Island, 50

Virginia Company, and venture capital, 5

Voltaire (François Marie Arouet), 14, 135

War Hawks, 158

War of the Spanish Succession, 21, 29

Warren, Commodore Peter, and Louisbourg, 41

Warville, Brissot de, 63, 67, 74, 109

Washington, George, and empire, 3, 77
and the case of Captain Asgill, 87–88; 91, 96–97

Washington, George, and Lafayette, 104–109, 120
and neutrality, 122–123, 128, 131, 132, 133, 134
and hero worship, 135–136, 137–142, 155, 160–161, 179–180

Webster, Daniel, 160–161

Webster, Noah, and patriotism, 96, 97n

Weems, Parson Mason L., and the Washington myth, 138–142, 167

Weld, Isaac, English traveller, 126, 128–130, 136, 146

West Indies, 19, 21, 23
and piracy, 32, 33, 44, 53–54, 66, 73, 81, 91, 104, 106, 119

Whigs, and patriotism, 1, 2, 13, 15, 21, 39, 60, 87

Winthrop, John, 7
and M. La Tour, 8–9; 11, 12, 58

Wood, William, and New England, 7

Yorktown, 106

Young, Arthur, writer on empire (1759), 54–55, 143

A B C D E F G H I J   5 4 3 2 1 7 0 6 9